THE NEW INSTITUTIONAL ECONOMICS

THE NEW INSTITUTIONAL ECONOMICS

Edited by

VEDAGIRI SHANMUGASUNDARAM

Published on behalf of
INDIAN ECONOMIC ASSOCIATION

DEEP & DEEP PUBLICATIONS PVT. LTD.
F-159, Rajouri Garden, New Delhi - 110027

THE NEW INSTITUTIONAL ECONOMICS

ISBN 978-81-8450-310-4

Typeset by THE LASER PRINTERS, 8/15, 3rd Floor, Subhash Nagar, New Delhi-110027.

Printed in India at NEW ELEGANT PRINTERS, A-49/1, Phase I, Mayapuri, New Delhi-110064.

Published by DEEP & DEEP PUBLICATIONS PVT. LTD.,
F-159, Rajouri Garden, New Delhi-110027. Phones: 25435369, 25440916.
E-mail: ddpbooks@yahoo.co.in • ddpubs@gmail.com
Sales Showroom: 2/13, Ansari Road, Daryaganj, New Delhi-110002
Phone/Fax: 23245122

Contents

SECTION V

NIE AND FINANCIAL REFORMS

Foreword

Since 1994, when the undersigned was elected as the Hony. Secretary and Treasurer of the IEA, efforts were made to publish theme-wise edited volumes of IEA Conference/Seminar papers as due to space constraint, it is not possible to include many good papers in the Annual Conference Volumes. Ultimately in 1997, during 80 years of the IEA, a plan was formulated to publish such volumes since 1994 Conference which, with active co-operation of IEA Presidents Dr. G.S. Monga and Prof. Ajit Kumar Sinha, could materialise in 1999. This is continuing till now with co-operation from successive IEA Presidents and Secretaries. The present volume is an outcome of such papers contributed to the IEA 86th Conference held at the Sibaji University, Kolhapur in 2003.

The New Institutional Economics is an edited volume consisting of 21 selected papers contributed in one of the technical sessions of the IEA 86th Conference. These are grouped in five sections viz. (a) NIE: The Framework, (b) NIE and Issues in Development Studies, (c) NIE and Agricultural Development, (d) NIE and Gender Issues, and (e) NIE and Financial Reforms. One can obtain an idea of the growing literature in this emerging and important area of economics from this volume.

We are thankful to the contributors of these articles without whose co-operation the publication of this volume could not be possible. Thanks are due to Prof. Vedagiri Shanmugasundaram for the editorial process and the introduction. We also thank Shri G.S.

Bhatia of Deep & Deep Publications Pvt. Ltd., New Delhi for publishing this volume in an elegant manner. The delay in publishing this volume for unavoidable reasons is regretted.

Kolkata

PROFESSOR RAJ KUMAR SEN
President (2003-04)
Indian Economic Association

List of Contributors

1. **Prof. Vedagiri Shanmugasundaram,** Former President, IEA, Former Vice-chancellor, Manonmaniam Sundaranar University, Director, IASR, Chennai.
2. **Prof. Nirmal Sengupta,** Visiting Professor, IGIDR, Mumbai.
3. **Dr. N. Jaganathan,** CBM College, Coimbatore.
4. **Dr. D. Namasivayam,** Annamalai University, Annamalainagar.
5. **Dr. M.K. Dasgupta,** (Former) Reader & Head, Economics Dept., B.N. Mahavidyalaya, Itachuna, West Bengal.
6. **Dr. Bharati D. Dave,** Bhavnagar University, Bhavnagar.
7. **Ms. Savita Bhagat,** DAV Centenary College, Faridabad.
8. **Dr. Bhagabata Patro,** Berhampur University, Berhampur.
9. **Dr. Purushottam Sahu,** Gopalpur College, Ganjam.
10. **Sri U. Ch. Panigrahi,** Gopalpur College, Ganjam.
11. **Dr. Shrawan Kumar Singh,** Jagan Institute of Management Studies, New Delhi.
12. **Dr. V. Loganathan,** (Former) University of Madras, Chennai.
13. **Dr. K. Jothi Sivagnanam,** University of Madras, Chennai.
14. **Dr. Y. Gangi Reddy,** National Institute of Rural Development, Rajendranagar, Hyderabad.
15. **Dr. Ratan Kumar Ghosal,** Professor, Commerce Department, University of Calcutta.

16. **Dr. Paramjit Nanda,** Guru Nanak Dev University, Amritsar.
17. **Dr. P. S. Raikhy,** Guru Nanak Dev University, Amritsar.
18. **Dr. Sandeep Kumar,** D.D.U. Gorakhpur University, Gorakhpur.
19. **Dr. Nisar Ahmad Khan,** Aligarh Muslim University, Aligarh.
20. **Dr. Falendra K. Sudan,** University of Jammu, Jammu.
21. **Prof. Yasodha Shanmugasundaram,** Former President, IEA, Former Vice-Chancellor, Mother Teresa University, Kodaikanal, Director of Research, IASR, Chennai.
22. **Dr. P. Arumugam,** Bharathiar University, Coimbatore.
23. **Sri A. Balasubramanian,** (Research Scholar), Bharathiar University, Coimbatore.
24. **Dr. Ghanshyam Upadhyay,** Bhavnagar University, Bhavnagar.
25. **Dr. C. Thangamuthu,** Bharathidasan University, Tiruchirapally.
26. **Dr. M.K. Datar,** IDBI, Mumbai.
27. **Dr. Parikshit K. Basu,** Charles Stuart University, Bathwest, Australia.
28. **Sri Ashutosh Kumar** (Research Scholar), IGIDR, Mumbai.
29. **Sri Debesh Bhowmik,** Pritinagar, West Bengal.

Scope and Significance of New Institutional Economics

VEDAGIRI SHANMUGASUNDARAM

The choice of the theme *'New Institutional Economics'* is in a way a tribute to the pioneers who launched Indian Economics as a distinct subject of study. In the early issues of the Indian Journal of Economics (IJE) of the Indian Economic Association (IEA) has in 1950s moved to Allahabad University, discussed this theme in its many facets of sociology of religion, state, class and caste, landed property and land tenure, usury *et. al.* Marx and Veblen like, the study of Adam Smith and his legacy, Marshall, Pigou, Keynes and the rest also came for study along with it. Now we have Ronald Harry Coase (Bom: 29th December 1910), Douglass C. North (Born: 6th November 1920) Robert William Fogel (Born: 1st July 1926), all of them anointed by the Nobel Foundation to complete the cycle. John Harriss, Janet Hunter and Colin M. Lewis of the London School of Economics have in the company of Douglass C. North attempted to apply the New Institutional Economics to what they termed *Third World Development*. It could well have been applied to emerging Human Resource Economics. With a feel for Indian Economics John Harriss may well do this. Economics is the subject of art and science of the possible in given conditions institutional or otherwise.

We need understanding of what Institutions are, how varied they are to which schools they conform, what were Indian contributions to their understanding, how and in what climate the theories and their exponents evolved and what message the

Indian learning has for the world and what the rest of the world scholarship is learning to grapple with the realities of Indian Economics. These are issues of theory and practice of economics for our profession of teaching and research.

The logic of classification is pedagogic. That economics is an universal science was an exploded belief in the *raison d'etre* for Indian Economics ably developed by the three 'D's —Dadabhai, Digby and Dutt and later by Gilbert Slater, C.J. Hamilton, Percy and Vera Anstey, J.C. Coyajee, M.C. Ranade, M. Visvesvaraya, V.G. Kale, T.K. Aiyer, Arcot Ramaswami Mudaliar, John Mathai, R.K. Mukherjee, in nearer times Mahatma Gandhi, Vinoba Bhave, Periyar E.V. Ramaswami, Ambedkar, B. Natarajan, B.V. Narayanaswami Naidu. Not all of them were of the academia. They studied poverty, rural indebtedness, prohibition, village communities, land tenures, social oppression, unemployment, costs of economic and legal institutions and transactions, and all village and state, agrarian and emerging market behaviour pattern in Indian setting. They were institutional thinkers almost eight decades before Ronald Coase, Douglass C. North and Ronald Fogel were spotted for Nobel recognition recently. Gandhian Theory of Trusteeship, in market economy bids fair to reach Keynesian claim of *General Theory of Employment, Interest and Money* in a free society. It is not surprising that it is now widely known and published that M.K. Gandhi is a name among the greats nominated for Nobel Award but not given the Prize.

Ethics in Economics is an early theme of the orientlists in times of peace, without forsaking the art of the possible during war. Kural, Dhammapada, Kautilya, Gita, Bible, Koran and the like have such institutional theories and precepts. That was before machines, robots, digital speed, bio-technology, new legal and financial Institutions, Governmental codes, other National, Multinational and Global practices, beliefs, possibilities and necessities of modern times and transactions arose. Wars and peace processes, inventions and enterprises, cultural and religious institutions, concepts of equality, equity, justice, freedom of movement and migration of men and materials are powerful factors in the emergence of rich economics of suppression resulting in entrenched poverty. Governance by the state as much as private and public sector practices, Role of accounting of fair and foul practices often determined the rise or fall of national economies. And now regional and global institutions probe into these causes of the wealth or poverty of nations. Institutional economics, both old and new, get a lease of life for study and research.

Markets and non-markets, rationalism and irrationalism, universality or specificity, positive and welfare, micro and macro concepts are classificatory tools for the cultivation of for what is in the end holistic economics. We have thus many tools in the broad firmament of New Institutional Economics for discussion.

The nine branches of NIE have many able exponents.

(i) New Economic History has been strengthened by North, and Fogel, (ii) New Social Economics is made widely known by Becker, (iii) Political Economy of Public Choices has been developed by Buchanan, Tullock and Olson, (iv) Institution of Collective Action has the votaries Ostrom, Olson and Hardin, (v) Major contributors for the Institution of Transaction Costs are Coase, North and Williamson, (vi) Social Capital outlined by J.R. Hicks, K.J. Arrow has been developed further by Putman and Coleman, (vii) Institution of Property Rights has growing literature, making it the centre piece of market economy by North, Coase and Alchian, (viii) Information Economics has major contributions from K.J. Arrow, Stiglitz, and Stigler, and (ix) Legal Economics of Institutions was pioneered by Posner and strengthened by Richard A. Posner, R.D. Cooter and G.S. Becker.

In his recent contributions Douglas C. North of Washington University, St. Louis, the foremost exponent of evolving NIE, has outlined five institutional changes which help us understand the dynamic social and political economy of the world, (i) continuous interaction of institutions; (ii) competition which forces investment in new skills and knowledge; (iii) identification of new skills and knowledge which are cost effective and essential; (iv) mental constructs and mental models of the players in socio-political framework; (v) economies of scale. Complementarities and matrix of net worked relations which obtain in the short-run and long-run as perceived at any given time. The rate of learning and employing the lessons determines the rate of growth and sustainability of economies. The inclusive growth which one discusses in many developing economies, is to the fore because of the complex of events both economic and non-economic, which are studied together in NIE. Economic institutions give the rules of the game. Political institutions give the teeth to enforce. The allocation of resources and the end products which emerge to satisfy wants within a state, depend in the global age, on the efficiency world level institutions which make for peace and orderly civil society permeating all nation states.

The subjects covered by the authors of papers presented in the IEA 87th Conference, range over this vast terrain, often overlapping, some of them innovative and most of them with a feel for Indian Economics. Papers on theory and methodology are few. Self-help, common property rights, informal and legal financial institutions, gender, community, technology, NGO institutions, markets and price mechanisms, social institutions like family, marriage, dowry, gender discrimination, affirmative action, legal frameworks, religious more, corporate and household savings, national, transnational and multinational platforms, capital markets and their under OIE and NIE, environmental critique of NIE, Indian varieties, beliefs and habits of economic and human resource content like vegetarianism and teetotalism, sports and leisure time pursuits, entrepreneur in NIE, Monetary institutions—old and new, gender issues of OIE and NIE are among the contributions. How many of them would make Douglas C. North and Ronald Fogel think of visiting India turning their attention to oriental thought and Indian Economics? This time alone with tell. Classical Economics with simple supply and demand theory in aggregates, yielded place to marginal theory and several linkages of neo-classical economics with many assumption unstated and assumed, especially rationality and perfect knowledge of men and matters of institutions, and behaviour patterns. Making hidden forces of economics which are equally powerful, is the central force of NIE, Maximizing gain or optimizing it *per se* is not laudatory. A robber can maximize his gain by habitual sealing. A buyer can maximize his gain by giving a forged cheque or stolen money. Such behaviour patterns will make the society unworkable, if practiced widely. Ethics, social values, political rights and duties, and whole set of evolved institutions over time make the civil economic order. This NIE commends, largely supporting the markets to function under representative government with balancing forces of legislature, executive, judiciary and the new pillar Responsible Press and Media. Rule of law within a state and new international economic order under the world governance by the United Nations agencies make for a egalitarian economic regimes in all parts of the world.

It is not by accident that forex reserves of India have in 2008 touched near US$ 350 billion while in early 1990s India pledged their gold reserves to the Bank of England to bail herself out of the foreign exchange mess. And her oriental neighbour China is in four time's hold of US dollars. Institutional and structural reforms initiated by Manmohan Singh, C. Rangarajan and pursued later have changed face of Indian economy. The sympathy for and condemnation of the under-developed and poor India is turning into admiration, all of a sudden. The hidden institutional trappings which held India in bondage were not known or visible to visiting economists and well heeled pundits of the IMF or World Bank and their kindred in India, till now: there were exceptions like Arthur W. Lewis, Joseph Eugene Stiglitz, T.N. Srinivasan in Princeton and Yale Universities of USA. The American Economy finds the I.T. sector of India efficient and cost-effective, a phenomenon of institutional economics submerged in thought and discussions some decades back. Transparency and accountability of the governing class, release of the energies of the people by education and health care institutions, judicious combination of rationality and faith, self-help, self-confidence and self-respect in global transactions, are values and institutions which are turning round the long moribund Indian Economics. John Hicks in his revisit to Keynesian Economics said that Economics was British Economics till 1945 and American Economics thereafter. Does it not seem the economics of the 21st Century is Oriental Chinese, Japanese and Indian Institutional Economics.

We have altogether 21 papers included in this volume. Like reformation in the west, Arya Samaj, Brahma Samaj and similar reformist institutions in many parts of India, have been curative socio-economic forces. The papers contributed cover most of these subjects. Papers are from several universities and colleges in India, though some more foundations and schools of economics could be more visible. And to fill the gaps in the whole scheme of New Institutional Economics in Comparison with Old Institutional

Economics and market systems, more authors could add new dimensions and make for a fuller text for a publication on Indian Critique of New Institutional Economics.

Time is the ring master in the cycle and circus of holistic economics. Its cultivation is full of possibilities for offering basic and applied understanding of Indian Economics from early times, in all its twists and turns in market, planning, evolutionary avatars, tracing the thought process in the study of which let us start from the early age of Kautilya and Kural, before moving to historical realism and real politic of the massages and tools of modern times.

The present volume is distributed over five sections preceded by a foreword by Professor Raj Kumar Sen which is both profound and punctilious so characteristic of his understanding of the profession and practitioners of Economic Sciences, especially in the recent decades by his prolific study and personal knowledge of them. I am all admiration for Professor Sen, whose long and sustained devotion to the near century old Indian Economic Association, is commendable. The IEA is old but not very old Institution considering the over two thousand old foundation of Indian economics built by Tiruvalluvar of the Dravidian and Kautilya of the Aryan races. The Foreword adds to the visions of the contributors, and this introductory piece on expanding scope and every increasing significance of the relatively more holistic discipline of New Economics, becoming newer and newer, and also curious in ever increasing measure to non-economists, by the perplexity of its width and depth.

Section I is on the New Institutional Economics and its framework, covering "The New Institutional Economics: Its Perimeters and Promises" by Nirmal Sengupta, "Theoretical Approaches of the New Institutional Economics" by N. Jaganathan and D. Namasivayam and "Conventional Economics in the New Institutional Framework" by M.K. Dasgupta. **The next Section II is on NIE and Issues in Development Studies.** The themes and authors are: "Role of Institutions in Economic Development" by Bharahti. D. Dave, "Relevance of New Institutional Economics for Developing Countries" by Savita Bhagat, "Development Implications of Institutional Changes in India: A case study" by Bhagabata Patro, Purushottam Sahu, U. Ch. Panigrahi, "New Institutional Economics and Economic

Reforms in India" by Shrawan Kumar Singh, "Local Government in India: The New Institutional Approach" by V. Loganathan and K. Jothi Sivagnanam, "Educational Initiatives of PRIs and Community in Education Development of Poor; Experience from Kolhapur, Maharashtra" by Y. Gangi Reddy, "Institutional Failure, Corruption and Economic Underdevelopment" by Ratan Kumar Ghosal. **The Section III is NIE and Agricultural Development.** "New Institutions for Meeting Agricultural Development: Challenges under Globalisation" by Paramjit Nanda and P.S. Raikhy, "New Institutional Economics and Agricultural Policy Issues" by Sandeep Kumar, "Sharecropping: A Rational Institutional Response" by Nisar Ahmad Khan, "Institutional Change, Transaction Costs and Natural Resource Management" by Falendra K. Sudan. **NIE and Gender Issues Constitutes the Section IV.** "New and Old Institutional Economics and Gender in India" by Yasodha Shanmugasundaram, "New Institutional Economics Approach to New Household Economics" by P. Arumugam and A. Balasubramanian, "Economic Implications of Marriage Institution with Reference to Women's Empowerment" by Ghanshyam Upadhyay. **NIE and Financial Reforms are covered by the Section V.** "New Institutional Economics: Its Relevance to the Financial Sector" by C. Thangamuthu, "Financial Sector Reforms in India: An Institutional Economics Perspective" by M.K. Datar and Parikshit K. Basu, "Formal Financial Institutions and Rural Credit Provisioning in India: A Micro-economic Model of Default Mitigation" by Ashutosh Kumar, "International Financial Institutions, European Central Bank and the International Monetary System" by Debesh Bhowmik. Many other contributions at the IEA Conference covered issues to fill the gaps left by aforementioned articles.

We have covered a rich fare of contemporaneously significant studies on the fast emerging sphere of institutional economics which builds on the classical and neo-classical economics to usher in the first major revolution of linking the theories of received economics with evolving sociology and political theories. The list of participants and authors of papers to the 87th Indian Economic Conference is long and impressive. Out of them this selection covers in broad categories, some related themes in the following pages. The application of the pair of blades of the editorial scissors is the most unenviable task which the fellow economists will understand. This is a joint effort of the printer and publisher, the editor coming on the margin in the world of commercial publications. The complete list of authors who made their contributions to the IEA conference is found in the Conference Volume available with the IEA Secretary-Treasurer Dr. Anil Kumar Thakur. The readers will find this volume a major introduction to some of the themes of NIE. Here both useful and thought-provoking. We are deeply thankful to the authors whose contributions are based on erudition and reflections on state of the art. They have made this publication possible. We reproduce this selection of contributions presented by the authors to the Annual Economic Conference on New Institutional Economics held between 29 and 31 December, 2003. We are grateful to the Conference President Professor Raj Kumar Sen, who combines economic expertise with legal training and competence-skills indispensable in equal measure for NIE. The then Secretary and Treasurer Professor A.D.N. Vajpai is a senior academic functionary as the former Vice-Chancellor of Awadesh Pratap Singh University, Rewa, Madhya Pradesh. Their ready acceptance and permission to bring out this publication help wider audience.

SECTION I

NIE: THE FRAMEWORK

The New Institutional Economics—Its Perimeters and Promises

NIRMAL SENGUPTA

THE NICHE

Herbert Simon (1991) wrote an interesting story. A Martian looked at our planet from their spaceship. He (or was it she?) could see human relations. To him organizations appeared as green areas, market relationships as red lines and contractual relationships as blue lines. The Martian reported back to his home base a description of planet Earth as full of green areas of various sizes along with some large regions with numerous red and blue lines. Ever since I read this story I have felt a kind of professional intimacy with Simon's Martians. They were social scientists. While technologists see structures and demographers people, social scientists on Earth specialize in 'seeing' human relations. Economists among them however, are a race of colorblinds, at least till recently, who could see only the red lines. The study of

*Visiting Professor, Indira Gandhi Institute of Development Research (IGIDR), Mumbai and Malcolm Adiseshiah, Professor for Policy Studies, Madras Institute of Development Studies, Chennai.

new institutional economics (hereafter NIE) is the long awaited surgery to cure this congenital defect of particularly, neoclassical economics.

What exactly is NIE? Oliver Williamson was the first to coin this term followed soon by Douglass North. The urge to add a prefix, is understandable[1]—way back in 1975 they needed a trademark to announce that they have a distinct product, which though was study of institutions did not follow an already established approach. But there can be many different approaches with claims of being new. It was Williamson who pointed out that his brand of NIE was not the same as that of North. Yet, the two of them are together in developing NIE. What then is NIE? Is it merely an assortment of approaches of everyone who would like to be called a new institutional economist? My answer is an emphatic 'no'. I list here four distinct features, closely related, that are characteristics of NIE studies.

What differentiates new institutional economics from the 'old'? Hodgson (1998: 181) the finest connoisseur of the 'old' institutional economics, draw the distinction as:

> The distinctive "new" institutionalist project has been identified as the attempt to explain the existence of institutions by reference to a given model of individual behaviour, and on the basis of an institution-free "state of nature." The procedure is to start with given individuals and to move on to explain institutions.

While Hodgson is critical, others, including myself, may consider this as a positive feature. Leaving aside the conflicting assessments, let us look at this as a distinctive mark of "new" institutionalist project. Essentially reductionist, this approach keeps NIE close to the neoclassical economics, thereby benefiting from the proven analytical strength of the mainstream economics. What may be the ultimate outcome of the NIE project is not certain. It may bring in substantial modification of the neoclassical economics or may result into a distinct paradigm. Even if the latter is the case, the new paradigm will have to emerge from within the neoclassical approach. This is where the NIE differs from the older institutionalists, whose contributions started as distinct and parallel streams and were faced with the daunting task of developing a new theory from the scratch. Whether the NIE (and many other modern institutionalists) approach is the right choice or not will be decided by the future. But this undoubtedly, is a well-designed and promising research agenda.

The second important feature is the subject of study—a single social institution at a time. Earlier institutional studies had dealt with totality of institutions, in a society or in a situation. Rare exceptions were confined to the analysis of money or market as institutions. In contrast, many studies in new institutional economics trend address a particular contract or a particular method of governance. 'Why did a firm exist', Coase (1937) asked. Instead of employing them, the producers could purchase the services of workers in markets! Coase's answer was simple—vertical integration of contracts and relationships, as is possible in firms, minimize the (transaction) costs of search, negotiation, monitoring and enforcement of those contracts. Firms exist because it is cheaper to organize some activities internally in a hierarchic set-up (governance structure) than it is to conduct that activity in the marketplace. Much has been written about Coase's 'discovery' of transaction cost. But that 1937 paper should also get the credit of pioneering studies of a single institution, a firm in Coase's work. As against the garbled institutional setting as a whole, the structure of Coase's arguments—analyzing the transaction cost for comparing the relative efficiencies of different forms of institutions and organizations—opened up the possibility of analyzing a specific institutional phenomenon. Some other modern institutional studies that follow this approach acknowledge their debts[2] to this article.

The third distinctive feature is best expressed in Coase's Nobel Lecture. NIE is essentially, the study of the institutional structure of production'.[3] Coase wrote (1991):

> The firm in the mainstream economic theory has often been described as a "black box". And so it is. This is very extraordinary given that most resources are used dependent on administrative decisions and not directly on the operation of a market. Consequently, the efficiency of an economic system depends to a very considerable extent on how these organisations conduct their affairs. . . . Even more surprising . . . is the neglect of the market or more specifically the

institutional arrangements which govern the process of exchange. As these institutional arrangements determine to a large extent what is produced, what we have is a very incomplete theory.

These are some of the characteristic features of NIE studies. Arguably, these are not unique to it. Several other streams of modern institutional research share these characteristics. Various commentators have included one or the other of these streams in 'new institutional economists', e.g. economics of imperfect information (viz. Bardhan, 1989), collective action theory (viz. *Nabli and Nugent*, 1989) and positive political theory (viz. *Klein*, 1999; *Dixit*, forthcoming). One possible reason is that these names describe branches professed to remain confined to specific fields, while an all-purpose institutional theory like NIE may unite them under a single head. I feel a deeper assessment is necessary, for NIE scholars also insist upon certain other characteristics, which may not be shared by all the studies included under these branches. The fourth characteristic of NIE studies is their analytical approach. Though still nebulous, the NIE scholars are trying to develop a distinct analytical approach which assign considerable importance to informal arrangements, private ordering outside law, trust-based self-enforcement, social relations serving as (relational) contracts, etc. In the last two decades there is an explosion of institutional studies. Transaction cost, information issues, property rights and contracts are now the subjects of discussion in many different branches. The same set of institutional and organizational phenomena are addressed by both NIE and many other modern approaches to institutional studies. From time to time attention has been drawn by NIE scholars to subtle differences in analytical approaches. This is therefore, a crucial fourth characteristic feature of NIE.

Thus, for example, franchise relations have been analyzed by many scholars (viz. *Dnes*, 1996; *Brown*, 1998; *Lafontaine and Slade*, 1999). In this context, Williamson explains (2000: 609-610), one approach will be "to conduct an *ex ante* bidding competition and award the right to serve the market to the group that tenders the best bid" accepting that "the future will take care of itself once the assets have been privatized in this way." The NIE approach in contrast, will be "looking ahead and uncovering *ex post contractual hazards*, thereafter working out the ramifications for alternative modes of governance.... Because franchise bidding works much better for some natural monopoly industries than others . . . the use of franchise bidding will be reserved for those industries where comparative net benefits can be projected—but not otherwise. Privatization, it turns out, is not an all-purpose solution (italics present author)." Or take the case of 'Law and economies', which has flourished as an independent subject acknowledging organic links with NIE. Law does not operate costlessly, a fact that relates it to transaction cost economics. In Posnerian approach of law and economics the courts, as the official agents of the state, settle disputes. NIE in contrast, argues that in many instances participants are able to devise more satisfactory private solutions to their disputes.

Methodological issues define lines of differentiation with some other branches which are closely linked. Evolutionary economists do not follow methodological individualism[4] and usually distant themselves from NIE. This is partly due to the fact that evolutionary economists have neglected certain research agenda which would have brought them and the NIE closer (*Foss*, 2001). In spite of some good start by Schotter and Sugden research in evolutionary game theory[5] has not found much recognition in NIE school; the current NIE literature shows a marked preference for incentive compatible mechanism design than evolutionary games. Emphasis on empirical validity led NIE to be keenly interested in experimental economics, though this is considered as a separate branch.

DEFINING THE SCOPE

NIE is far from well developed. Though some textbooks are now available that introduce the elementary matters, it will be grossly inadequate to introduce NIE only by that limited scope. Among its merits, NIE scholars are trying to define and redefine scope of NIE studies to match the wide variety of institutions and organizations in real life. As the exercise matures more and more research gaps are identified. Though it makes the deficiencies of current state of understanding increasingly conspicuous, the exercise also paves the way for a rich theory to emerge in due course. Even at present there is considerable scope of doing good research. In the next section I will introduce a few areas from the Indian scene, as examples. My third agenda in this section is discussion of certain methodological imperatives that are regarded as the ultimate test for inclusion in NIE School. This is not a methodology in true sense of the term but certain principles that are becoming distinctive marks. I prefer to start with this matter, which Williamson (2000) in a recent article called 'the key good ideas' that are associated with the NIE:

(i) Human Actors are characterized by bounded rationality, opportunism and some amount of foresight, even though not perfect.
(ii) Scope of analysis is feasible organizational alternatives characterized by functional flaws and implementation costs as against ideal types.
(iii) Analytical method is one of moving 'from simple to complex', starting with closer to ideal governance structures and exploring alternative modes of governance suitable under different less-than-ideal situations.
(iv) Operationalization, complete with formalization and empirical testing.
(v) A theory of development that is under construction. NIE studies accepts that formal models need to be tested in empirical situations and can be accepted only when they pass the test. An appropriate theory of development requires rejection of inadequate and improper formal models.

Transaction cost economics though is the backbone of NIE, has wider adherents. Apart from transaction cost, property rights and contracts are the major themes on which current researches on NIE are built. The Mission Statement of the International Society for New Institutional Economics[6] (ISNIE) lists the topics of interest as: the organization and boundaries of the firm, structure and performance of contractual arrangements, the determinants and impacts of property rights and transactions costs on resource allocation and governance institutions, the causes and effects of government regulatory and competition policies, the structure and effects of legal, social and political institutions on economic performance, the role and response of organizations to innovation and technological change, and the nature of economic development and transition economies. Until recently, categorization of these works was being done under two heads: 'institutional environment' and 'institutional arrangement' or 'governance structure'. Recently, Williamson (2000) has developed a more inclusive scheme consisting of four levels:

(1) Social embeddedness level: informal constraints like norms, customs, traditions, religion.
(2) Institutional environment level: formal rules like law, property right, executive, legislative, judicial and bureaucratic functions of the government.
(3) Institution of governance level: aligning governance structure with transactions.
(4) The fourth level where the neoclassical analysis works—including resource allocation and prices.

Williamson hopes that in economics a zero level analysis explaining how mechanisms of mind take shape, will develop in due course.

It is now possible to appreciate why the different contributions in NIE also read so very different. They belong to different levels, or address different issues connecting several levels, which demand different kinds of discourses. Among the well-known NIE works, Coase's seminal papers (1937, 1960) may be included in level 4, being critical of neoclassical economics within its own territory. Williamson's early contributions (1975, 1985, 1996) belong to the third level. North's book (1990), *Institutions, Institutional Change, and Economic Performance*, is a first step to developing a coherent framework connecting all these levels while his earlier works may belong to level 2. Numerous other studies primarily concerned with levels (2) and (3) exist. Empirical works are in abundance in NIE. Both Coase and North, though better known for their theoretical writings, have done some very valuable empirical works. Shelanski and Klein (1995) reviewed more than a hundred NIE empirical studies conducted even before 1993. For some later works one may consult Alston *et. al.* (1996), Menard (2000), World Bank (1995) as well as the papers read at the Annual Conferences of the ISNIE available from their website (http://www.isnie.org/).

Because of the multiple levels and the consequent need for different discourses, a single textbook for studying NIE is almost impossible. The widely read *Institutions, Institutional Change, and Economic Performance* (North, 1990) is a must for familiarization with the broad field[7]. But out of necessity, its exposition is completely different from the distinct style of research that has become the trademark of NIE. The first few chapters of Williamson's (1985) *The Economic Institutions of Capitalism*, is still the best introduction for the laymen. My suggestion for textbooks is: a chapter (ch. 20) in Kreps (1990) and the recent book by Furubotn and Richter (1997). Milgrom and Roberts (1992) provides an excellent comparative assessment instead of a chapter or book dedicated to NIE studies. For further reading one may consult ISNIE or Ronald Coase Institute websites.

RELEVANCE FOR INDIAN SITUATION

In India, a few empirical studies of transaction cost have been done in recent years (*Varde et. al.*, 2001, 2002, *Taneja and Pohit*, 2002). One may recall that the task force on taxation reforms (Kelkar Committee) dealt at length with transaction cost reduction. Trade Facilitation, one of the so-called Singapore Issues in WTO is essentially concerned with transaction cost reduction[8]. However, such issues rest at the fringes of the Indian economy reinforcing the belief that NIE is concerned with the rise of the western world (*North and Thomas*, 1973), the firm, the market, and the law (*Coase*, 1988) or the economic institutions of capitalism (*Williamson*, 1985). There is a doubt whether this theory has any use for understanding the major problems of developing countries like India. NIE scholars do not seem to be too willing to address the problems of the developing world (*Shirley*, 1997). In contrast, some other branches of modern institutional theory have shown much greater interest, e.g. studies of sharecropping (viz. *Singh*, 1989) or Akerlof's (1976) on caste. Recently John Harriss in his Radhakamal Mukherjee Memorial Lecture (*Harriss*, 2003: 17) questioned the utility of the NIE in explaining underdevelopment.

My position is very different from that of my friend Harriss. I feel that NIE has much to offer even for explaining the historical period of the Indian economy. It is true that the economic institutions of capitalism, the firm, the market, and the law, did not develop as well in India as in the western world. The usual explanation, including that of Harriss, use dual economy framework. In another variant, the 'mode of production debate' argued that the nexus of feudalism (or semi-feudalism) proved to be too strong to be easily broken. By admitting the possibility of market failure the NIE literature permits an alternative explanation—that the market did not develop here can well be a case of market failure. The facts are very much in favor of this argument. India has been open to market influence for more than two centuries. By certain combination of events, a trading company, the East India Company came to run the government in India at a time when the traders were still not in hegemony in England. The governance systems the trading Company introduced at the beginning were so extremely market-oriented that no reformer of that period in the Western World would even think of it in his wildest imagination. Under the Farming System (1772), estates were auctioned to the highest bidders. Under the infamous Sunset Law, if an estate owner failed to pay as per the contract within the sunset of a specified date his estate was auctioned again. When this system failed the Company opted for another governance structure—the Permanent Settlement for hundred years (the Zamindari system). When its limitations were noticed they introduced still another—the Ryotwari system. Profit considerations of the trading company, in the form of land revenue earnings, were at the roots of all these choices. The essential distinctions were that in the Permanent Settlement the relational contracts in the countryside survived behind the zamindars while in the Ryotwari system the Company government aspired to replace those by formal contracts. Their successes and failures were determined by the incurrence (and non-incurrence) of necessary transaction costs (*Sengupta*, 2001: 107-133). The consequences were both market failure and failure of modern system of governance in various ways. That countries like India have been a part of the capitalist world for a long time was the position of Marx as well as that of the Dependency Theory. How long would it take for capitalism to radically alter the institutions in colonies? Marx believed it would be fast. That did not happen. The Dependency Theory explained the perpetuation of underdevelopment as part and parcel of capitalism though could not provide any analytical tool for explaining specific phenomena or historical events. I found that NIE approach of explaining perpetual underdevelopment (as well as developments) as market and governance failures can be used even to explain the distinct courses of developments in zamindari and ryotwari areas.

NIE approach is useful for explaining not just the history but also some complicated present-day realities of Indian agriculture. I studied (*Sengupta*, 2001: 167-217) several such modern issues. Here, let me cite one example—the possibility of transforming traditional irrigation management systems of Bihar (*Sengupta*, 2001: 214-217). In Bihar those are still community managed where farmers contribute communal labour. A transition has occurred in south India—in parts of south India after the nineteen seventies those are managed by farmers' cooperatives engaging wage labourer. Why was there no such change in Bihar? I found transactions cost advantage dictates the choice. However, the advantage is on the decline because of social phenomena like caste conflicts. One may note that there is a sharp contrast in the behavioural assumptions made by my friend Harriss and me. Implicit here in my approach is that the farmers are intelligent; whether to accept a new opportunity or not is decided by them on considerations of cost efficiency. Harriss opined, it was a "...paradox of agriculture in Bengal, where cultivators failed for a long time to take opportunities offered by groundwater irrigation" (*Harriss*, 2003:16). He did not inquire whether farmers of Bengal considered groundwater irrigation an 'opportunity'. The likelihood of severe Arsenic problem that has appeared recently after extensive groundwater irrigation was not unknown to farmers of Bengal. I did not study Bengal but I studied the salinity problems in several other parts of India and found (*Sengupta*, 2002) that almost everywhere the 'ignorant' farmers were very reluctant to take up modern irrigation wherever such problems could arise. One great merit of applying the NIE framework will be to relieve the researchers of an old institutional belief of irrationality of every bit of folk wisdom.

Among other areas of application, the ultramodern economic institutions of capitalism are far from insignificant in India today. For example, let us consider the importance of franchise system. It is said that franchising today accounts for 4 percent of India's gross domestic product and is fast expanding. All around us are NUT, APTECH, Pepsi and Coke, Cable TV network and Cell

Phone outlets. The DAV schools have a long history of successful franchising in education services. Others have followed the lead. In the emerging IT industry in nineteen eighties India was one of several countries with certain advantages. It was the franchising innovation in IT education that consolidated India's advantages and gave the country its current position in software. Today franchise accounts for 95 per cent of IT education in India. In just about two decades the leading private sector organization, NUT Ltd., has gone from being a one-location training outfit to a Company with only about 40 wholly owned centers along with 2200 franchised centers within India. Another giant, Aptech has 2150 franchisees in India. These are global players. NUT is present in 38 countries, Aptech in 52. Overseas operations too are managed through franchise avenue. In Cable TV the current controversies on regulation is too well known. The Finance Act 1994 defined franchise in India as business format franchising only. Franchise agreements are now charged to service tax.

CRITICISMS: VALID AND VOID

In the final section I mention some criticisms of the NIE. Various kinds of questions have been raised from both outside and within the NIE research—I have already introduced some. This is not a place to make a thorough assessments of all the issues raised nor is it an exhaustive list. While studying NIE literature and the literature about NIE, readers will find a healthy tendency of making critical assessments found in many contributions. Reflecting my own understanding the exposition here pertains to the points that appealed me most. I have chosen not to indicate the references always because some of these criticisms were raised by several scholars.

Stigler's unkind remarks about the disregard shown by the Coase theorem[9] to differences in wealth or power need mention even after so many years because this is still an oft-repeated criticism.[10] Its replies unfortunately, are not so widely known. Coase (1991) himself had agreed to those remarks but drew attention to the fact that formal models always suffer from such problems. The essential purpose of his work was to show that 'institutions have neither substance nor purpose' in a world without transaction cost. This criticism is taken care of simply by making explicit assumptions about the setting (viz. *Milgrom and Roberts*, 1992: 38-39). Herbert Simon charged the NIE with lacking sufficient empirical support. I have already noted the mass of empirical works. Posner (1993) opined that NIE has contributed more in the way of terminological changes than in significant theoretical advances. I have already discussed that I benefited in more substantive ways. Many others will concur.

Lack of a comprehensive theory and model is a weakness acknowledged by many NIE scholars. I am rather willing to remain patient in this matter. Current tendency in modern institutional economics is to conjure up theories and models by making some modifications in standard neoclassical theories and models. These resulting mixes however, are internally inconsistent (*Furubotn and Richter*, 1997: 442)—in some matters the components are relieved from unreal neoclassical assumptions but in some others they retain the same old limitations. The slow growth in NIE theories may be a reflection of its cautious (overcautious?) attitude to reflect real world situations.

One of the most serious problems of NIE, the efficiency issue, is indeed, such a problem of internal inconsistency. Implicit in NIE is a notion that the actual relations observed are efficient in the sense of transaction cost economizing. This is inconsistent with the bounded rationality assumption for, economizing presumes knowledge of all different forms (omniscient individual). Recently Williamson (2000) has qualified efficiency concept in NIE as that this is about comparative efficiency within the known forms. Then the question arises 'known to whom'. Even here the implicit assumption is that the choice set, though limited under bounded rationality, is still a common knowledge to all the agents and is not constrained by procedural rationality.

The predominance of efficient forms even under bounded rationality may arise in two ways: competition leads to *selection* of efficient form (Alchian), learning leads to *adoption* of efficient form (evolutionary games). Both of these imply that the efficient form may prevail after a *sufficiently long* time. The NIE empirical studies do not specify if either of these evolutionary explanations were assumed or whether the sample chosen had made any allowances for time needed for adjustments by selected units. In fact, evolutionary matters are rarely considered in NIE studies.

Most of NIE is rather static and follow the conventional equilibrium analysis approach.

At the root of this is a lack of clear definition of institutions and organizations. Not just the NIE, most of the modern institutional economic studies fail to make it clear whether they are theorizing on an individual unit, a representative entity or a population characteristic. For showing the importance of transaction cost in a theoretical analysis it does not matter whether the firm analyzed is a single unit or a typical firm representing the whole population of firms. In empirical analysis conducted over several firms this is a serious issue and estimation methods must make, at least implicitly, some assumptions about the homogeneity of firms. On the one hand cultural features like norms and conventions, shared by many individuals in a population, are institutions. On the other hand, a law is also called an institution. Even a place of research, like where I work, is regarded as an institution. One may feel that these are only in popular parlance; the research organization should be rightly called an organization. But in actual uses, even in analytical papers, clear distinctions are not always made (*Nelson*, 1995: 80-82). Witt (2001: 53-54) notes that the absence of population thinking is a general weakness of studies following methodological individualism.

In defense of NIE empirical works, it must be noted that the field is new and starting from data availability and hypothesis formulation, explorations are going on in every area. The NIE scholars themselves have made some excellent assessments of the methods used.[11] NIE has tremendous potential for policy-making (*Shirley*, 1997), and some excellent works exist. The problem here is that numerous institutional features are related. It is often difficult to isolate the most relevant aspects from among them. A hierarchy of factors is still awaited.

Achievements of the NIE are not exactly nominal. Coase's work received its due recognition after an inordinate delay. But lately, recognitions received by the NIE are fast piling up. The criticisms must be seen in this perspective. To a great extent these are internal criticisms reflecting a healthy dissatisfaction with the state of affairs and a widespread urge to improve. Much of it is directed to develop concepts and theories that are better adapted to the complex reality. Economic models have a tendency to quickly fossilize into certain moulds proliferating at a regular distance from the reality. Until now NIE scholars have shown some amount of contempt for such tendency. It is still a long way to achieve the goal of constructing a meaningful economic theory of institution. However, the developments in NIE School is worth watching because here there is a group of scholar who seem to be willing to do the arduous work needed for building such a theory.

Notes and References

1. Earlier, being led by similar consideration, another group of American institutional economists: Veblen-Dewey-Ayres were named 'neoinstitutionalist' (Dopfer ed. 2001: 197).
2. Coase's pioneering analysis (*Coase*, 1937) is credited as the 'precursor' of economics of information (*Stiglitz*, 2000: 1459 fn 40).
3. To the classical economists the primary purpose of economic studies was discovering the mysteries of production. The marginalists, while laying the foundation of mathematical economics, shifted its focus to rational behaviour of a single consumer because here they found a problem readily amenable to the mathematical tools at hand. Production process was assimilated after a couple of decades but as a mirror image of consumption. A fundamental difference between the consumption and production processes is—one is a private action, the other a joint one. A consumer can decide his best option all by oneself, but a single individual in a production process cannot. The recognition of this fundamental difference would have made it imperative for the neoclassical economics to develop as an analysis of systems of interaction. All processes of production and exchange need to be analysed in their institutional contexts (*Sengupta*, 2001:221-2).
4. Armen Alchian however, is an exception. He is respected name in NIE but rarely cited in evolutionary economics school.
5. Later development of evolutionary game theory has shifted the inquiry of its application to studying learning theories as against institutions.
6. See their website http://www.isnie.org/. Also see the website of The Ronald Coase Institute (http://www.coase.org/) engaged in capacity building of younger scholars in this field.
7. North's encyclopedic study elicits a tendency to treat it like a gospel, much like the treatment met by the older institutionalists (e.g. *Fiori*, 2002). Application in empirical work and critical assessment of North's theory on the basis of empirical findings will be more in the spirit of NIE. I did make an effort (*Sengupta*, 2001) to study a single institution through many different phases, under different kinds of governance, as self-sustaining informal relations and also as ripe for institutional

change. It is also a critical assessment of several features of North's theory.

8. We (*Sengupta and Bhagabati*, 2003) did a study of trade facilitation issue in WTO perspective.
9. This is not the 1937 article but Coase's other famous work, "The Problem of Social Cost" published in 1960 (included in *Coase*, 1988).
10. In the same vein Bardhan was critical of the absence of power relations.
11. Klein (1999) has an excellent assessment. The later collections of empirical works too include valuable assessments.

REFERENCES

Akerlof, George A., 1976: "The Economics of Caste and of the Rat Race and Other Woeful Tales," *The Quarterly Journal of Economics*, 90 (4): 599-617.

Alston, Lee J., Eggertsson, Thrainn, and North, Douglass, C. ed. 1996: *Empirical Studies in Institutional Change*, Cambridge, Cambridge University Press.

Bardhan, Pranab, 1989: "Alternative Approaches to the Theory of Institutions in Economic Development" in Bardhan, P. ed., *The Economic Theory of Agrarian Institutions*. Oxford. Clarendon Press.

Brown, W.O., 1998: "Transaction Costs, Corporate Hierarchies, and the Theory of Franchising." *Journal of Economic Behaviour and Organization*. 36: 319-329.

Coase, Ronald H., 1991: "The institutional structure of production", Lecture to the memory of Alfred Nobel, December 9., *American Economic Review*, 1999 (82): 713-719.

Coase, Ronald H. ed. 1988: *The Firm, the Market, and the Law*, Chicago, University of Chicago Press.

Dnes, A. 1996: "The Economic Analysis of Franchise Contracts—Survey Article." *Journal of Institutional and Theoretical Economics*. 152: 297-324.

Dixit, Avinash, "Lawlessness and Economics: Alternative Modes of Economic Governance", forthcoming. (http://www.princeton.edu/~dixitak/home/Chapterl.pdf).

Dopfer, Kurt ed., 2001: *Evolutionary Economics: Program and Scope*, Boston, Kluwer Academic Publishers.

Exim Bank (Export-Import Bank of India), 2003: "Transaction Costs of Indian Exports: A Review", prepared by Planning & Research Group of Exim Bank, Mumbai.

Fiori, Stefano, 2002: "Alternative Visions of Change in Douglass North's New Institutionalism", *Journal of Economic Issues*, 36(4), December, 1025-1043.

Foss, Nicolai, 2001: "Evolutionary Theories of the Firm: Reconstruction and Relations to Contractual Theories", in Dopfer ed. *op. cit*.

Furubotn, Eirik G. and Rudolf Richter, 1997: *Institutions and Economic Theory:*

The Contribution of the New Institutional Economics, Ann Arbor: The University of Michigan Press.

Harriss, John, 2003: '"Borderland of Economies': Institutions, Politics and Culture in the Explanation of Economic Change", *Indian Journal of Labour Economics*, 46(1): 15-26.

Hodgson, Geoffrey M. 1998: "The Approach of Institutional Economics", *Journal of Economic Literature*, Vol. 36 (March), pp. 166-192.

Klein, Peter G. 1999: "New Institutional Economics", http://encyclo.findlaw.com/0530book.pdf.

Kreps, David M., 1990: *A Course in Microeconomic Theory*, Princeton, Princeton University Press.

Lafontaine, F. and M.E. Slade, 1999: "Incentive Constraints and the Franchise Decision." in *Advances in Business Applications of Game Theory*, K. Chatterjee and W. Samuelson (eds.), Kluwer Academic Press.

Menard, Claude, ed. 2000: *Institutions, Contracts and Organizations: Perspectives from New Institutional Economics*, Northampton, MA, Edward Elgar.

Milgrom, Paul and Roberts, John, 1992: *Economics, Organization, and Management*, Englewood Cliffs, New Jersey, Prentice-Hall.

Nabli, M.K. and Nugent, J.B. (1989): The New Institutional Economics and its Applicability to Development. *World Development*, 17, 1333-47.

Nelson, Richard R. 1995: "Recent Evolutionary Theorizing about Economic Change", *Journal of Economic Literature*, 33 (March): 48-90.

North, Douglass C. and Thomas, Robert Paul, 1973: *The Rise of the Western World: A New Economic History*, Cambridge, Cambridge University Press.

North, Douglass C., 1990: *Institutions, Institutional Change and Economic Performance*, Cambridge, Cambridge University Press.

Posner Richard A., 1993: "The New Institutional Economics meets Law and Economics", *Journal of Institutional and Theoretical Economics*, 149: 73-87.

Sengupta, Nirmal, 2001: *A New Institutional Theory of Production*, New Delhi, Sage Publications.

Sengupta, Nirmal, 2002: "Salinity Prevention By Rainwater Harvesting", Keynote address, Indian Society For Ecological Economics, 2nd Biennial Conference, Bhopal, December 2001. Published as "Traditional *vs.* Modern Practices in Salinity Control", *Economic & Political Weekly*, 37(13), March 30.

Sengupta, Nirmal and Moana Bhagabati, 2003: *A study of Trade Facilitation Measures From WTO Perspective*, Report for the Ministry of Commerce and Industries, unpublished.

Shelanski, H.A. and Klein, Peter G., 1995: 'Empirical Research in Transaction Cost Economics: A Review and Assessment', 11, *Journal of Law, Economics, and Organization*, 335-61.

Shirley, Mary M., 1997: "Pressing Issues for Institutional Economists: Views from the Front Lines", Paper presented at the ISNIE Conference, September 19-21, St. Louis (MO), Washington University (mimeo).

Simon, H.A. (1991). "Organizations and markets", *Journal of Economic Perspectives*, 5, 25-44.

Singh, Nirvikar, 1989. "Theories of sharecropping", in Bardhan, P. ed. *The Economic Theory of Agrarian Institutions*, Oxford, Clarendon Press.

Stiglitz, Joseph E., 2000: "The Contributions of Economics of Information to the Twentieth Century Economics", *Quarterly Journal of Economics*, November, 1441-78.

Taneja, Nisha and Sanjib Pohit, 2002: "Characteristics of India's Formal and Informal Trading with Nepal: A comparative Analysis," *Indian Economic Review*, 37(1), 69-89.

Varde, V. *et. al.*, 2001: "Dwell Time Study of Import-Export Cargo," Agricultural Finance Corporation Ltd, Mumbai. (Mimeo).

Varde, V. *et. al.*, 2002: "Study of Process Re-Engineering at Mumbai Port," Agricultural Finance Corporation Limited, Mumbai (Mimeo).

Williamson, Oliver E. (1985), *The Economic Institutions of Capitalism*, New York, NY, Free Press.

Williamson, Oliver E., 2000: "The new institutional economics: Taking stock, looking ahead", *Journal of Economic Literature*, 38:595-613.

Williamson, Oliver E. and Scott Masten ed. 1999: *The Economics of Transaction Costs*, Adelshot, Cheltenham, Edward Elgar Pub.

Witt, Ulrich, 2001: "Evolutionary Economics—An Interpretative Survey", in Dopfer ed. *op. cit.*

World Bank (team led by Mary Shirley), 1995: *Bureaucrats in Business: The Economics and Politics of Government Ownership*, New York: Oxford University Press.

Theoretical Approaches of the New Institutional Economics

N. JAGANATHAN AND D. NAMASIVAYAM

New Institutional Economics (NIE) has emerged as an important paradigm in economics. The aim of NIE is to explain and understand the institutions of society, drawing on theoretical and empirical tools from mainstream economics. By subjecting a vast range of market and non-market institutions to scrutiny, NIE brings still wider areas of social life within the domain of economic analysis. In this connection, an attempt is made in this paper to analyse the different approaches of New Institutional Economics. Sections one and two explain the basic concepts and the different theoretical approaches of NIE respectively. Section three contains the criticisms of NIE.

1. BASIC CONCEPTS IN NIE

All human interactions require a degree of predictability. Individual actions become more predictable when rules—or institutions—bind people. Institutions are needed to facilitate economic life. Indeed, the type and quality of institutions make a great difference to how well the members of a community are able to satisfy their economic aspirations and how fast the economy grows. In short, economic practices are embedded in rules, routines and conventions.

Institutions are the rules of human interaction that constrain possibly opportunistic and erratic individual behaviour, thereby making human behaviour more predictable and thus facilitating the division of labour and wealth creation. They are taken to be the formal and informal rules which govern or at least influence the behaviour of participants of a society as they interact in political and economic activities. The formal rules include laws and regulations as interpreted and enforced by political authority. The informal rules are the shared beliefs about acceptable and unacceptable behaviour enforced by conscience, a result of socialization, based upon the actual and expected reactions of other members of the society. Both the formal and informal rules reflect or embody views about fairness, legitimacy, good and evil, right and wrong.

There are internal and external institutions. *Internal* institutions evolve from human experience and incorporate solutions that have tended to serve people best in the past. Examples include customs, ethical norms, goods manners and conventions in trade, as well as natural laws. *External* institutions are imposed and enforced from above, having been designed and established by political and administrative agents. An example is legislation. External institutions are enforced by explicit formal sanctions (through the law courts and legitimated use of force—the police).

Institutional Economics examines the two-way relationship between institutions and individuals. It is concerned with the effects of institutions on individuals, as well as the transformation of institutions through individual practices. In addition, institutional economics is inter-disciplinary: it engages, borrows and draws on other social sciences such as sociology and political economy. It is appropriate to analyse values: institutions influence how people attain their own personal objectives and are able to realise their fundamental values (such as freedom, justice, security and prosperity). Shared fundamental values in the community support cohesion and motivate people to act within the institutional framework. In that sense, institutional economics draws upon moral philosophy.

NIE expands neo-classical economic theories by incorporating property rights and transaction costs into neo-classical economics to explain economic behaviour. The origin of property rights and transaction costs stems from Coase (1960). The term *"New Institutionalism"* is usually reserved for the work of Ronald *Coase,* Armen *Alchian,* Harold *Desmsetz* and Oliver *Williamson,* and others on the transactions costs and the property rights paradigm. It stresses the need to explore how the definition and enforcement of property rights influence the manner in which economic agents behave.

NIE is an approach to give the importance of Institutions, to which the neoclassical approach gives little attention. New institutional economics is not an approach that conflicts with the classical micro-economic approach, but it has led to gradual adjustments in the latter, from 1970s onward, by adding the institutional component to it. Because of its roots in neoclassical economics it is often called neo-institutional economics.

2. THEORETICAL APPROACHES IN NEW INSTITUTIONAL ECONOMICS

Even though the core concepts of NIE are transactions cost and property rights, the four theoretical streams of NIE are given below:

1. The Property Rights Theory.
2. The Transaction Costs Theory.
3. The Agency Theory/Principal-Agent Theory/Imperfect Informations Theory.
4. The Collective Action Theory.

The division into these four streams suggests a clear distinction between them, but in reality they are interwoven and overlap each other, and many assumptions are implicit. Transaction costs, for example, are a central part of the property rights theory. And the agency theory connects the transaction costs theory with the property rights theory. The division, as strict as it seems, does not everyone fully agree with it, for example, regards the agency theory as a part of the property rights theory. Nevertheless, this division forms a useful analysis of NIE.

2.1 Property Rights

Property rights are rules that define or delimit the range of activities granted to individuals in specific assets. This includes the right to use an asset, the right to derive income from an asset, the right to transfer ownership of an asset, and the right to exclude others from using this asset. This does not mean that these rights are unrestricted; the government can attenuate them by legal restrictions. The central assumption behind the property rights paradigm is that the better the property rights are delineated and the lower the transaction costs, the better the parties involved are capable of internalizing externalities. According to the institutional economists, the existence of transaction costs is a fundamental element in the emergence and evolution of property rights.

Property rights structure the incentives present in an economic system which in turn influences economic behaviour of each economic agent. That is, property right, by defining who has the right to use, change and bequeath a given resource, is an institution which internalises externalities. Property rights can be seen as the institutional arrangements that constrain or direct competition over scarce resources. The emphasis on property rights shows that it is the rights to use a property that are owned instead of the property itself. It is not the resource itself which is owned; it is a bundle, or a portion, of the right to *use* a resource that is owned. In its original meaning, property referred solely to a right, title, or interest, and resources could not be identified as property any more than they could be identified as right, title, or interest.

2.2 Transaction Costs

Transaction costs can be defined as all costs of entering into an agreement or contract: Searching for trading partners, negotiation, verifying information, monitoring, controlling and enforcing the contract including eventual litigation expenses. Thus, *ex ante* costs (before signing the contract), *ex post* cost (after signing the contract) and the costs of signing the contract itself are transaction costs. The features (or attributes) of a transaction determine the size of the transaction costs, and therefore affect the choice of a coordination mechanism (e.g. through the market or a hierarchy). Some of the most important features are asset specificity (the more specific an asset, the more the supplier and demander are dependent upon each other), the uncertainty, the frequency and the scale of transactions. The transaction costs include all the costs connected not only with the use of institutions but also with the creation or change of institutions.

Transaction costs are applied by Coase in two different, but closely related ways. In the nature of the firm (*Coase*, 1937), he actually asks the basic question. Why does a firm exist? He asks this question because the firm is a coordinating mechanism, and according to the neoclassical economists the market is so useful in coordinating exchange. He argues that the size of transaction costs determines the choice for the coordination mechanism. The choice for market forms of coordination or for more hierarchical forms such as the firm (market *versus* hierarchy) can be brought back to the more basic business-like decision between 'make' or 'buy'.

The other way in which Coase applied transaction costs is through an economic analysis of property rights of goods and services. In which he explained the relationship between externalities, property rights and transaction costs. It seems that only his second approach incorporates property rights, and the first approach is about how coordinating mechanisms emerge and evolve. The first approach (also) deals with the way in which the attributes of the transactions in *properly rights* affect the emergence and evolution of organizations. And if that property rights regimes are coordinating mechanisms, then both the transaction costs and the property rights theory are very much linked.

An important implication of transaction costs is the breakdown of fundamental theorems of welfare economics. The purpose of institutions is to economize transaction costs. An institution which for given relative prices and technology minimizes transaction costs is efficient. Property rights, the state, money, capital markets and the legal system are institutions that save transaction costs and facilitate the development of a modern market economy.

2.3 The Agent Theory/Principal Agent Theory/Imperfect Information Theory

The agency theory is that there is a hierarchical system, in which the authority of hierarchically superior actors, seen as the principals, is often delegated to inferior actors, the agents. These agents have to execute the delegated activities in the name of the principal. This theory suggests that the agent has a significant discretionary decision margin. This is so in the first place because it is impossible for the principal to watch over all the activities of the agent, and, because the agent might have its own interests, the principal is not guaranteed the optimal outcome he is pursuing. And in the second place, there is an asymmetric division of information between the principal and the agent. The agent often has more specialized knowledge and is, because he performs the work, closer to the information sources. This all leads to a tension between the agent who has more information and has his own interests, and the principal who tries to pursue his own or his organization's interests and therefore tries to monitor the agent. Initially, the principal-agent theory was an approach to organizational matters in the private sector only, but gradually it has also been applied to the public sector.

This theory can be regarded as a specification of the property rights and the transaction costs theory and seems only applicable in special intra-organizational matters, namely principal-agent relationships.

This theory stresses the importance of missing, incomplete and asymmetric information as well as risk in shaping the relations between agents and providing the scope for institutions. This theory is principal-agent or contract theory, which analyses the optimal design of contracts between two parties that possess factors of production in different proportions and hence are able to achieve mutual gains from entering into a contract. Often, the trade-off between insurance and incentives in contract design is in focus. Imperfect information theory is based on three central assumptions: (i) Individuals (including peasants) are self-motivated, rational and adapt to circumstances, (ii) Information is costly to achieve and process, (iii) Institutions adapt to reflect the information (and other transaction) costs. Thus, institutions are. not to be taken exogenous, but are endogenous, and changes in the environment may lead, with a lag, to changes in institutional structure.

2.4 Collective Action

The focus of collective action theory is collective decision-making. It analyses the factors that promote and retard cooperation within groups to achieve a given goal. Olson was interested in how people cooperate to form interest groups to lobby the state to supply public goods. The major obstacle to collective action is that individuals' free-ride on others' effort towards providing the common good. Free-riding occurs when there is disutility from effort and when individual effort is difficult to monitor and enforce. Under these conditions it is difficult to assign rewards and punishments that provide individual group members with incentives to provide effort towards the public good.

Collective action theory has frequently been applied to analyse issues of natural resource management at the local level. When a group of people collectively own or use a limited resource, it is a collective action problem to develop and maintain institutions for resource management. Also, organising investment and sharing costs of resource improvement entail collective action problems

3. CRITICISMS

The selected and important criticisms of the different approaches of the NIE are given below:

3.1 Degree of Hierarchy Reduces Efficiency

Many new institutional economists believe that property rights regimes evolve towards efficiency. Changes in regimes are provoked by technological innovations and the opening up of new markets.

But the use of the concept of efficiency does not imply that it is understood and used in an unequivocal way. Because, property rights have no general applicability, but must be narrowed to special groups. The government establishes rules, which have to be obeyed, even though they are not necessarily efficient for society. The restricted applicability to close-knit groups reduces efficiency. Institutions, in the commercial world in reality, seem to be quite robust and path dependent and not very sensitive to the degree of efficiency realized.

3.2 Inefficiency in Constrained Optimization

The new institutional economics defined efficiency as constrained maximization. Efficiency conditions are seen as the properties of a determinate (equilibrium) solution implied by a given theoretical construct. On this view, a system's solutions are always efficient if they meet the constraints that characterize it. Therefore, an allocation is efficient when it is maximized within the constraints. But the optimal efficiency cannot be achieved due to the institutional constraints and bounded rationality. Moreover, the assumption behind constrained optimization is that constraints are given and unavoidable. But in practice not every constraint is unavoidable for everyone. So, the discussion is what is avoidable and what is unavoidable. This becomes especially important when related to personal qualities and tastes of individual decision-makers. This is highly subjective and therefore difficult to determine. Efficiency in the above sense is hard to operate.

3.3 Process Inefficiency

There are many transaction cost economists who regard transaction costs, although this reasoning often seems implicit, as the determinants of efficiency. This approach deals with the minimization of the (transaction) costs of the process towards that output. So, this approach could be characterized by the term process efficiency.

Transaction costs have a significant heuristic value whether they are measured or not. Heuristic in this sense means that the exact quantity cannot be determined, but their order of magnitude can be approximated, especially when different sums of transaction costs of different property rights regimes are compared with each other. In addition, transaction costs do not necessarily have to be expressed in money, but can also be expressed in time, energy and efforts. This allows saying that more about the efficiency of a property rights regime. But, the determination of transaction costs is not a routine job. Moreover, no-one who has tried to measure them has come with completely satisfying results.

3.4 Assumption of Individuality

The criticism is directed to one of the basic assumptions, namely, the assumption of individuality. In reality many decisions are made by groups, and groups do not always follow the same logic as individuals do. In groups people do not always have their own critical opinion regardless of what others in their surrounding think. Nevertheless, the aggregation of individual interests forms the interest of the organization. This organization acts like an individual actor with its own single interest. For example, a municipality may exercise individual property rights in land, just like a household, and is legally not any different from that household. If one regards an organization as an individual actor one could also argue that the assumption of methodological individualism does not have to be rejected. Even then, it is more difficult to maintain the assumption of methodological individualism.

3.5 Immobility of Resources for Inefficient Allocation

The Coase theorem has a limited applicability to landed property, because of the immobility of land. Because, he argues that one of the main requirements for efficient allocations of resources is the mobility of all the resources. Many assets like buildings and infrastructure (e.g. a canal) are tied to the land they are built upon, by physical nature or law. So, these resources cannot be put to the most efficient use (with regard to the output mix). Therefore, the Coase theorem in its pure form is not very useful. Moreover, many planners in Europe are not very concerned with the (land) economics of planning. Many have written more on equity, fairness and aesthetic matters.

3.6 Transaction Costs Fit for Every Thing but for Nothing

The distinction between transaction cost economics and imperfect information approach is not always clear. This is because information problems are one component of transaction costs. Transaction cost theory, to the extent it relies on unobservable and unquantifiable transaction costs, cannot be falsified. Indeed, a common criticism of NIE is the failure to rigorously define and measure transaction costs, and instead to rely on theoretical constructs. Transaction costs risk becoming a fit-all concept useful for explaining everything, and thereby nothing.

3.7 Inherent Limitation in the Fundamental Analysis of Institutions

Transaction cost and imperfect information theory are often used for functional analysis of institutions and thereby understanding the role performed by given institutions to reduce transaction costs, to compensate for missing markets and to improve economic efficiency. Yet, one should be conscious of the limitations inherent in functionalist approaches. By pointing to the purpose of a specific institution, no one explained it. For example, while rightly arguing that property rights in land serve important purpose of internalisation of environmental and farming externalities, no one explained how property rights develop and change over time and the social processes needed to create them. Bardhan brings out this point very clearly when he criticises transaction cost and imperfect information economics.

3.8 Institutions are always Optimal is Absurd

The assertion that institutions are always optimal seems absurd when confronted with reality. Without careful empirical analysis (which is rare) functionalist explanations may become justifications for irrational or non-functional institutions. Theories purporting to explain institutions functionally fall short by failing to consider inertia, friction, vested interests, agency and collective action problems. In sum, the role of history and politics is ignored.

The new institutional economics have made some major changes to the neoclassical theory. But the new institutional economics have not caused the end of the neoclassical paradigm. Some of the hard core elements that exist in Neo-Classical and Neo-Institutional approaches are stable preferences (wealth maximization), rational choices (although often bounded) and equilibriums. Neo-institutional economics (NIE) resolved some major shortcomings of the neoclassical approach even though it has a few shortcomings.

REFERENCES

Alchian, A.A. and H. Demsetz (1973): "The Property Right Paradigm", *The Journal of Economic History*, 33, 16-27

Bardhan, P. (1989b): "The New Institutional Economics and Development Theory: A Brief Critical Assessment", *World Development*. 17(9), 1389-90.

Coase, R.H. (1937): "The Nature of the Firm", *Economica*. 4, 386-405.

Coase, R.H. (I960): "The Problem of Social Cost", *Journal of Law and Economics*, 3, 1-44.

Neelakantan, S. (1992): "New Institutional Economics and Agrarian Change—A Premier", Indian Economic Society Trust Publication, New Delhi, 22-25.

Nocholas Faysse (1994): "Recent Results of NIE as a Basis of Analysing Common Pool Resources", Research Paper, New York.

Rasmus Heltberg (1998): "New Institutional Economics: A Survey of Property Rights and Natural Resource Management", *A Survey of NIE and Development Issues*, New York.

Williamson, O.E. (1999): Public and Private Bureaucracies: A Transaction Costs Economics Perspective", *Journal of Law, Economics and Organization*, 15, 306-42.

Conventional Economics in the New Institutional Framework

M.K. Dasgupta

I

By institutional economics we understand a type of economic analysis which emphasises the role of social, political and economic organization in determining economic events. The conventional economic analysis either in the classical framework or in the neo-classical structure completely ignore the non-economic environment in which individuals make decisions. In the classical and neo-classical analysis we study the relationship between the economic variables which are basically objective in nature. However, in the econometric studies the impacts of stochastic components are included in the measurement process such that the effects of some sorts of non-economic factors are measured. The emphasis on the role of institutions in economic affairs is a criticism of conventional economics in the classical or neo-classical framework. The movement of economic analysis introducing institutions of social, political and economic organizations flourished in the early 20th Century under the influence of T.B. Veblem and W.C. Mitchell (1874-1948). The movement gained momentum through a bunch of economists during 1950's under the leadership of G.K. Myrdal who have emphasised the importance of the social and political structure within which the economy operates and attempted to use a broader method of economic analysis encompassing the disciplines of politics and sociology.[1]

II

Now the question arises that why economists are continuously searching for the new direction for institutional framework. We may try to find out answers from historical perspective. The basic economic problems of production and distribution were first analysed theoritically by Physiocrats assuming an institutional framework where three following fundamental conceptions prevailed:

(i) the conception of natural rights,
(ii) the idea of beneficient Providence, and
(iii) the doctrine of *laissez-faire*.

The ideas of Physiocrats were the reaction against the institution of the then state dominance, the characteristics of which were the French nobility and monarchy, the economic and social evils of the monarchical state. Actually the Physiocrats were in revolt against art, artificial wealth and political artifices of wealth getting. Similar type of state dominance under the king and church in England inspired Adam Smith to lay the foundation of the new Science-Economics under the institution of *laissez-faire*. Even though Adam Smith played the role of a critic of Physiocracy, he was undoubtedly indebted to Diderot, Akembert, Turgot and Quesnay. Adam Smith accepted the originality of the theoretical ideas of the Physiocrats as the then new institutional economics which developed: (i) the idea that every social phenomenon was subject to 'natural law', (ii) the idea that self-interest was the prime source of human motivation and could bring about the social optimum, (iii) the concept of free competition resulted in the establishment of *bon prix*, and (iv) the idea of indispensability of landed property. Both Adam Smith and the physiocrats were valiant proponents of economic liberalism. Economic variables under such institutional frame work will be working on the basis of complete free choice of individuals whose preferences were communicated by the market to profit maximizing firms. They again go through the price system which is fixed by the *invisible hand* for purchasing inputs and supply final goods to the consumers who being the price takers show their preferences for purchasing commodities and the whole process of circular flow continues smoothly. Thus the state intervention was considered futile by the followers of Adam Smith and the whole group of classical economists. *Laissez-faire* or uncontrolled capitalism was accepted as ideal institutional framework under the perspective of the economy controlled by the french nobility and monarchy, England's church and king, From the days of Adam Smith institution as free enterprise system flourished and a generation allowed themselves to be covered by the spectre of a relentless monolith of the free world.

With the alternative institutional system emerging in East Europe and some other countries under the leadership of the Soviet Union just after the Second World War, young generation every where were no longer automatically adopting the overall perspectives of commodity society as the unquestionable limits of their own aspirations. The ardent supporters of uncontrolled capitalism chose to treat economics as a respectable science and make extra ordinary gradation into pure theory, monetary economics, international economics, industrial economics, labour economics, development economics, welfare economics and so on. All these categories have a set of assumptions:

(i) Capitalism is accepted as the socio-economic institutional structure.
(ii) Absence of irreconciliable conflicts of interest between social groups.
(iii) Passionate Individualism.
(iv) The state is an impartial arbitrator, not committed to any particular class or group.

With the assumption of free competition and absolute freedom of individual, all statements about society, are reduced to those about privatized, self-seeking individuals. The neoclassical economists shifted their focus of attention from fundamental social issues to efficient allocation of resources assuming capitalism essential social and economic institutions. Again new institutional periphery was searched for, as in the Capitalist framework the economists became sycophants of inequality, alienation, commodity fetishism, destruction of the environment, imperialism, racism, and the subjugation of women. The basic idea of neo-classical school is related to the neo-classical value theory which becomes essentially a theory of the allocation of scaree resources in a static economy. Further the modern neo-classical economics may be said to incorporate most of the central ideas of its founders, viz. J.M. Clark, F.Y. Edgeworth, I. Fisher, A. Marshall, V. Pareto, L. Walras and K. Willsell who used marginal analysis (the concept of marginal utility and marginal productivity) to analyse the pricing of goods, services and factors of production in competitive markets. They emphasised that the market prices of goods and factors were related to their scarcities. In particular, they studied the possibility of a set of market prices which ensured the equality of supply of demand in all markets. The idea of perfectly Competitive economy in equilibrium, which may be attributed especially to Walras, is central to the neo-classical scheme.

Thus the existence of the competitive market is the pre-condition for achieving optimal allocation of resources. However, Pigou's Wealth and Welfare questioned this basic assumption particularly in that case where there are technological externalities. These are goods for which no market can be formed. In that case is state intervention to be saught? Professor K.J. Arrow, however, rests faith on neo-classical theory especially in its compretive form and hence change of institutional framework under state guidance is unnecessary according to him. He believes that "The neo-classical theory, in its competitive form, can be and has been given a rich formal development. Parenthetically, one cause for the persistence of neo-classical theory in the face of its long line of critics is precisely that for some reason of mathematical structure, the neo-classical theory is highly manipulable and flexible, when faced with specific issue, it can yield meaningful implications relatively easily . . . . In its most formal statement, we simply use for analysis the equilibrium conditions of the individual agent and of the market, without inquiry as to how they come to hold."[2] But professor Arrow was very much conscious about the two basic limitations of neo-classical system, the first being the existence of unemployment which is clearly a direct contradiction to the notion of the smoothly clearing market, and the second one is the differential levels of economic development which point to a difficulty with the other fundamental concept, the conditions of optimization. He mentions, "If countries differ in their production possibility sets, then firms occupying similar economic problems are facing different constraints on their optimization. This does not contradict the fundamental assumption of optimising behaviour, but it does raise severe questions about its interpretation. The simplest hypothesis is to take the technological conditions as data, possibly varying over time due to exogenous changes in scientific knowledge. But here we are asserting that two contemporaries have different access to productive knowledge, clearly, we are saying something about the conditions of transmission of knowledge across national boundaries, and of course the same questions arise among firms or workers within a single economy. The constraints on the firm's optimization begin to seem more like variables to be explained than like constraints exogenously given."[3]

III

The search for new institution because of the incompatibility of classical or neo-classical economics under uncontrolled Capitalism with the objective of human welfare in the form of higher employment opportunities, reduction of inequality and alienation, restoration of environment, removal of racism and religious fanaticism, bringing *'liberté, égalité, pour'* weaker sex, etc. has been felt by social reformers. New era started after the October revolution which declared that all resources belonged to the common people and all decisions regarding consumption and production would be undertaken by the state. Thus the two extreme forms, first one being the uncontrolled capitalism, the second becomes perfect socialist economy or command economy, were prevalent during the three decades starting from the twenties of the twentieth Century. But as a substitute of 'Free-enterprise' economy socialist economy faced several constraints The post-revolution Soviet Union went through crucial economic problem viz. to procure surplus grains for the urban areas and the heavy industries programme of the post revolution government.

With the breakdown of socialism in Soviet Russia, in 1990's World attention goes towards market economy and the supporters of capitalism start eulogising it without mentioning the basic conditions of capitalist development which have been violated time and again. The basic conditions for the success of market economy depends heavily on: (i) consumer's sovereignty, (ii) right to information, and (iii) minimum ethical values. Unfortunately all these conditions were never fulfilled. Further, entrepreneural efficiency has been accepted as complementary to corruption and monopolisation which is the total distortion of the market economy. With the tremendous progress of science and technology, the rate of return on capital has been increased many times. But quality of life of a vast majority of population have been continuously deteriorating. Particularly the less developed countries are suffering from poverty, unemployment, inflation and stagflation and institutionalisation of corruption.

On the other extreme side the perfect command economy though ensured a large number of basic amenities to the people often suffered from low level equilibrium trap, yet the party dictatorship brought bureaucratisation and ultimately corruption and crime against humanity. Consumer's sovereignty as a rule has never been accepted, and the complete cover up of the transparency system of right to information led to severe distortions. Further, the aspiration level which have been glaringly exhibited under capitalism, can never be achieved under socialism. This often has brought frustration among the common people. Under such circumstances the world became the witness of the breakdown of socialism in U.S.S.R. and in other East European countries. In view of this abnormal phenomenon, the revival of capitalism in its original Adam Smithian form has been propagated by the proponents of the capitalism. But the question of Schumpeter "can capitalism survive" has not been seriously considered. His "Crumbling walls" are sufficient for non-acceptance of capitalism in its original form.

IV

A search for new direction has been started since the thirties of this century. Two alternatives: (i) Market Socialism, and (ii) Mixed Economy in democratic framework have been suggested. In case of market socialism, socialistic economic system leaves the day-to-day running of the economy to the market mechanism. In the 1930s Lange originally put forward the notion which has been experimented first in Yugoslavia and later in many East European countries, theoretically expounded by Ota Sik but with time bound success. On the other hand, mixed economic system in a democratic framework has been experimented in some countries. Again a large number of distortions have been generated particularly in the less developed countries like India and development has been severely retarded. Under such circumstances a search for new direction—an alternative approach is extremely urgent. In this respect one thing must be remembered that the extreme form of market economy or complete *laissez faire* system was never existed. Control was there. The question is control by whom and to what extent. Is it a state control ? Or it is a control of a cartel. Whatever may be the type of control, the distortions could not be avoided and Schumpetarian optimism for transformation of capitalists into socialism without violent revolution and without losing the good features of capitalism is belied. The search for new direction comes of the basic institutional frameworks on which it must depend on. By the following theoretical model we try to explain the features of the new direction.

After Soviet Revolution the economists could not come out of the two basic Institutional framework that is (i) complete free market economy (F), and (ii) absolute controlled economy (C). They only suggested to a coexistence of both F and C and then try to find out a feasible region so as to reach a maximized zone. Mathematically it is possible to reach the optimum profit both for a single objective criterion and a multiple objective criteria by applying classical linear programming method or a more sophisticated method of fuzzy goal programming technique. In this endeavour they try to reach a solution in FOC zone.

To have a solution suppose the bounded region POQ is more reliable where OP and OQ limit the impossibility of F and C. Then either mixed economic system in a democratic framework or a market socialist structure as prescribed by Oscar Lange exists. But in both cases we have experienced that serious distortions are observed. Thus we need a third axis which will give better index of development free from other distortions. Suppose Z is the third

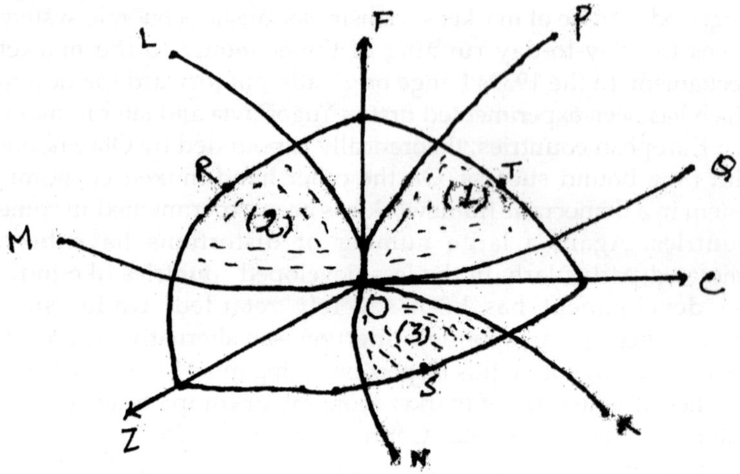

axis, though it is not completely free from the influence of F and C. Thus Z is in some way or other depends either on the two. Suppose we define Z in such a way as it depicts an institution where ruling group maintains a minimum ethical quality. We further define the minimum ethical quality as follows: (i) The ruling group can not be bribed (as for example the involvement of ruling group in Bofors case or in security scandal on in Tehelka case is an impossibility), (ii) They maintain neutrality in policy framing (pressure from any group within or outside the country can not change the accepted policy), (iii) Nepotism in publicity life does not occur (no minister, at least project their sons and daughters as future business magnet or future minister), (iv) They do not give false promises to win election, (v) Politician-criminal nexus will never occur. Many other values may be added or deleted at a particular point of time.[4]

Defining Z in that way we may say Z = z (F, C). Now whatever may be the institutional framework the quality of the ruling group in Z is always acceptable. Hence the feasible zones, LOM and KON are preferable to the zone POQ.[5] The probability of higher optimum points in the regions '2' (LOM zone) and '3' (KON zone) is greater than that in the region '1'. For the last three hundred years it has been found that the feasible points in the Zone POQ, if nearer to the F axis brought innumerable social maladies inspite of its tremendous initial success. Similarly for the points in the same zone nearer to C-axis could not satisfy the aspiration level of people as evident from the breakdown of Soviet Union and other East European countries. As institutional framework both failed to fulfil the minimum expectations of the people. The institutional framework under F, however, has been charged with built-in exploitative nature which ultimately commits crime against humanity. But that under C is basically more humane in nature, but certain endogenous factors lead it to commit the same crime. Thus control or no control it matters little, the zones connected with the Z-axis would definitely bring better results.

The three arbitrary points, T, R, S, on the highest available level on the bounded zone show optimality in the three zones. Then we say RpT and SpT. R and S are indifferent. From the history of capitalism and socialism the points in the zone FOC bring severe distortions through monopolization, bureaucratization and criminalization. But either of the two P or C, coupled with Z in which primitive forces like might is right, survival of the fittest struggle for existence chicanery is the best policy, etc. are controlled by the quality people with ethical values. Thus all the points in the feasible region of FOC are less preferable to those in both the regions FOZ and COZ. Obviously the optimum points R and S are logically preferable to T.

V

Finding the feasible region and having obtained the optimum points we should try to explain the characteristics of the optimum points. If Z-axis and C-axis form the feasible region, worker's dominance is established but in the region ZOF, entrepreneural efficiency and competition will dominate. In that region the workers do not understand that the surplus value generated by them has no relevance on their level of living. It is simply utilized by the capitalists as profit. It is never reinvested for the improvement of the standard of living of the workers. Still the quality of ruling class protects their interests. Whatever may be the relations between worker's entrepreneurs and other parasite classes they can not go away from the three feasible regions as shown in the diagram. Thus from the foregoing analysis We find that the search for new institutional economics is for optimizing the basic goals suggested since the time of French revolution

'Liberté, egalité, Fraternité,' which thought to ensure basic minimum needs by removing the bondage of common people both politically and economically. This type of institution can only exist with quality ruling group. Otherwise the institutional set-up of the economy would make hardly any difference.

Notes and References

1. Allocation and its commodity fetish manifestation, under capitalism, go well beyond the strictly economic sphere. Berger and Pullberg (1966) explain how in Marxian thought this is conceived to extend through all human experience "the autonomization of the economic is paradigmatic of the autonomization of the whole range of social relations. In other words, there are not only fetished commodities, but there is also fetishized power, fetishized sexuality, fetishized status. Just as the fetishism of commodities finds its theoretical experience in a refied political economy so the other species of fetishization are theoretically formulated and thereby mystified in reified political science, reified sociology, reified psychology and even scientific philosophy."
2. *Collected Papers of Kenneth J Arrow*—Reprinted paper No. 12, Vol. 4, pp. 155.
3. *Ibid.*, p. 156.
4. J.A. Schumpeter apprehended that crumbling walls would never allow Capitalism to grow without compromise. His explanation of crambling walls led him to the view that Capitalism may well be transformed into socialism without violent revolution (Schumpeter (1966): *Capitalism, Socialism and Democracy*).
5. The dependency of each axis makes the limiting lines nonlinear and there are simultaneous relations as F = F (z, c) and C = C (Z, F) which break the linearity assumption.

References

Arrow, K.J. (1974), *Limited knowledge and Economic Analysis*—Presidential Address, Eighty-sixth meeting of the American Economic Association, New York. Reprinted IASR Press, Chennai, India.

Arrow, K.J. and Hahn, F.H. (1971), *General Competitive Analysis*.

Berger, P. and Pullberg, S. (1966), 'Reflection and Sociological Critique of Conciousness', *New Left Review*, Vol. 35.

Dasgupta, M.K. (1998), "Market Failure and Breakdown of Socialism, A Search for New Direction", *Market Capitalist and Socialism* (ed.) R.K. Sen, New Book Stall, Kolkata.

Dobb, M. (1969), *Welfare Economics and Economics of Socialism—Towards a Commonsense, Critique,* Cambridge University Press.

Dorfman, R. (1967), *Prices and Markets,* Prentice-Hall.

Dutt, B., Panda, S., Pattanaik, P.K. (1986): "Exact Choice and Fuzzy Preferences", *Mathematical Social Sciences,* Vol. II.

Friedman, M. (1967), 'Value Judgements in Economics' in S. Hook (ed.), *Human Values and Economic Policy,* New York University Press.

Fellner, W. (1949), *Competition Among the Few,* Knopf.

Galbralth, J.K. (1958), *The Affluent Society,* Miffin.

Goodman, D.A. (1974), *A Goal Programming Approach to Aggregate Planning of Production and Work-force,* Management Science.

Lerner, A.P. (1944): The Economics of Control, McMillan, New York.

Myrdal, G. (1953): *The Political Element to the Development of Economic Theory,* Routledge and Kegan Paul.

Scitovsky, Tibor (1962): "On the Principles of Consumer's Sovereignty," *American Economic Review.*

Schumpeter, J.A. (1966) *Capitalism, Socialism and Democracy,* Unwin University Books (Eleventh impression).

Dobb, M. [illegible] Cambridge University Press.

[illegible] (1967) [illegible] Prentice-Hall.

[illegible] Patnaik, P.K. (1990) 'Exact Choice and [illegible]', [illegible] Vol. [illegible]

[illegible], M. (1967) 'Value Implications in Economics' in S. Hook (ed.) [illegible] Values and Economic Policy, New York University Press.

[illegible] (1975) [illegible]

[illegible] (1978) [illegible]

[illegible] A Framework [illegible] of [illegible] Economic Science

[illegible] (1936) [illegible] Macmillan, New York.

[illegible]

[illegible]

[illegible]

SECTION II

NIE AND ISSUES IN DEVELOPMENT STUDIES

Role of Institutions in Economic Development

Bharati D. Dave

Introduction

The term 'new institutional economics' (NIE) was originated by Williamson (1975). NIE, which began to develop as a self-conscious movement in the 1970s, traces its origins to Coase's analysis of the firm (*Coase*, 1937). The new institutional economics is an attempt to incorporate a theory of institutions into economics. It builds on, modifies, and extends neoclassical theory to permit it to embrace some problems, which could not be tackled earlier. What it retains and builds on is the fundamental assumption of scarcity and hence competition—the basis of the choice theoretic approach that underlies micro-economics. What it abandons is instrumental rationality—the assumption of neoclassical economics that has made it an institution-free theory. How does this new institutional approach fit in with neo-classical theory? It begins with the scarcity hence competition postulate; it views economics as a theory of choice subject to constraints; it employs price theory as an essential part of the analysis of institutions; and it sees changes in relative prices as a major force inducing change in institutions. How does this approach modify or extend neo-classical theory? In addition to modifying the rationality postulate, it adds institutions as a critical constraint and analyzes the role of transaction costs as the connection between institutions and costs of production. New institutional economics is in real sense an interdisciplinary approach combining many disciplines such as economics, law, organization theory, political science, etc. to understand the institutions of social, political and commercial life. "But its primary language is economics." (Klien Peter, G., p. 1) Can this approach help us in understanding the development process in a better way? This note proposes to briefly survey some of the works that link institutions and development. Section I discusses the concepts of institutions and organizations. Section II pays attention to functions and quality of institutions and put up briefly some of the very recent studies published by IMF. Finally a summary and implications in Indian context are briefly narrated.

I

Institutions

It may be useful to begin with Davis and North's (1971) distinction between the 'institutional environment' and 'institutional arrangements'. The former refers to the background constraints, or 'rules of the game', that guide individuals' behaviour. These can be both formal, explicit rules (constitutions, laws, property rights) and informal, often implicit rules (social conventions, norms). While these background rules are the product of—and can be explained in terms of—the goals, beliefs and choices of individual actors, the social result (the rule itself) is typically not known or 'designed' by anyone. Institutional arrangements, by contrast, are specific guidelines—what Williamson (1985), calls 'governance structures'—designed by trading partners to mediate particular economic relationships. Business firms, long-term contracts, public bureaucracies, non-profit organizations and other contractual agreements are examples of institutional arrangements.

In brief institutions are humanly-devised constraints that structure human interaction. They are composed of formal rules, informal constraints, norms of behaviour, and self-imposed codes of conduct, and the enforcement characteristics of both. The institutional environment forms the framework in which human action takes place. 'Institutions reduce uncertainty by providing a structure to everyday life', writes North (1990, p. 3). "In the jargon of the economist, institutions define and limit the set of choices of individuals. Institutional constraints include both what individuals are prohibited from doing and, sometimes, under what conditions some individuals are permitted to undertake certain activities. . . . They are perfectly analogous to the rules of the game in a competitive team sport" (*North*, 1990, pp. 3-4).

However according to Hali Edision, "The term institution has been defined in different ways. Douglass North describes institutions very broadly, as the formal and informal rules governing human interactions. There are also narrow (and easier to grasp) definitions of institutions that focus on specific organizational entities, procedural devices, and regulatory frameworks. At a more intermediate level, institutions are defined in terms of the degree of property rights protection, the degree to which laws and regulations are fairly applied, and the extent of corruption. It is narrower than North's definition, which includes all the norms governing human interactions. Much of the recent research into determinants of economic development has adopted the intermediate definition." (*Hali Edison*, 2003, p. 36)

Organisations

But then what are organizations? Again according to North, "Organizations are the players: groups of individuals bound by a common purpose to achieve objectives. They include political bodies (political parties, the senate, a city council, a regulatory agency); economic bodies (firms, trade unions, family farms, cooperatives); social bodies (churches, clubs, athletic associations); and educational bodies (schools, colleges, vocational training centers. (*North, ibid.*, p. 5)

Having briefly introduced new institutional economics, institutions and organizations, section II discusses role and quality of institutions and deep determinants of development including institutions.

II

Functions of Institutions

Most of the recent work on institutions and economic growth has focused on the importance of a particular set of institutions, namely, those that protect property rights and ensure that contracts are enforced. One can call them market-creating institutions since, in their absence, markets either do not exist or perform very poorly. But long-run economic development requires more than just a boost to investment and entrepreneurship. It also requires effort to build three other types of institutions to sustain the growth momentum, build resilience to shocks, and facilitate socially acceptable burden sharing in response to such shocks. These institutions might be called—

Market regulating: namely, those that deal with externalities, economics of scale, and imperfect information. Examples include regulatory agencies in telecommunications, transport, and financial services.

Market stabilizing: namely, those that ensure low inflation, minimize macroeconomic volatility, and avert financial crises. Examples include central banks, exchange rate regimes, and budgetary and fiscal rules.

Market legitimizing: namely, those that provide social protection and insurance, include pension systems, unemployment insurance schemes, and other social funds.

Quality of Institutions

In the recent period a lot of attention is paid on the quality of institutions, as quality of institutions is considered more important for faster growth. Thus according to Acemoglu (2003), "Good institutions have three key characteristics; enforcement of property rights for a broad cross-section of society, so that a variety of individuals have incentives to invest and take part in economic life; constraints on the actions of elites, politicians, and other powerful groups, so that these people cannot expropriate the incomes and investment of others or create a highly uneven playing field; and some degree of equal opportunity for broad segments of society, so that individuals can make investment, especially in human capital, and participate in productive economic activities" (*Acemoglu*, p. 27). He is of the opinion that such good institutions are non-existent in many societies even to day, which is one of the main reasons for relatively underdeveloped conditions of these economies.

How is institutional quality measured? According to Hali Edison (2003), "Recent empirical analyses have typically considered three relatively broad measures of institutions—the quality of governance, including the degree of corruption, political rights, legal protection of private property and how well such laws are enforced; and the limits placed on political leaders. The measures themselves are not objective but, rather, the subjective perceptions and assessments of country experts or the assessments made by residents responding to surveys carried out by international organizations and non-governmental organizations.

The first of these measures—the aggregate governance index—is the average of the six measures of institutions developed. These measures include: (1) voice and accountability—the extent to which citizens can choose their government and have political rights, civil liberties, and an independent press; (2) political stability and absence of violence—the likehood that the government will not be over-thrown by unconstitutional or violent means; (3) government effectiveness—the quality of public service delivery and competence and political independence of the civil service; (4) regulatory burden—the relative absence of government controls on foods markets, banking systems, and international trade; (5) rule of law—the protection of persons and property against violence and theft, independent and effective judges, and contract enforcement; and (6) freedom from graft—public power is not abused for private gain or corruption."

"A second measure focuses on property rights. This measure indicates the protection that private property receives; yet another measure, constraints on the executive, reflects institutional and other limits placed on presidents and other political leaders. In a society with appropriate constraints on elites and politicians, there is less fighting between various groups for control of the state, and policies are more sustainable." (*Hali Edison, ibid.*, p. 36) The study finds that institutional quality does have a significant effect, not only on the level of income but also on growth and the volatility of growth.

Deep Determinants of Level of Development

Economic development is no longer regarded as a gradual, inevitable transformation from local autarky to specialization and the division of labour. Instead, development is seen as a response to the evolution of institutions that support social and commercial relationships. Economic growth thus depends on the degree to which the potential hazards of trade (shirking, opportunism and the like) can be controlled by institutions, which reduce information costs, encourage capital formation and capital mobility, allow risks to be priced and shared and otherwise facilitate cooperation.

Discussing the causes for the level of economic development, Dani Rodrik and Arvind Subramanian (2003), considers three main deep determinants of level of development. First geography. Geography is the key determinant of climate and of natural resource endowments, and it can also play a fundamental role in the disease burden, transport costs, and extent of diffusion of technology from more advanced areas that societies experience, it influence on agricultural productivity and the quality of human resources. A second view emphasizes the role of international trade as a driver of productivity change and income growth. We call this the integration view because it gives participation in the large global economy. A third view centers on institutions—in particular, the role of property rights and the rule of law. In this view, what matters are the rules of the game in a society, as defined by prevailing explicit and implicit behavioural norms and their ability to create appropriate incentives for desirable economic behaviour. This view, associated with Noble Prize winner Douglass North (1990), has recently been the subject of a number of econometric studies, in particular by Daron Acemoglu, Simon Johnson, and James Robinson (2001).

Discussing interrelationship between these three variables, the above authors agree that causality is very complex. The difficulty. lies in disentangling the complex web of causality involving these factors and income levels. Geography is the only one of these deep determinants that can be treated as exogenous or not influenced by income. In order to highlight the interrelationship the authors present the following chart.

Authors find that the quality of institutions is the only positive and significant determinant of income levels. Institutions are

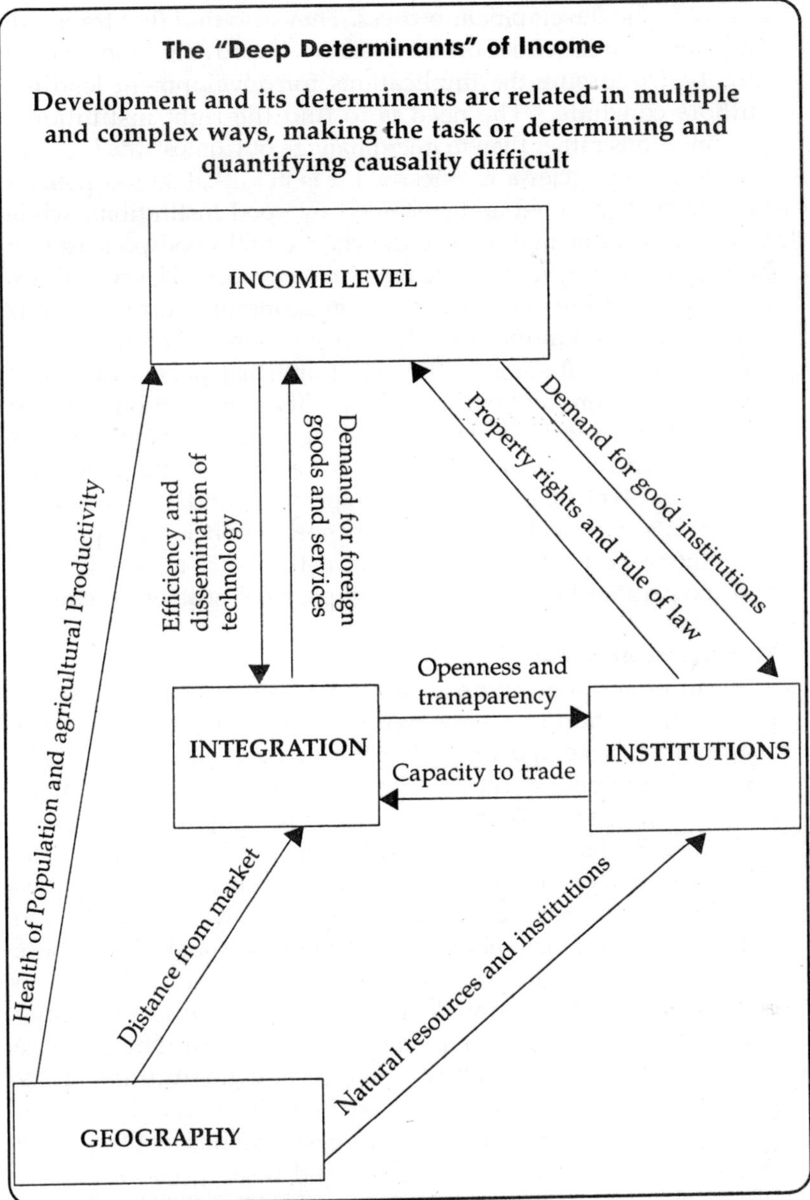

Source: Dani Rodrik and Arvind Subramanian, "The primacy of institutions (and what this does and does not mean)", "Finance & Development", pp. 31-34, June 2003.

critical to the development process. They also find that trade can have an indirect effect on incomes by improving institutional quality. Discussing the implications for development lending, authors conclude, "The need is to find the right institutional preconditions rather than to micromanage outcomes" (*ibid.*, p. 34).

As far as policies are concerned it is held that sound policies need to be supported and sustained by good institutions, while weak institutions may reduce the chance that good policies will be adopted or may undermine policy effectiveness. Hence, policies are important but their influence on economic performance is already reflected in the strength of institutions. The foregoing is a brief account of some of the IMF published papers that have found institutions and particularly quality of institutions a major determinant of level of development, etc. In fact, recent papers have argued that institutions explain nearly everything about a country's level of economic development and that resource constraints, physical geography, economic policies, geopolitics, and other aspects of internal social structure, such as gender roles and inequalities between ethnic groups, have little or no effect.

The Broader View

'institutions only' approach is attractive as it provides a single factor explanation to a very complex problem. Secondly, if the argument is accepted the rich have no responsibility to help financially the poor countries. The poor must develop institutions and they will grow. This sort of thinking is opposed by many including Sachs (2003) who writes, "The problem is that the evidence simply does not support those conclusions. Institutions may matter, but they don't matter exclusively. The barriers to economic development in the poorest countries today are far more complex than institutional shortcomings". He further writes, "In other worlds, sub-Saharan Africa and other regions struggling today for improved economic development require much more than lectures about good governance and institutions. They require direct interventions, backed by expanded, low technological productivity, and resource limitations that trap them in poverty. Good governance and sound institutions would, no doubt, make such interventions more effective." (*ibid.*, p. 38). He is of the opinion that good institutions certainly matter, and bad institutions can sound the death knell of development even in favourable environments. But poor physical endowment may also hamper development. Development thinking and policy must return to the basics: both institutions and resource endowments are critical, not just one or other. The point is that the poverty trap is real: countries can be too poor to find their own way out of poverty. These countries need massive international aid.

By freeing our thinking from one-factor explanations and understanding that poverty may have as much to do with malaria as with the exchange rate, we will become much more creative and expansive in our approach to the poorest countries. And, with this broader view, the international institutions can also be much more successful than past generations in helping to free these countries from their economic suffering.

Larger Perspective

The world Bank's World Development Report, 2003: Sustainable Development in a Dynamic world argues that often appropriate policies are known but not implemented because of distributional issues and institutional weakness. What is needed, it says, is for policy-makers to focus on institutions (rules and organizations, informal and formal) to get the government, non-governmental organizations (NGOs), and the private sector to manage a broad portfolio of assets—not just human and physical capital but also environmental assets (such as freshwater and fish stocks) and social assets (such as trust), if social groups feel secure, and have a stake in the future, they will take a long-term perspective, establishing a link between poverty reduction and institutions for sustainable development. By facilitating the management of environmental and social assets, institutions underpin sustainable development.

Highlighting the need for institutions for greater social stability and sustainable development (*Christian Eigen-Zucchi et. al*, 2003) conclude, "Although many of the institutions needed for strong income growth and asset accumulation are equally important in fostering social and environmental assets, the institutional underpinnings of sustainable development are somewhat broader. They rest on greater access to information and knowledge and the ability to form broader partnerships. Without these additional institutional elements, society risks fragmentations, and the environment is susceptible to degradation, ultimately imperiling both income growth and well-being" (*ibid.*, p. 43).

Summary and Implications for India

The foregoing has briefly put up a sketch of new institutional economics which retains the assumption of scarcity and abandons concept of instrumental rationality of neo classical economics. Concept of institutions as humanly devised constraints on their interactions and its narrower interpretations are also explained. Organizations are seen as formal groups of persons having some common interests. Functions of institutions for the purposes of sustained rapid growth are: Market creating, Market regulating, Market stabilizing and Market legitimizing. Quality of institutions is extremely important for rapid growth. Good institutions must have at least three qualities: Protection of property rights, constraints over the powers of the elite and a sort of equal opportunities for all. The problem of measurement of quality of Institutions is also discussed briefly. Deep determinants of development are explained in some detail. They are geography, International trade and Institutions. It is found that institutions and quality of institutions play a major role in economic development. Broader view emphasises that institutions may matter but they do not matter exclusively. World Bank and other scholars want Institutions for larger perspective of social justice and sustainable development.

In the Indian context the New Institutional Economics has widened horizons on many fronts. Firstly, it has opened wide areas of research in model building and empirical research in microeconomics. Secondly, some of the major macroeconomic problems such as low interest-saving controversy, fiscal profligacy, etc. need to be understood with clear model and empirical content. Perhaps New Institutional Economics can come to our help. It is now clear that for rapid growth and social justice much more needs to be done on various fronts. We need rule abiding citizens, honest and efficient public servants and corruption free politicians. All these can be understood within the framework of New institutional Economics and suitable policy adopted and social awakening created for rights and duties of everyone. Let a clear understanding of values, rules, traditions and norms be established in all economic and social walks of life and accepted and followed by all. This will ensure sustainable development with social justice.

REFERENCES

Acemoglu Daron, Simon Johnson, and Dames Robinson (2001): "The Colonial origins of comparative development: An empirical investigation," *American Economic Review*, Vol. 91 (December), pp. 1369-1401.

Christian Eigen-Zucchi, Gunnar S. Eskeland, and Zmarak Shalzi (2003), "institutions Needed for More than Growth", *Financed Development*, June.

Christain *et. al.*, *Ibid.*, p. 43.

Coase, Ronald H. (1937), 'The Nature of the Firm', in Coase, Ronald H. (ed.), *The Firm, the Market, and the Law*, Chicago, University of Chicago Press, pp. 33-55.

Dani Rodrik and Arvind Subramanian (2003), "The primacy of institutions: (and what this does and does not mean)," pp. 31-34, *Finance and Development*, June.

Dani Rodrik and Arvind Subramanian, *ibid.*, p. 34.

Daron Acemoglu (2003), "Root causes", *Fiance and Development*, June, p. 27.

Davis, Lance E. and North, Douglass C. (1971), *Institutional Change and American Economic Growth*, Cambridge, Cambridge University Press.

Hali Edison (2003), "Testing the Links: How Strong are the links between Institutional Quality and Economic Performance?" *Finance & Development*, June, Vol. 40, No. 2.

Hali Edison, *ibid.*, p. 36.

Jeffrey D. Sachs (2003), "Institutions Matter, But not for Everything: The Role of Geography and Resource Endowments in Development shouldn't be Underestimated", *Finance & Development*, June.

Jeffrey D. Sachs, *ibid.*, p. 38.

Klien Peter, G. (1999), "New Institutional Economics," *New Institutional Economics*, p. 459.

North, Douglass C. (1990), Institutions, Institutional Change and Economic Performance, Cambridge, Cambridge University Press.

Williamson, Oliver E. (1975), Markets and Hierarchies: Analysis and Antitrust Implications, New York, NY, Free Press.

Williamson, Oliver E. (1985), *The Economic Institutions of Capitalism*, New York, NY, Free Press.

World Development Report, 2003.

Relevance of New Institutional Economics for Developing Countries

SAVITA BHAGAT

INTRODUCTION

Several remarkable developments have taken place in the realm of economics in the last two decades. Prominent among them are those which highlight the shortcomings of neo-classical economics and its assumptions about an economy with a perfect setting for all the players with full information. It is common knowledge that markets are at best imperfect providing asymmetric information to the participants. The issue of economic growth, which assumed greater importance after the depression of 30s, exposed the weaknesses of markets all the more. Neo-classical economists worked with three factors of production, i.e., land, labour and capital (including entrepreneurship). But the different growth patterns observed in different countries and regions led to the exploration of some missing factors without which differences in growth could not be adequately explained. This formed the basis of New Institutionalism.

Institutional economics comes in 'new' and 'old' versions. The 'old' institutional economics of Veblen, John Commons, and Wesley was dominant in university departments in the US between the First and the Second World War. Its followers in Europe included Gunnar Myrdal, K.William and Kapp. More recently, there has been spectacular rise of 'new' institutional economists such as Ronald Coase, Douglass North and Oliver Williamson. This has had a major impact on both economic theory and economic policy.

The purpose of this paper is to analyze the basic differences in the approach of neo-classicals and institutionalists and then look into some of the serious problems inflicting developing countries, which are posing a serious threat to their material advancement and its sustenance. Then an effort has been made to study the applications of NIE in ameliorating the suffering of people in poor counties and its success in various parts of the world. For this purpose the paper has been divided into four sections. In section I the origin of the institutionalist school of thought and the conditions which led to its coming to the fore are reviewed and in section II the issues of poor countries which are not only of concern to them but should be equally disturbing for the rich countries because of increasing interdependence in a rapidly shrinking world, have been taken up and in section III various instances of successful grafting of institutions have been deliberated. And in the end are given the conclusions of the paper.

SECTION I

Adam Smith in his Wealth of Nations was concerned more about specialisation, trade and size of the market. A comprehensive study of the theory of development is missing in the classical scheme of things. The Classicals were more concerned with the attainment of full employment. The visibility of the issue of development diminished greatly in the writings of neo-classical economists, almost disappearing from mainstream economics during the last half of the 19th century. This resulted from the preoccupation of economists during this period with obtaining a good understanding of the role played by fully developed markets in the resolution of resource allocation and income distribution problems. The assumptions of earlier economists were:

- Man is basically an economic entity and has no other desire than promoting his own self-interest.

- His self-interest is promoted by the largest production of wealth, i.e., goods with value in exchange for the least trouble.
- Such pursuit of private goods promotes the general well being of society.
- Free and unlimited competition among individuals is the only safe and natural regulator in the market.
- All customary and state regulation is encroachment on natural liberty.
- Every individual knows his interests best and has the capacity and desire of acting according to his knowledge.
- There is perfect freedom and equality in power of contract between individuals.
- Capital and labour are ready to move from one place to another in the hope of better remuneration.
- There is universal tendency of wages and profits to seek a common level.
- Demand and supply mutually tend to adjust to each other.

Institutional economics is the school of thought which flourished in US in the 20's and 30's which saw evolution of economic institutions as part of the broader process of cultural development. T. Veblen laid the foundation for institutionalism with his criticism of the traditional economic theory. He tried to replace the concept of people as the makers of economic decisions with a more realistic image of people as influenced by changing customs and institutions. Institutions are rules of games in a society. They are humanly designed constraints that shape human interaction and structure incentives in human exchange. Institutions shape the way societies evolve. Economies perform differently because of difference in institutions. They are the key to understanding historical change. The Neo-classical model describes the output of an economy as a function of the quantity and costs of a set of inputs, i.e., land, labour, capital and entrepreneurship, given some production function derived from technical knowledge. But this formulation has proved to be misleading since if it were true for all societies, they would all be rich. In fact, costs of production is a function of the traditional costs of production and costs of transaction.

The school of thought represented by North Douglass has

proved that institutions matter in the development of an economy. The reason why some economies perform better than others and why over a period of time some countries have shown remarkable progress while others have remained laggards, is the impact of the prevailing economic, social and political environment represented by institutions.

There can be formal as well as non-formal institutions. Instituions are arrangements between people of civilised society through which they transact their business. The nature of laws, courts, rules and regulations, written as well as unwritten, traditions and customs—all are part and parcel of institutions. Hence, they limit and define the choice set of neoclassical theory. Our interest is not in the institutions per se but in their consequences for choice individuals make. To the degree that individuals believe in the rules, contracts and property rights of the society, they will be willing to forgo the opportunities to cheat, steal and engage in opportunistic behaviour. The gains would not be worth the pains. They will abide by the rules of contract. Conversely, if individuals do not have faith in the rules or regard them as unjust or simply live up to the standard wealth maximising behavior given by neo classicals, the costs of contacting, that is, transaction costs will increase.

The issue of development came to the fore only after the great depression of 1930's. The length, breadth and intensity of depression made economists think about the issues of sustainable development. The question that chiefly concerned Keynes was why a mature price system economy should suffer depression. His perspective on the issue differed greatly from the neoclassical line of thinking. The neoclassical formulation of three factors—land, labour and capital—tried to explain the working of price system and allocation of factor income in the economy. They were not analysing secular change in the economy. Reference to other sources of growth along with labour and capital were no doubt initiated in the works of Schumpeter (for example, his concept of entrepreneurial spirit is linked to institutions), Solow and Lewis. But they have taken institutions to be exogenous and transitory in nature. Solow's work on the US economy showed that increase in GNP could not be fully explained by quantities of labour and capital but that something else was behind the growth that was responsible for the shift in the production function. Events through time cannot be understood without knowing the institutional setting. Institutional setting changes the production function.

Economic historians of the Industrial Revolution have concentrated upon technological change as the main dynamic factor of the period. Generally, however, they have failed to ask what caused the rate of technological change to increase during this period: often it would appear that in arguing the causes of technological progress they assume that technological progress was costless or was spontaneously generated. But in reality, an increase in the rate of technological progress will result from either an increase in the size of the market or an increase in the inventor's ability to capture a larger share of the benefits created by his invention (Intellectual Property Rights). The degree of sophistication of property rights is an institutional phenomenon. The size of the market is less so but markets take an institutional guise if they are viewed not as abstract concepts of neo-classical theory but as institutional arrangements through which trade is organised.

SECTION II

Development requires that people are able to realize their potential. They have sufficient motivation and incentives to acquire more assets and strive for enhancement of assets—material, non-material and natural resources—on which the prosperity of the country depends. The issue of development is not only the concern of those countries whose people are living in sub human conditions but poverty of poor economies is posing a threat to the rich countries also because of globalization and increasing interdependence.

Complex and inefficient institutions are a common problem, especially for the poor people in poor countries. In Mozambique, for example, registering a new business requires 19 steps and five months, and costs more than the average per capita annual income. By contrast registering a new business in Australia requires only two steps, two days, and two percent of the average annual income per capita. In Slovenia resolving a dispute over a returned cheque can take up to four years, in Singapore it takes just 35 days.

In many countries, legal systems fail to serve the needs of poor people who are unable to pay legal fees or read complex judicial documents. The excessive load on judicial system is quite clear from a newspaper report in India that even if no fresh case is taken up, it will take another hundred years to clear the backlog. Justice delayed is justice denied is a very apt saying in the case of our own country. For prosperity to usher in, it is very necessary to win people's faith and confidence in the system, which is so far woefully lacking and is the biggest stumbling block in the way of development. People's cooperation with the establishment comes from trust that the existing institutional framework has not been able to guarantee. Institutions should not only be just but them must seem to be so. The Bar Council of India has drawn up a list of 131 High Court judges in whose courts relatives are appearing as lawyers. Thus law has become a family business in India, shaking people's faith in the judiciary

Institutions in the form of rules and regulations including informal ones that coordinate human behaviour are essential for sustainable and equitable development. There are protective institutions that define and support control rights in terms of access to and use of assets central to human well-being. A special subset of protective institutions is private property rights. This entails right of use and decision-making for an owner, typically including rights to sell or lease an asset. In a modern state, this commitment requires an active obligation of enforcement from the government (police or judiciary) and the assurance that the government itself respects those rights.

The security of property rights is closely associated with the rule of law—so that people are clear as to what will be respected as theirs. The dispersed interests of thousands of owners, for instance, were potentially threatened by well-placed and powerful individuals as it happened in the case of Enron. Protective institutions protect the interests of diverse interests but they are not perfect. So somebody has to monitor the monitor as well.

When these institutions function well, they enable people to work with each other to plan a future for themselves, their families and their communities but when these institutions are weak or unjust, the result is mistrust and uncertainty. If people want to change their destiny, institutions have to be modified. To take an example, Indians who are mediocre in their own country, go abroad and perform excellent in foreign lands. It is the right kind of opportunities, incentives, rules, laws and codes of conduct that allow people to flourish there. It does not mean that they are very efficient economies in every respect. The progress they have achieved has been at the cost of irreversible damage to the environment, for instance. The right kinds of institutions were not developed there for saving critical natural resources. The burden of follies committed by developed world is falling on the poor countries as well. The irony of the situation is that in rich parts of the world, at least they have material prosperity but in developing economies they are losers on both the fronts. Neither have they decent standards of living nor have they been able to protect the richness of natural resources. Clean drinking water, clean air and forest resources all are facing the danger of extinction because of lack of protective institutions.

Institutions keep on evolving. The right kind of institutions are those which are able to pick-up signals about needs and problems (information, feedback, anticipation of future problems) and balance different interests by forging agreements (transparency, voice forums for negotiations) by avoiding stalemates and conflicts. They must also be able to execute and implement solutions (commitment and enforcement mechanism). Learning from the successes and failures of other countries' experiences in institution building can provide valuable guidance. But copying institutional models without considering whether they are needed by the people they are supposed to serve, and without gauging the capabilities of governments and citizens, will waste scarce resources.

For example, in the early and mid-90s, Zambia tried to establish stock markets by building stock exchanges and training people to staff them. However, there were so few listed companies and so little trading that the exchanges could not generate the fees to be self-sustaining. In hindsight, it is clear that conditions were not yet ripe for the creation of stock markets and the effort would have been better spent on other needs, such as improving accounting and information systems. In the development business there is a tendency to label approaches that have worked well in one or more countries as 'best practice' and then try to transplant these in other countries. But we should not lose sight of the fact that when it comes to institutions, one size doesn't fit all.

It is very difficult to have the right kind of institutions just by trying to transplant successful institutions of the other countries. Initial difficulty is in designing suitable institutions for economic agents to work in their best interests. More important is protecting and nurturing them. Because institutions govern behaviour, when they are strong they are social assets, when weak they become liabilities.

In primitive societies in matters of personal exchange, individuals either exchange in repeat dealings with others or otherwise have a great knowledge about the attributes and characteristics of others. The transaction costs of working in such a framework are very low. Cheating, shirking and opportunism—all features that underline modern industrial organizations- are limited or are absent. Under such conditions, norms of behavior are seldom written down. There are few formal laws. However measured transaction costs are low in such countries and production costs are high, because specialization and division of labour are limited to the extent of the market that can be defined by personal exchange. At the other extreme we have a world of specialized interdependence where exchange ties extend both in time and space. Under this impersonal kind of exchange, in which there are no repeat dealings, transaction costs can be very high. There are gains to be made by indulging in cheating shirking etc. As a result we have devised formal contracts and elaborate monitoring and enforcement mechanisms. Institutions reduce uncertainty and even as the network of interdependence caused by growth of specialization widens, we can have confidence in the outcomes that are remote from our personal knowledge. This is only possible with the development of third party to exchanges, namely government, which specifies property rights and enforces contracts. The rise of impersonal rules and contracts means rise of the state and with it unequal distribution of coercive power. This provides the opportunity for individuals with superior coercive power to enforce the rules to their advantage regardless of their effects on efficiency, i.e., rules will be devised and enforced on behalf of the interests of the politically advantageous class but they will not lower the costs of transacting in toto.

To quote Douglass, political systems have an inherent tendency to produce inefficient property rights that result in stagnation or decline. Even when rulers want to have rules with efficient consequences, survival will dictate a different course of action because efficient rules can offend powerful interest group in the polity.

Poor countries' major need is to improve productivity and income levels to usher in prosperity. This growth needs to be achieved not by endangering the ecosystem but rather by strengthening the institutional framework for saving natural resources for the coming generations. But the ground reality of many of these countries is a cause for concern. In many developing countries:

- Productivity is low, growth is stagnant and unemployment is high.
- The number of people living on less than a $1 a day is 1.2 billion.
- Income inequality between rich and poor countries and within countries is more than what is it was a decade ago.
- Political system is far from responsive and countries are torn by civil conflict.
- Environmental resources are under great pressure. Water resources, clean air and forest cover along with flora and faunas are on the verge of extinction.
- The financial resources to address these problems are not adequate.

The current path of development, it is agreed, is not sustainable. Now it is no longer a question of public vs. private, because experience has shown that if markets are not perfect, states are also imperfect. Both systems have belied the hopes of the people. It has to be a proper balance of business, government and civil society. For the assets most at risk—the natural and social—markets can not provide the basic coordinating functions of sensing problems, balancing interests and executing policies and solutions. Assets that are public goods or common property goods such as clean air, forests, water and fisheries, are a challenge to manage sustainably. The poor depend most on environmental resources and if they lack voice and a stake in society, these assets are eroded and the ability to solve economic, social and political problems also diminishes. Making progress on sectoral issues requires first a better understanding of the local conditions and a better ability to diagnose local problems. Secondly, some distributional issues must be resolved, e.g., the division of water among various claimants, division of land in various uses and for whom. Without institutions that represent the interests of the powerless, dispersed groups, these sectors are prone to be captured by vested interests and efficient solutions won't be implemented in that case.

The rule of law and good governance is the first requirement for better management of resources. Schooling, health care, provision of environmental assets and land reforms, all generate assets for the poor. An open and verifiable flow of information is important to tighten accountability in government, unlike our country where even one year after the passage of the right to information bill by Delhi Assembly, the people are not even aware of it.

There is a role for everybody in the development process. Governments can improve the accountability of public agencies and provision of information about social and environmental problems, balance interests fairly and come up with solutions. If institutions structure human behavior in such a way that the organisations' efficiency is increased, it is called an institutional fit. If however existing rules and regulations are preventing members of the organisations to carry out necessary activities, we call this institutional misfit. Civil society organizations can make the voice of the powerless heard and provide independent verification of public, private and non-government performance. Therefore, in several countries government ministries and civil society are working together to strengthen and expand community-based initiatives.

SECTION III

Provision of protective institutions and institutions which try to include the marginalised and disenfranchised sections of the society in the development process in various parts of the world, is showing results. Some striking examples as given in the World Development Report 2003 are as follows:

- A community-based health and malaria eradication programme was launched in 1992 in Ethiopia with 714 volunteers serving more than 1.7 million people in some 2000 villages.

- In Orissa the international NGO CARE is setting up micro-enterprises to produce insecticide-treated mosquito nets to reduce malaria and to help poor villages generate more income.
- Private banks in Lebanon are sponsoring NGOs to promote micro savings in remote mountainous areas. Vans go to villages, collecting savings, making small loans and depositing the savings in the nearest bank branch.
- El Salvador, Thailand and Uganda have established small courts that rely on simplified, sometimes merely spoken procedures. The simpler procedures resolve disputes faster and at lower costs than regular courts.
- Some 80 percent of economically active women in Sub-Saharan Africa are into agricultural activities. Forward-looking institutions are responding with changes in attitudes and service delivery. Bangladesh's Grameen Bank and Morocco's Zakoura Foundations offer micro-credit for women and schools for girls. Agencies and communities recognizing the high returns from raising women's status are coming together with NGOs to reach women directly with information, education and access to credit.
- In many Latin American countries a national park may be created with a simple presidential decree, but dismantling a park requires the approval of both the President and the legislature.
- In a study in Udaipur district of Rajasthan it was found that local level networks between individual agents located in different formal sectors of the economy over an extended period of a decade or so, created well-specified institutions for the management of common property. This resulted in decrease in distress migration from semi arid regions to urban areas. With clearly spelt out principles of inclusion in the group that was bound by a system of commitments to protect and privileges to share in the outcome of that protection, the role of commons as a provider of insurance and sustenance during drought came into play more clearly. In particular villages where institutions were stronger and well established migration decreased substantially.

- A vibrant civil society and such institutions as a democratic legislature can provide for dynamism in every sphere including that in rule-making. Amartya Sen's findings are that democracy helped by free speech plays a key role in eliminating famine and getting effective disaster relief.

CONCLUSIONS

The development of poor countries no doubt depends on their own social, political economic and environment embedded in the form of good institutions, good governance and good policies. Government, business and civil society have to work together in developing and nurturing good institutions and an effective system of checks and balances can reduce the possibility of misuse of institutions by vested interests. Government can provide property rights through rule of law and Civil society and media can play an important monitoring role in improving accountability and reducing incentives for corruption in government. When citizens have access to independent sources of information, meaningful channels for political participation and legal protection against retribution, they can become a strong political force for improved performance of public agencies. Higher national income can contribute to better institutional quality and better institutions can contribute to greater national income since good institutions facilitate investment. According to one study, better voice and accountability would raise national income by a factor of 2.5. Institutions assist in coordination but encouraging the emergence of good institutions is itself a coordination problem. The main message of institutionalism is that sustained development requires a broad thriving portfolio of assets, and that managing this broad portfolio requires better institutions. Wherever positive changes have taken place they are because of better quality of institutions:

- An important element in political discourse in Western Europe and North America in the 20th century has been "to give everyone a stake in the society."
- One of the remarkable examples of institutional transformation towards an inclusive society is that of

South Africa's transition from white rule to pluralistic democracy founded on the principles of human rights.

- The miraculous growth in the last decade in China can also offer a lesson or two for other developing countries. In their context it has been pointed out that—
  (a) gradual reforms have generally produced better results than 'big bang' or shock therapy;
  (b) it is better to proceed through experimentation in limited regions and then extend it to other areas if the experiment turns out to be successful;
  (c) pragmatism suited to local conditions rather than untested theories/doctrines, guide the policy-makers;
  (d) appropriate legal and regulatory institutions are crucial for the functioning of markets;
  (e) existing institutions should not be destroyed without putting new ones in place. But there is no need for a hasty introduction of a supposedly perfect or best practice institution; and
  (f) local participation, autonomy, decentralisation and grassroot organisations are needed for wide dispersal of benefits. In China many reforms originated locally (rather than centrally). In an unprecedented move, 12,000 farmers in a village filed a class action law suit against the local government for levying excess fee and won a ruling in favour of farmers in the local court.

In order to meet local needs, the locals' participation in the development process is no doubt much talked about. It is said that mobilising people in order to channelise their energies to socio-economic reconstruction and involving them all in the activities of communities through new institutions, reducing the work of the government and making people responsible for their destiny is a must for development. Introducing Panchayati Raj Bill was a step in this direction in India. But the working of the recently constituted Gram Sabhas in Scheduled areas in Madhya Pradesh shows that people are not even aware of the position and status of these Gram Sabhas and that these institutions are also being coopted by the powerful local interests. Mere legislation will not serve the purpose of empowering the disadvantaged. An enabling environment is to be created, marginalised sections are to be protected and included in this process and the government has to be a facilitator rather than a provider. To quote Roosevelt, the test of our progress is not whether we add more to the abundance of those who have much: it is whether we provide enough for those who have little.

The ever-growing interdependence of the world has shown that good institutions at the global level are also equally if not more important for the prosperity of the poor countries. As within a country we were talking about voiceless and marginalised people whose concerns are not taken into account, similar is the case at the global level with financial, trade and other dispute-resolving institutions. Right kind of institutions at the international level that are not only just in their conduct but also seem to be so, are the urgent need of the day. If creative and productive energies of the people of the less developed countries are to be unleashed, internal as well as external institutions have to be suitably modified. Might is right when not justifiable in the national context, is equally abhorrent and untenable in the international context.

REFERENCES

Alok Ray (2002), "The Chinese Economic Miracle—Lessons to be Learnt, *Economic and Political Weekly*, September 14-20.

Douglass North (1989), "Institutions and Economic Growth: An Historical Introduction" *World Development*, Vol. 17, No. 9, pp. 1319-32.

Harold Demstez, "*Dogs and Tails in the Economic Development Story*," Prepared for the Second Annual Conference of 'International Society for New Institutional Economics', 1998, Paris.

Kanchan Chopra (2002), "Social Capital and Development Processes: Role of Formal and Informal Institutions," *Economic and Political Weekly*, July 13-19.

Mustapha K. Nabli and Jeffery B. Nugent (1989), "The New Institutional Economics and its Applicability to Development", *World Development*, Vol. 17, No. 9, pp. 1333-47.

Yatindra Singh (2002), "Decentralised Governance in Madhya Pradesh, Experiences of the Gram Sabha in Scheduled Areas," *Economic and Political Weekly*, October 5-11.

—— (2003), *Sustainable Development in a Dynamic World: Transforming Instituions, Growth and Quality of Life*, The World Bank, Washington, DC.

Development Implications of Institutional Change in India: A Case Study

BHAGABATA PATRO, PURUSHOTTAM SAHU AND U. CH. PANIGRAHI

Continuous failure of the economists to explain the slow growth of many developing countries (except East Asian countries) demanded examining the efficacy of the social, political and economic institutions in playing their designated role in the process of economic development. Absence or non-performance of these institutions have resulted in lesser mobility of human and physical capital due to inadequate information base. Their marginal return on capital, thus, continued to remain low due to absence of opportunities. In the old traditional society even though there is lesser personal mobility, yet there exists extraordinary information flow and communication among individuals due to personal relationship. But as economies grow, trade and commerce expands between relatively unknown faces giving rise to the need for specific institutions to acquire and share information on a wider scale. Two type of institutions appears to be necessary to cope with the latest situation of the complicated markets. One is to facilitate information on the quality of goods and services produced by different organisations and the other is necessary to monitor the transactions entered in the process of trade. (*World Development Report*, 1998-99)

In the background of this environment one of the contentious issue at the moment is the role of the State in the process of economic development. While there is no difference of opinion among the economists with regard to the need of the state, yet what exactly is the function of the state is subject to widespread debate throughout the world. Most of the World bodies since the nineties advocate for regulatory role of the state in spite of their full knowledge that market itself always is against the poor. In India such an circumstance. This possibility is more when individuals are more self-oriented than community-oriented.

THE PROCESS OF BARGAINING AND INSTITUTIONS

The emergence of institutions in a historical perspective is to create order and reduce uncertainty in the process of exchange (North, 1991). Institutions provide an incentive to carry out production activities in an economy. The process of bargaining of individuals through institutions can be translated into a game theoretic exercise. Individuals cooperate and bargain in an easier way when they have complete information about the past performance of the rivals and when the number of players are small. Effective institutions smoothens the bargaining process and reduce transaction cost. For this purpose both political and economic institutions are equally important. In a small village economy, the process of bargaining is very easy but emergence of long distance trade poses two direct transaction cost problems. One is the appointment of agents to accompany the traded goods and finalize the terms and conditions of sale. The second one is to come to an agreement and enforce it by protecting the goods and services in the process of transportation from one place to the other.

DEVELOPMENT IMPLICATION OF INSTITUTIONS

The new endogenous theories of economic development now recognizes that transaction cost and information network directly influences the efficiency in resource allocation. Indirectly, this governs the ownership structure and property relations. Most of the developed western countries have complex institutional structures for enforcing property rights, formal contracts and guarantees, corporate hierarchy, vertical integration, limited liability, bankruptcy laws, etc. This reduces the uncertainty of social experimentation is going on and we have decided to give an important role to the nongovernmental agencies to supplement the developmental role of the government agencies. The purpose of this paper is to evaluate the performance of a single NGO with regard to a specific scheme in a particular village. The conclusion that follows from the analysis is almost applicable to other NGOs working in the development field.

MARKET IMPERFECTION AND EFFICIENCY

The later part of the twentieth century witnessed a strong debate on the issue of efficiency aspect of a perfectly competitive market. In a seminal paper Ronald Coase (1960) challenged the classical idea that Pareto-efficiency always requires competitive market. He concluded that efficiency will be optimal only when the market is imperfectly competitive and individuals are allowed to negotiate and reach a compromise for the benefit of each other (*Farell*, 1987). It dispenses the heavy assumption of perfect competition but assumes that no mutually beneficial agreement is left out. This means the Coasean argument believes in lesser formal institution like government but emphasizes on more participatory organizations like co-operatives, self-help groups, community development blocks, etc. where people interact and decides the provision of public or merit goods. The only problem likely to emerge in the event of so many people to co-operate is the failure to reach at a consensus. In such a situation, the government may intervene to act as a 'referee' and regulate the way negotiations take place. This means the role of the government should be that of a facilitator rather than a direct development agent. The inefficiency in the bargain process is still likely to exist if the individuals taking part in the negotiation failed to take decision clearly in a given interaction and allow productivity gains of larger scale (*Meir*, 1995). Explaining as to why physical and human capital are better utilized in certain economies, Benhabib and Jovanovic (1991) stated that differences in growth rates can persist because of better capacity to absorb knowledge which depends on the institutional features of the economy. Institution according these economists refer to corporate, legal or bureaucratic structures or even attitudes to work. It is used to describe non-market interactions, i.e. allocation of resources through administrative methods (*Bardhan, Datta-Chowudhary, Krishnan*, 2000).

Government as an institution has deep involvement in development strategy. It succeeded in East Asian Countries but failed in many other places to generate a tempo of economic development. This obviously mean that in other countries the government failed to identify the goal to which its' activities are directed. Bardhan and others (2000) identify it to be the creation of a flexible economy and concluded that decentralized institutions that have a comparative advantage in absorbing and processing specific types of information impart the greatest flexibility to the economy.

NON-GOVERNMENTAL, NON-PRIVATE INSTITUTIONS

Non-governmental and Non-private institutions are identifies as a class of intermediate institutions in the nature of alliances, communities and coalitions. By having interaction among themselves, these institutions provided the required public good in an economy taking into account the wider interest of the society. Strong alliances among these organizations can help to build up a fabric as a common information base.

The evolution of an appropriate form of institutions depends on historical circumstances and long-run relationship among different organizations. Interaction between individuals and deliberations in different formal and informal gatherings give rise to different types of institutions. The role of the government in such circumstances is to facilitate autonomous formation of institutions. There are certain advantages of opting for decentralized institutions over hierarchical institutions. The final choice is, therefore, should based on encouraging transparency in transactions, fruitful use of localized information, multiplicity of attainment and characteristics of population and mechanism of countervailing economic and political power (*Bardhan and others*, 2000).

CHANGE OF INSTITUTIONAL STRUCTURE IN INDIA

In the Indian development scenario, there has been a constant endeavor to bring in the non-governmental institutions to the forefront of implementing development programme. This is perhaps due to the historical failure of the governmental institutions to provide public goods in an efficient manner. The Tenth Five Year Plan (2002-07) stated in clear terms that efficiency in governance requires efficient institutional structure. Further, the efficiency of the institutions of an economy, on the motherland depends on their adopted procedure of delivery mechanism and supportive framework. This is valid both for governmental and non-governmental institutions participating in the development process. The plan clearly stated 'it is expected that the state yields to the market and the civil society in many areas where it, so far, had a direct but distortionary and inefficient presence.'

The Tenth Plan assumes an institutional set-up which can be presented in a chart given below.

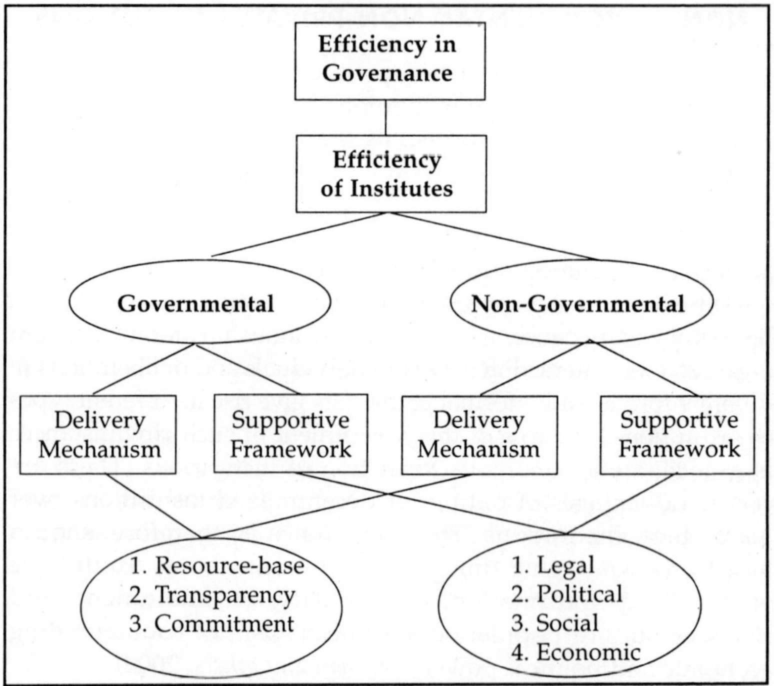

It declared some aspects of governance and contingent instruments to be taken up on priority basis. These are identified as:

1. Involvement of people in all stages of planning,
2. Decentralisation of administration to the possible lowest level,
3. Ensure right to information,
4. Improving reform in the revenue system and mobilization of other resources,
5. Greater role to the civil society,
6. Changing the attitudes of civil service, and
7. Reform in procedure, etc.

A CASE STUDY OF A NON-GOVERNMENTAL INSTITUTION

The debate of identifying a suitable institutional set-up for the purpose of promoting economic development of the country has been on some time and in the nineties planners expressed their anguish on the manner in which the governmental institutions are working and advocated for greater market freedom and access to non-governmental institutions. As a result, there has been a great spurt in the number of non-governmental institutions and it spread like an industry everywhere. In the last one decade, these institutions were given with the responsibility of implementing several development programmes. It is appropriate now to evaluate the performance of these institutions with regard to their social relevance to design an appropriate policy for them.

The present study pertains to a housing scheme namely, Samagra Awas Yojana (SAY) which is a centrally sponsored scheme. This scheme was launched in the country in the year 1999-2000. In Orissa, a total of 25 blocks are brought under this scheme. The Rangeilunda block of Ganjam district is a block implementing the scheme.

TABLE 1

Composition of Households in the Village New Boxipally

Caste	*Total Households*	*Population*		
		Male	*Female*	*Total*
ST	—	—	—	—
SC	5	7	10	17
OBC	291	612	567	1198
Minority	—	—	—	—
General	7	14	14	28
Total	303	643	600	1243

Source: Field Survey.

A total of 303 household units were covered under scheme in the year 2001. The Gram Vikas a leading district level NGO is implementing the scheme. The average family size is 4 per family.

FEATURES OF THE SCHEME

The details of the scheme is given in Table 2.

TABLE 2

Features of Samagra Awas Yojana in New Boxipally Village

Description	*No. of Units*	*Peoples' Contribution*	*SAY Assistance*	*Other Sources*
Housing	325	9543463	—	8775000
Toilets/Bath rooms	325	369525	1300000	812500
Water supply system	1	47100	350000	16000
Drainage system	1	25500	125000	0
Community hall	1	2717	60000	100000
Roads	1	—	165000	0
Support to livelihood activities	325	1625000	0	3250000
Corpus fund	325	325000	0	0
Motivation and training cost	1		0	200000
Technical supervision cost	1	—	0	1750000
Total		11938305	2000000	150475000

Source: Office of the DRDA, Ganjam.

INVESTMENT PATTERN

The Investment pattern of the project reveals four different sources of funding. 41 percent of investment is peoples own contribution while another 41 percent is raised through loan. The grant component of the project is 17 percent of the total. The details of the investment is given in Table 3.

TABLE 3

Investment Pattern of the Scheme

	Investment	*Per cent*	*Per family*
Peoples' own Fund	11938305	41	36733
Loan Fund	12025000	41	37000
Grant Fund	5022500	17	15454
Total	28985805	100	89187

Source: Office of the DRDA, Ganjam, 2003.

PROGRESS OF THE PROJECT

The progress of the project in financial and in physical terms is given in Table 4. The survey reveals total completion of the houses to the extent of only 40 percent. There are about 30 percent cases where the houses were not started at all. The rest beneficiaries are in the intermediate stage of construction.

TABLE 4

Progress of the SAY Project in New Boxipalli Village

Item	*Achievement*	*Percentage*
Expenditure incurred	34,07,293	
Total Houses in the Project	303	
Houses fully completed	124	40
Houses in progress	40	13
Houses at the foundation level	50	17
Houses not started	89	30

Source: Field Survey.

CONCLUSIONS

The numerical data given in the analysis and our field experience have generated many interesting observations. These are:

1. The performance of the Non-Government institution is in no way different from the similar type of schemes implemented by the governmental agencies. The partial achievement reflects this point.
2. The Agency implementing the project has presence in the village earlier. Hence, the extent of success of the project is somewhat satisfactory. For a completely new NGO, this extent of achievement may not be possible.
3. It is reported by the beneficiaries that they are not aware of the grant component of the project. The scheme entails a 17 percent subsidy and lack of awareness about this by the beneficiary means, the implementing agency might have utilized the money for their own administrative purposes which is not permissible under the scheme.
4. Most of the poor beneficiaries were of the opinion that the IAY scheme which involves only subsidy of around Rs. 22,000 is better than this. The reason for this is that the amount is given in the shape of grant whereas in SAY it is loan only.
5. The other associated items like provision of septic latrine and safe drinking water has worked well as revealed from the field survey.

REFERENCES

Bardhan, P., Datta-Choudhury, Mrinal, Krishnan, T.N. (2000), *Development and Change*, Oxford University Press, New Delhi.

Farell, Joseph (1987), "Information and the Coase Theorem," *Economic Perspectives*, Vol. 1, No. 2.

Jain, S.P. and Raju, K.N. (2002), "Institutional Framework for Development of Backward Rural Areas," *Kurukshetra*, Vol. 50, No. 10.

Meir, G. (1995), *Leading Issues in Economic Development*, Oxford University Press, Delhi.

Misra, Suresh and Dhaka, R.S. (2001), "Institutional Mechanism for Participatory Rural Development," *Kurukhetra*, Vol. 49, No. 12.

North, D.C. (1991), Institutions, *Journal of Economic Perspectives*, Vol. 3, No. 1.

Rutherford, Malcolm (2001), Institutional Economics: Then and Now, *Journal of Economic Perspectives*, Vol. 15, No. 3.

World Bank (1998-99), *World Development Report*, Oxford University Press, New Delhi.

New Institutional Economics and Economic Reforms in India

Shrawan Kumar Singh

I

According to Warren J. Samuals (1987) institutionalism has served the dual functions of providing critiques of mainstream neoclassical (and Marxian) economics and producing an alternative conception of the economy and of doing economic research and analysis The precise relationship of heterodox institutional economics to orthodox neoclassical economics is complicated by several considerations: (i) the awkward sociological status of heterodoxy within the discipline, (ii) the ambivalence within institutionalism as to the relationship, (iii) some institutionalists feeling that the two are complementary and others that the two are mutually exclusive; and (iv) the presence within institutionalism of two different and to some extent conflicting traditions. Both accept that actual economic performance is a function, *inter alia,* of both technology and institutions.

In contrast with mainstream economics, which maintains that the central economic problems are the allocation of resources, the distribution of income, and the determination of the levels of income, output and prices, *institutional economists assert the primacy of the problem of the organization and control of the economic system, that is its structure of power.* Thus, whereas orthodox economists tend strongly to identify the economy solely with the market, institutional economists argue that the market is itself an institution, comprised of a host of subsidiary institutions, and interactive with other institutional complexes in society. In short, the economy is more than the market mechanism: it includes the institutions which form, structure, and operate through, or channel the operation of, the market. *The fundamental institulionalist position is that it is not the market but the organizational structure of the larger economy which effectively allocates resources.*

But institutionalists are generally less concerned with price and resource allocation *per se* and more with the problem of the organization and control of the economy, that is, with performance seen as specific to power (rights) structure, as well as to technology. Institutionalists thus are interested, for example, in the formation and role of institutions, and the interrelations between economic and legal systems and between power and belief system. In the real world such questions have to be worked out both within institutions and through contests over institutional adjustment and reformation.

The central features of institutional thought are its holism and evolutionalism. Thus, the further principal themes of institutional economics include the following (Warren J. Samuels, 2003):

(i) A theory of social change, an activist orientation towards social institutions, through focusing on both the substantive impact of institutions on economic performance and the processes of institutional change, treating institutions not as something to be taken as given but as man-made and changeable, both deliberatively and non-deliberatively.

(ii) A theory of social control and collective choice, or a theory of institutions, a focus on the formation and operation of institutions as both cause and consequence of the power structure and socialized behaviour of individuals and sub-groups, and as the mode through which economies are organized and controlled. Instead of focusing on the mechanics of choice from within opportunity sets, a focus on the formation of opportunity sets; instead of a focus on unfettered market freedom, a focus on the total, complex pattern of freedom and control, that is, on the formation and operation of the system of control through which both actual opportunity sets and freedom are formed.

(iii) A theory of the economic role of government, as a principal social process through which both itself and other institutions of economic significance are in part formed and revised. Instead of treating government, law, and the system of rights as either given and/or exogenous, these are treated as both dependent and independent, and always critical, not merely aberrational, economic variables.

(iv) A theory of technology, as defining and determining the relative scarcity of all resources, as a principal force in the evolution of economic structure (including the operation of institutions) and performance, and as the basis of the logic of industrialization marking the mentality as well as the practices of modern economies.

(v) The fundamental principle that the real determinant of resource allocation is not the market but the organizational—institutional, power—structure of society.

(vi) An emphasis on facets of the value conception which transcend price, on the values represented in and given effect by the habits and customs of social life, on the pragmatic, instrumental values ensconced in the transcendental notion of the life process of man and society, and on the constructive values latent within and given effect by the working rules of law which are both the foundation and the product of the power structure of society. Included are attempts to understand the process by which values are changed, in contrast to the orthodox assumption of given values; that is, to consider within economics such questions as where the values come from, how they are tested, and how they are changed.

The institutionalist solution to such problems is that of Gunnar Myrdal: to avoid the pretence of value-free economics by making all, or substantially all and certainly the operative, value premises explicit and by generating appraisals thereof. Accordingly, institutional economists have tended to avoid recourse to methodological individualism and to abstain from puzzle-solving research in the context of models devoid of institutional embodiment and stressing equilibrium, optimality, and purely competitive markets. They have rather attended to theoretical and empirical analyses of real-world problems, such as the operation of particular institutions, business-government relations, and the conditions of economic development. Insofar as they have dealt with economic variables at fundamental conceptual levels, such as government and rights, they have at least tried to do so in both analytically credible and non-presumptive ways.

"The best known contemporary version of the institutionalist conception of the economy has been that of John Kenneth Galbraith. Following the course and down by Veblen, and grafting it on to a version of Keynesian economics, Galbraith has explored the corporate nature and planning modes of the business system and the impact of what he considers to be technological imperatives, the social formation of individual preferences underlying demand functions, the power and continuous interaction of the state and the corporate core of the economy, and the factors and forces which influence the formation of opinion and policy of the public sector. In such fields as labour economics, industrial organization, economic development, law and economics, agricultural and natural resource economics, and macroeconomics, institutionalists, through their primary attention to power structure and belief system, in the context of the overriding concerns with social change and social control have produced understandings or pictures of economic reality quite different from those of neoclassical economists. Altogether this work has constituted an alternative analysis of the economic system, especially of capitalism but also of socialism, and a critique of both existing economic systems and orthodox school of economics" (*Samuels*, 1987).

II

In any discussion on economic reforms, there ought to be three strands: (i) Why were reforms necessary and what was wrong with the earlier system? (ii) what reforms have been introduced, and (iii) what remains to be done?

Economic reforms were intended to enable Indian industry to develop an *outward orientation, and to allow freer play to market forces.* Indian industry was to become more competitive, acquire modern and up-to-date technologies so that costs could be controlled and quality improved, establish production capacities that would allow cost advantages, become export-oriented, and through investments by international companies tie in with the growing intra-firm trade of multinational companies. *The new policies placed overwhelming reliance on private initiative and enterprise* to achieve these objectives. Public investment expenditures would over time play a secondary role.

There are essentially two aspects to economic reform, relating to internal and external economic policies. Each, in turn, has two aspects. *In international policy-making,* one aspect is *debureaucratisation and easing of controls; the other pertains to privatisation of public enterprises,* following the neo-liberal philosophy of *laissez-faire* and *reliance on the market for all investment decisions, with minimum government intervention in the economy.* The New Economic Policy is a set of policies and administrative procedures introduced in July 1991 to bring about changes in the economic direction of the country. It has two major components: *Stabilisation and Structural Reforms.*

The *stabilisation* part has three components: (i) Management of Balance of payments; (ii) Control of inflation; and (iii) Fiscal Correction. *Structural Reforms* part has seven components: (i) Exchange Rate Adjustment; (ii) Liberalisation of Imports; (iii) Relationlisation of Tariff Structure; (iv) Delicensing /Removal of Licensing Restrictions; (v) Financial Sector Reforms; (vi) Disinvestment of Public Sector Shares; and (vii) Foreign Direct Investment.

Though these policies and procedures have a macro-economic thrust, their impact on micro-level economic activities can not be ignored. From this point of view the new economic policy will have its repercussions on the entire gamut of economic development. It is important to understand clearly what the economic reforms package is and equally important what it is not. The three-pronged approach of stabilisation, restructuring and globalisation of Indian economy has major implications for the functioning of the economy and its future direction. They imply a complete and a sudden break from the past, and several issues arise relating to:

(a) the desirability of the pattern of development sought; (b) the timing of the various policies and, more importantly, their sequencing; (c) the relative importance attached to the different aspects of policy, in as much as domestic *priorities relating* to the provision of education, health, employment, *globalisation* of the economy; and (d) the likely impact *of the package of policies.*

It must be noted that while *the stabilisation policies are intended to correct the lapses and put the house on order in the short-term, the structural reform was intended to accelerate economic growth over the medium-term.* Structural reform policies can not succeed unless a degree of stabilisation has been brought about. But stabilisation by itself will not be adequate unless structural reforms are undertaken to avoid the recurrence of the problems faced in the recent period.

What, after all, is Washington Consensus? In Williamson's view, it was a policy-frame based on ten areas of reforms. These ten principles are: *(i) fiscal discipline; (ii) right public expenditure priorities; (iii) liberating interest rates—more broadly, financial liberalization; (iv) tax reforms; (v) competitive exchange rate; (vi) trade liberalization; (vii) liberalization of foreign direct investment; (viii) privatization; (ix) deregulation; and (x) property rights.* The term "second-generation reforms" builds on the importance of institutions in permitting a market economy to function effectively. This concept lies at the heart of the concept of "second-generation reforms". Williamson argues that institutional reform should not content itself merely with politically boring esoterica, "like creating budget offices or Securities and Exchange Commissions". Institutional reform involves far more—such as reform of judiciary, the labour laws and the civil service. Such second-generation reform is vital even to ensure the success of the first-generation of reform, since it creates the necessary institutional infrastructure. The second-generation of reforms involve a whole series of new painstaking initiatives in regard to *governance in general.* While a reform process may succeed in all over dimensions, it will ultimately be judged by how it arrives at the goal of better income distribution together with higher growth. In this connection, John Williamson makes a specific mention of remedying inequality by increasing access to education.

III

One of the factors that is likely to play a key role in India's economy is privatisation. By whatever called—*privatisation, disinvestment or sell-off*—it will surely determine the country's future in a broad socio-economic aspect. Though much has been written on the topic it remains a highly-debated issue even among the economists. The PSUs were set-up more as an instrument of social welfare. Hence, to successfully implement privatisation or disinvestment without disturbing the socio-economic framework can be a Herculean task. The issues are (Gowthaman Muruganandan, 2003):

(i) *Corruption:* The concept's (privatisation) success depends a lot on how policy is framed. One reason given for privatisation is *corruption*. It is held by the "reformers" that the PSUs are corrupt. Looking from the other side of the coin, it is the same government officials who decide on matters relating to disinvestment. The question is who will take the responsibility for ensuring that those who decide on privatisation are not corrupt, (ii) *Control:* Another aspect to be considered is *control*. At least the key sectors—water, electricity, railways—should be left untouched. If one were to argue that the regulating bodies, such as the RBI and SEBI, will prevent scams, one would do well to remember the various stock scams. Also, it is possible for any industry, which enjoys monopoly, to create an artificial scarcity or at least control the demand and supply position in the market, (iii) *Efficiency:* It is also held that the privatized sectors are far more efficient than the PSUs. If that is the case then why have some corporate giants disappeared, (iv) *Under-selling:* Then there is the risk of under selling the PSUs. (v) *Human resource:* For any industry to succeed the human resource involved in the same is more decisive than all other assets put together. One should also understand that once the private parties take over the public sector there will be no more reservations for the weaker sections, (vi) *Public Welfare:* But is sell-off the only answer? One has to consider the after effects of its sale. One has also to understand that if the Metropolitan Transport Corporations have been incurring losses for some time. Corporations are privatized the private player will quite stop all loss-making routes and reduce the number of buses. This will definitely affect the welfare of the local population. As privatisation goes on it will have a far-reaching consequences on the economy. Hence, to ensure sustainable socio-economic growth the process should be based on a pragmatic approach. The Government and its think-tank will have to display initiative in adopting a foolproof method if it is to go ahead with disinvestment, and reforms, in general, regardless of the time taken and the political conflicts involved.

Competition Commission is a big step in a country's journey towards a market system. The Competition Act is also a broad sweeping Act which has many potent provisions that can be used to safeguard consumers' interest. It again has not attracted the attention it deserves as it will examine industry practices, monopolistic or oligopolistic behaviour and fair trade practices. It will be interesting to watch its interface with the various regulated regimes, especially as regards pricing policies and also in the face of the trend of consolidation one is witnessing in many industries. Lack of preparedness to account for the effect of the Competition Commission may lead to costly unwinding later. The success of the Maruti disinvestments appears to have buoyed the prospect for an acceleration of the disinvestments process. By successfully establishing the viability of disinvestments, and showcasing the enormous benefits it brings to the people of India, the Government has clearly paved the way for large-scale progress on this score. Why is disinvestments important for the people of India? It reduces their tax burden, as simple as that.

The restructuring of ownership in public enterprises has always attracted internal opposition stemming from the loss of fiefdom that such divestiture entails not to mention the opportunity for rent seeking behaviour. But the exercise itself is an important component of public enterprise reform on which a broad national consensus has emerged. It follows then that the public need to have some knowledge of the forces that are seeking to undermine the process. More important, an understanding of the arguments could lead to a meaningful debate on the pros and cons so that future decisions on disinvestments would be the better for it. For a disinvestments exercise to maximize public proceeds, the field of competition among prospective bidders should be as wide as possible.

The *RSS* as well as the *Swadeshi Jagran Munch* (SJM), which shares the same parentage as the BJP, are *opposed to foreign investment, to globalisation, to the World Trade Organisation, to privatisation, all of which are part of the agenda of the ruling alliance led by the BJP.* Indeed, on many of these and other issues like labour law reform, RSS/SJM are closer to the left parties like the CPI(M) than the BJP. Besides the internal contradictions in the two major policies, the politics of economic policy also has to contend with opposing coalitions controlling the two houses of parliament. Since our democracy has not matured much beyond the scoring of points, this also hampers needed legislative changes. The end result is that the reform process seems to have come to a dead-end on several issues.

In terms of the resources constraint, perhaps the most important is the issue of subsidies to those who are not really needy. White Paper on subsidies a few years back argued that 75 per cent of the subsidies are aimed at not the really poor, but the relatively better-off. It is of course a moot factor what part of the balance is eaten up by middlemen before reaching the 'poor' over whose plight ritual tears continue to be shed in each policy announcement. With changes in subsidies even to the less-than needy not feasible under the current dispensation, the resultant pressure on resources means that the ability to fund primary schools, village roads, water supply and other rural infrastructure, etc. is crippled. Other financial time bombs are also ticking—even after the change in the last budget, the government's pension liability will keep growing for many years to come, and there is also the large gap between the return on employees provident fund and what the investment can earn.

Some argue that democracy is no bar to economic development and point to countries in Europe and the US. They forget that when these countries were developing, there was no universal suffrage, which came much later. In the world other than India, it seems, democracy has followed, not preceded, basic development.

Take the question of labour law reform which, to my mind, has become hurdle to job creation. It is worth nothing that despite 6 per cent per annual GDP growth for a decade, there has been hardly any increase in employment in the organized sector. Job protection seems to be coming at the cost of job creation. In theory, economic liberalization should lead to investments in areas where we have a comparative advantage. In our case, it has led to huge investments in say refineries. It is worth remembering that much of the rapid growth in China has come in the *'special economic zones'* (SEZs) in which job protection laws do not apply.

IV

Institutional Weaknesses

If financial constraints are one part of the political economy, major institutional weaknesses are another. Amongst these perhaps the *legal system* is at the top. The delays, the focus on procedures rather than substance, the unwillingness to reform have crippled the system to such an extent that even the guardians of law and order, namely the police, prefer 'encounters' to prosecution of criminals, and the otherwise vociferous human rights activists watch in silence. But the legal system is by no means the only one suffering from inefficiencies and poor governance. In this context A.V. Rajwade (2003) has sighted three examples:

(i) The US 64 fiasco

(ii) The case of Enron's power project in Maharashtra. Our political/administrative system seems incapable of sorting out the problem in any purposeful way; and (iii) The CBDT has started examining the issue of tax treatment of derivatives. How many years after trading in derivatives started? As if the system does not have a surfeit of tax disputes already! In short, are we not capable of proactive actions in almost any area? Can we only have governance by crisis?

What are the key challenges which need to be overcome to see the necessary economic changes through? N.K. Singh (2003) points out the following:

(i) There is the *fiscal challenge*. The combined fiscal deficit of the central and state governments remains unacceptably high. *Fiscal consolidation implies a more credible programme on downsizing of government*, rationalizing and better targeting of subsidies—particularly food and fertilizers—application of user charges and adhering to the time frame for phasing out kerosene and LPG subsidies. State governments have to seek fiscal rectitude in areas like curtailing of wasteful expenditure, putting a ceiling on fresh government employment, quickly implementing power sector reforms and privatizing loss-making public sector undertakings, even while adhering to the discipline of meeting their expenditure not through fresh borrowings or creation of contingent liability through creation of para-statal entities.

(ii) When will the government realize that people are not anti-reforms but are pro-growth? It is true that the fruits of growth do not automatically percolate to the poorer segments of society and the rural areas. While growth with equity and justice may be a rhetorical slogan, it is necessary that policies of *economic deregulation are coupled with credible social safety nets, reform of healthcare systems and improved infrastructure so that the benefits of reforms are felt by the average Indian*. For too long without being electorally tested, it has been wrongly assumed by governments in India that reforms are unpopular and impending elections have logic in postponing difficult measures. This approach is often prompted by strong vested and organized groups. But postponement of change is to the detriment of the people in general. The refashioning of a credible communication strategy is critical in shaping perspectives and bringing about a mindset change in the way reforms are perceived.

(iii) The growing regional divide and high pockets of poverty among states and within states is a matter of concern. The experience of resource transfer to address pockets of endemic poverty has met with limited success, and *issues of governance loom large in any discussion relating to balanced regional development*.

(iv) While the six successive governments since the

commencement of reforms in 1991 have *not reversed any major economic decisions*, the continuation of bipartisan support is critical to the passage of important legislations pending in Parliament. Political parties must cease to be nostalgic in terms of what they did in the past or persist with ideological barriers to permit the passage of these critical economic legislations during the tenure of this Parliament, and

(v) There is the issue of the *government living up to its own promise:* the promise of bringing about changes in labour laws, further rationalization of the reservation policy in respect of the small scale sector, a rapid reduction in import duties to bring them on par with other Asian countries, restructuring of railway projects and finances, a forward looking civil aviation policy need decisive action. If India can overcome these challenges, the next five years will catapult the country as a major economic power. This is achievable and political parties must realize what Shakespeare said: *"We know what we are but know not what we may be." The India to be must be our over-riding national goal.* (*Singh*, 2003).

The framing of an enlightened economic reforms programme is totally dependent on the level of technical skill of its architects and also their political maturity in view of the fact that the reforms essentially mean political adjustments that will have to be made as a result of existing, resizing, relocating and re-orienting different spheres of economic activity. Obviously, at some point, those with the technical skills and those with adequate political sagacity to tackle the attendant problems will have to comprise different sets of people.

V

This is the first time since Independence when there has been no decadal crisis. For the last five years or so, the government has no longer been coping with massive problems of the sort the previous governments used, problems that take a huge national effort and time to solve. In corporate terminology, it is the equivalent of a massive infusion of capital and technology that puts to rest fears of survival. The nature of coping has thus changed, in as much it is now of a more routine sort a management type of coping daily fire-fighting if you will rather than a huge effort merely to stay in business.

Happily, the change this has brought about is apparent in the outlook of some of the institutions within the government. It is already in evidence in the sector that was most affected by the previous cautiousness, namely, the financial sector. In the last 10 years, it has changed beyond recognition. The results are beginning to show—and one proof of that is the steady inflow of dollars. If foreign money is not sure of how good your financial systems are, it will not come in. *But not many politicians recognize that the nature of the problem has changed in a very fundamental way.* When one blames coalitions for slow reforms, it is not the fact of coalition itself that is at fault; the fault lies with the leaders of the smaller parties in the coalition (*Reghavan*, 2003a).

While worrying about economic reform, the country should equally worry about the *quality of governance* in its poorest states. This affects growth too. For as a recent survey showed, one of the principal constraints on the demand for consumer goods in India is the absence of electricity (*T.N. Niman*, 2003).

The economic reforms, introduced since the crisis year 1991, are an important landmark in the economic history of India. They transformed the closed, centrally-planned economy to an open, largely market-driven, one. The reforms included removal of industrial licensing, which abolished restrictions on investment and capacity expansion, de-reservation of industries reserved for the public sector, substantial opening up of foreign direct investment, and trade liberalization through elimination of quantitative restrictions and reduction in Customs tariffs. These and related reforms were aimed at promoting faster growth of the economy, aided by improved productivity and efficiency and at making the economy competitive both domestically and globally.

The revival in non-food bank credit reflects improvement in the industrial climate. Inflation has remained moderate, notwithstanding the shortfall in agricultural production and volatility in oil prices.

The prospects of further inflation in the light of West Asian developments, however, remain to be seen. As regards external front, the current account balance recorded larger surplus despite a reasonably well-distributed pick-up in imports. Capital flows remained stable both on account of FDI and non-resident deposits. This salutary development resulted in a record accumulation of around $83 billion of foreign exchange reserves. In the decade preceding reforms India had a growth rate of GDP of 5.6 per cent while the period from 1992-93 to 2002-03 showed a marginally higher rate of growth of 6.1 per cent.

The pre-reform decade had witnessed a substantial increase in public investment in infrastructure, particularly on power, transport and rural development, which was reduced in the 1990s. The fiscal reform of the 1990s was essentially achieved by a contraction in investment. Again, the revenue deficit in the pre-reform decade was only 1.65 per cent of GDP against 6.07 per cent for the reform period 1997-98 to 2001-02. The quality of fiscals reforms definitely leaves much to be desired. One aspect of economic development post-reforms is the decline in momentum in manufacturing growth. The fall in the share of industry in GDP is perhaps an unintended consequence of the reform process and calls for rectification. Policy innovations, which will increase the proportion of industry's share in GDP, seem necessary.

Industrial performance still continues to be hampered by physical infrastructural bottlenecks. There is the need for power sector reforms and correction of the cross-subsidies in the tariff structure. The emphasis should be on the need for extra investments in the power sector, be it in the public sector or the private, both to be supported by adequate tariff reforms. The report rightly stresses the role of credit in the growth of industry. There has been slowing down of credit to small and medium industry. There is need for greater concentration on cleaning up the institutions, including the State Finance Corporations. Credit flow is an essential precondition for economic growth. The sectoral shift in favour of services accompanied an almost stagnant share of industry and agriculture. The growth performance of the services sector has provided a modicum of resilience to the overall growth of the economy. The reform process, which involved liberalization of the financial sector, also provided an environment for faster growth of financial services. As a result, the share of services touched a high 50 per cent of GDP. A substantial fillip to the services sector also came from exports, such as software and call centers. True, the growth in services may be attributed, in part, due to growth of expenditure on public administration and defense, particularly in the backdrop of the Pay Commission's recommendations.

What should India do to get greater gains from globalization? Tenth Plan include lower government borrowing much less restrictive labour laws, phasing out of SSI reservations, lowering of our unusually high customs duties, quick reform of the power sector, reduction in 'transaction costs' in taxation, finance and infrastructure provision, decisive privatizations and so on. The problem is not with knowing what's to be done...but to do it. Until we DO sensible economic policies, half-hearted globalization will continue to yield half-baked results!

VI

An adequate growth programme needs to be anchored in two strategies: an investment strategy designed to kick-start growth in the short-term, and an institution-building strategy designed to provide an economy with resilience in the face of adverse shocks. The key to investment strategy is to get domestic entrepreneurs excited about the home economy. Encouraging foreign investment or liberalizing everything and then waiting for things to improve does not work. An effective strategy must accomplish two tasks: encourage investment in non-traditional areas, and weed out projects and investments that fail. For this, governments must deploy both the carrot and the stick. Learning what a country is (or can be) good at producing is a key challenge of economic development. The carrot is needed because there is great social value in discovering, for example, computer software can be produced at low cost, because this knowledge can orient the investments of other entrepreneurs. In turn, the stick is needed to ensure that these incentives do not lock in unproductive and wasteful investments. Economic growth requires most than eliciting a temporary boost in investment and entrepreneurship. It also requires effort to build four types of institutions required to maintain growth momentum and build resilience to shocks:

- *Market-creating institutions* (for property rights and control enforcement);
- *Market-regulating institutions* (for externalities, economies of scale, and information about companies);

- *Market-stabilising institutions* (for monetary and fiscal management); and
- *Market-legitimising institutions* (for social protection and insurance).

According to Dani Rodrik (2002), "Building and solidifying these institutions, however, takes time. Using an initial period of growth to experiment and innovate on these fronts can pay high dividends later on. A key point here is that institutional arrangements are, by necessity, country-specific. Discovering what works in any others. Such specificity helps explain why successful countries—China, India, South Korea, and Taiwan, among others—usually combined unorthodox elements with orthodox policies. It also accounts for why important institutional differences persist among the advanced countries of North America, Western Europe, and Japan in areas such as the role of the public sector, the legal system, corporate governance, financial markets, labour markets, and social insurance.

While economic analysis can help in making institutional choices, there is also a large role for public deliberation and collective choice. In fact, we can think of participatory democracy as a meta-institution that helps select among the "menu" of possible institutional arrangements in each area. Designing such a growth strategy is both harder and easier than implementing standard neo-liberal policies. It is harder because the binding constraints on growth are usually country-specific and do not respond well to standardized recipes. But it is easier because once those constraints are appropriately targeted, relatively simple policy changes can yield enormous economic payoffs and start a virtuous cycle of growth and institutional reform. Adopting this approach does not mean abandoning mainstream economics—far from it. Neo-liberalism is to neo-classical economics as astrology is to astronomy. In both cases, it takes a lot of blind faith to go from one to the other. Critics of neo-liberalism should not oppose mainstream economics—only its misuse.

There are no easy or simple links between economic freedom and growth. Some kinds of government intervention (complex and corrupt controls and procedures) can greatly slow down growth, but other interventions (universal education, good infrastructure, good governance) are essential for growth. Merely being an open economy (like some African sluggards) is not good enough: you need institutions that facilitate entrepreneurship and dynamism. The experience of China, India and Vietnam shows that the direction of liberalization seems far more important than its absolute level. Above all, it seems that many very different paths can lead to success. So much depends on local traditions and history that no single blueprint will succeed everywhere, and freedom to experiment and innovate seems to be vital.

India's development policy challenges could be grouped into two broad areas: (i) improving management of public resources by reducing Budget deficits, reallocating spending to more productive investments and enhancing the quality of service delivery, and (ii) improving the investment climate and raising productivity in industry, services, agriculture and rural development. The 10th Plan envisages a sizeable fiscal adjustment would be required to generate the level of public savings and provide space for the level of public and private investment, needed to generate eight per cent growth. Certain areas demand response, the failure of which would derail reforms and retard poverty reduction plans.

To achieve the planned growth target of 8 per cent, India will need to impart a fresh impetus to reforms. Fiscal adjustment, along with other reforms to improve the investment climate, will be essential to accelerate growth." It also pointed out that the continued deceleration in industrial growth was accompanied by slowdown in investment and deterioration in the fiscal position of both Centre and the States. To improve the investment climate and raise productivity, it would be necessary to address the market distortion and inefficiencies in industry and service sectors, tackle infrastructure bottlenecks, especially in power and transport, and boost agriculture and rural development.

References

Acharya, Sadkar (2003), "Half-hearted Globalisation," *The Economic Times*, January 2.

Choudhury, Ranabir Ray (2003), "Where are we headed?," *The Hindu Business Line*, July 7.

Desikan, R. (2003), "Should a Regulator be Regulated?" *The Hindu Business Line*, June 18.

Muruganandan, Gowthaman (2003), "Is Privatisation the way to go?," *The Hindu Business Line*, June 12.

Ninan, T.N. (2003), "Governance Matters," *Business Standard*, July 19/20.

Pani, Narendar (2003), "The Price of Political Vetoes," *The Economic Times*, March 14.

Rajwade, A.V. (2003), "The Economy: A Post-Budget Perspective," *Economic and Political Weekly*, April 5.

Ravimohan, R. (2003), "Acts and Inaction," *Business Standard*, July 18.

Reserve Bank of India (2003), *Report on Currency and Finance, 2001-02*, Department of Economic Analysis and Policy, Mumbai, April.

Rodrik, Dani (2002), "After Neo-liberalism what?," *The Economic Times*, November 19.

Samuels, Warren J. (1987), "Institutional Economics" (in *Palgrave's Dictionary of Economics*), Macmillan, Vol. I, pp. 864-966.

Singh, N.K. (2003), "Let it Grow," *The Hindustan Times*, June 4.

Srinivasa-Raghavan, T.C.A. (2003a), "From Coping to Managing," *Business Standard*, July 5/6.

—— (2003b) "The Limits of Economics," *Business Standard*, July 19/20.

Venkitaramanan, S. (2003), "Revisiting the Washington Consensus," *The Hindu Business Line*, May 12.

Venkat, Kumar (2003), "Making Globalisation Work," *The Hindu Business Line*, June 18.

Williamson, John (2003), "The Washington Consensus and Beyond," *Economic and Political Weekly*, April 12.

Local Government in India: The New Institutional Approach

V. LOGANATHAN AND K. JOTHI SIVAGNANAM

INTRODUCTION

This paper is an empirical attempt to examine the institutionalisation of rural local self-government in India. It focuses mainly on the issues and various aspects of institutionalisation of local self-government in India under the new dispensation. It is done within the theoretical framework of New Institutional Economics. To begin with, the paper examines the role and significance of institutions in economic development and economic reforms with a brief discussion of the concepts of 'institution' and 'New Institutional Economics' (NIE). Then it proceeds to examine the recent trend towards decentralisation and the significance of local self-government. Local self-government is examined both as a new institution as well as a development strategy. In doing so, emphasis is laid on differentiating the priorities for which the local self-government institution is designed and argues that development rather than privatisation should be the top most priority. Within this theoretical and conceptual framework, the Indian experience is examined.

INSTITUTIONS AND DEVELOPMENT

The role of institutions in economic development in general and reforms in particular have gained much significance in recent years. A proper set of institutions becomes essential for economic growth and development. Economic reform policies and development strategies never proceed independently of specific institutional and historical context. That is especially true of India and other Asian countries as there are innumerable social, economic and political institutions. Therefore, no generalized IMF or World Bank prescriptions are acceptable. Rather they have to be applied with suitable and thorough modifications in such a way that they are in perfect harmony with the existing institutions, which we have inherited from the past. For economic policies to bring about the desired results, there must be the right institutional and political underpinnings to these policies; otherwise, the reforms will be only partially successful or entirely fail or possibly even lead to outcomes that are worse than the initial situation (*Kahkonen and Lanyi*, 2000).

Within this frame, understanding these institutional and political underpinnings of development is necessary for the success of any reform as well as the development policies. This is more so in the developing countries where IMF-World Bank sponsored economic reform policy changes are in progress. Most of these countries are still dependent principally on agriculture and most of their population still lives in rural areas. The challenges of rural development administration become an even more serious challenge in the light of structural adjustment and stabilization programmes. The reform policies must carefully be designed against the background of existing social, political and economic institutions in rural areas in addition to creating new institutions to implement the reform policies. The following sections provide a brief discussion of the concepts of *institution* and *NIE*.

INSTITUTIONS AND NEW INSTITUTIONAL ECONOMICS

Institutions are the rules, laws, habits, traditions, mores, etc. that govern our social, economic and political lives. The term encompasses both formal arrangements (rules-of-game) and informal norms, customs, conventions, standard patterns or arrangements or operating systems which define the relationship between individuals and social groups. Formal arrangements are important carriers of such institutions as are governance regimes with codified rules and sanctions but institutionalisation can also take less visible forms (North, 1990). But such "less visible forms" are in fact more visible in developing societies. The list of such informal forms of institutions is long.

According to Richard Langlois (1986), "the NIE includes the evolutionary theory of Nelson and Winter and other work influenced by Joseph Schumpeter; the modern Austrian school, especially as influenced by the work of F.A. Hayek; the transactions cost economics of Oliver Williamson and certain aspects of the property rights literature inspired by Ronold Coase. There are other affinities and sources of influence, notably Herbert Simon and the behaviouralist school".

Douglas North, the 1993 Nobelist, defines the NIE as follows: *"The new institutional economics is an attempt to incorporate a theory of institutions into economics"*. The main difference between neo-classical economics and NIE is lies in their treatment of institutions in economic analysis. The institutionalist does not repudiate the basic methodology of neo-classical economics but assumes 'institutions' as endogenous variables and tries to provide better explanations within the neoclassical framework. Neo-classical economics however assumes 'institutions' as exogenous or given and proceeds with their analysis within such given institutional settings.

Institutions provide the incentive structure of an economy; as that structure evolves, it shapes the direction of economic change towards growth, stagnation or decline. If economics work well and perform well, it is because you have a set of institutions that provide incentive for people to be productive. As professor Lindbeck, the chairman of the 1993 Nobel Prize Committee put it: "the Soviet-bloc countries fell apart because they did not have institutions that functioned".

NIE can be applied to both individual and collective decision-making. However, its specialty is collective choice. Adam Smith's famous invisible hand celebrates the assertion that people need have no concern for each other and need not make any conscious collective decision. The best aggregate results will emerge from individual isolated choices. This 'homogenous individual globule of desire' (in Veblen's usage) calculates how to get the most for the least.

This mindless and relentless optimization drive becomes the basis for the neoclassical market mechanism. Such markets have miserably failed in several areas of public and social goods provision whose consumption is 'collective' and 'non-rival' in nature. Even in the case of many private goods, markets have failed in many rural areas of developing societies. Instead of focussing on market transactions, the institutional approach focuses on collective decisions about economic affairs and this mainly directs the analysis to the areas where voting for choosing among the alternatives is an ultimate requirement to arrive at collective decision and then to implement them. The following section examines the emerging trend of decentralisation and the importance of local self-government and its institutionalisation within this theoretical framework.

DECENTRALISATION AND DEVELOPMENT

Recent years have witnessed a worldwide interest in decentralization. Decentralisation, involves a statutory assignment of specific functions, necessary funds, and required personnel to local governments in such a way that it should facilitate to move governance more closely to the people. Decentralization and participation become the avowed objectives and part of the development strategy of many developing and transition economies. Multilateral donor agencies have also started to encourage this trend which started in eighties and gained momentum in the nineties.

POLITICS AND ECONOMICS OF DECENTRALIZATION

Reasons for this emerging trend are both political and economic in nature. To facilitate globalization, new institutions are needed to be created mainly to provide the necessary protection and foundation for a well functioning market economy. One such most discussed institution is 'privatization'—moves from a command economy to one of liberalized markets and free economic agents.

'Decentralization' has become another required institutional change because it is likely to be associated with a smaller public sector. Brennan and Buchanan [1980] claimed that decentralization is an effective mechanism to control Leviathan's expansive tendencies. They argued that, other things being equal, the size of the government sector (total government spending) varies inversely with the extent of fiscal decentralization.

Whatever may be the political and ideological reasons for the new enthusiasm in decentralisation at the national and international levels, there are strong and powerful economic rationale for decentralized provision of public goods and services in an efficient way and hence enhanced prospects for higher growth. The theory of fiscal federalism argues that public goods can be provided to meet the diversified needs of the people across all sub-central units in a cost-efficient manner through proper decentralization. This is possible because the benefit regions of many local public goods are much smaller and affect people only in those regions. The welfare gains are much greater, the greater the diversity in preference levels among persons in various areas. Then at local level more effective collective decision-making and greater popular control can be exercised over the precise manner in which the services are provided. Finally, the principle of benefit regions to the benefit, that is, the benefit incidence of various local public goods is subject to spatial limitations and therefore each service should be divided upon and paid for within the confines of the jurisdiction in which benefits accrue. Now recent empirical findings (*Huther and Shah,* 1998) prove significant positive correlation between the quality of governance as such and the degree of decentralisation in a sample of eighty countries (Table 1).

DECENTRALIZATION IN DEVELOPING COUNTRIES

In the developing and transition countries, *'decentralisation'* has acquired new attention as a reform policy and development strategy. The World Bank in its ever-growing efforts to create market-friendly institutions in such countries is recently interested in decentralisation because it thinks that the ultimate form of decentralisation is privatisation. But in developing countries like India where social and rural sector are still backward and further affected by the ongoing liberalisation, privatisation and

TABLE 1

Decentralization and Governance

	Correlation Coefficients
Citizen Participation	
Political Freedom	0.599**
Political Stability	0.604**
Government Orientation	
Judicial Efficiency	0.544**
Bureaucratic Efficiency	0.540**
Absence of Corruption	0.532**
Social Development	
Human Development Index	0.369**
Egalitarianism in Income Distribution (inverse of Gini coefficient)	0.373**
Economic Management	
Central Bank Independence	0.327**
Debt Management Discipline	0.263**
Openess of the Economy	0.523**
Governance Quality Index	*0.617***

* significant at the 0.05% level (2-tailed test)
** significant at the 0.01% level (2-tailed test)
Correlation of the Decentralization Index with Governance Quality Indicators (Sample size: 80 countries)
Source: Huther and Shah (1998).

globalization processes, decentralization is viewed mainly as a people-friendly institutional approach to development.

Not only that, in the case of India, local governments are not new institutions and they were in existence for many centuries before the World Bank's findings. In India, decentralised form of local bodies traditionally was institutions of self-governance and they really served the state-society relation at least at the local level. Now in the post-independent India, decentralisation has become a rural development strategy.

Hence the institutionalisation of local government should be viewed in continuity with the past as an important and effective development strategy at least within the framework of our country to meet its pressing development needs particularly rural development. Rural development has now acquired added emphasis and significance in the liberalized and globalized regime particularly to safeguard those who have been marginalised in such process. Thus the crucial relationship is not between decentralisation and efficiency but between decentralisation and development.

Finally, decentralization is not only an institutional means to reach economic and political ends but an end in itself. Thus apart from its instrumental value, decentralization has its own intrinsic value in developing countries where government, any form—federal, regional or local for that matter, has not yet fully reached many rural parts. Hence more than efficiency or tailoring the local public goods to suit the local preferences, these regions deserve the provision of some minimum ethically defined essential services like drinking water, primary health care, primary education, road, electricity, etc. Here, the ultimate purpose of decentralisation in India, and any developing country for that matter, is to ensure the efficient and effective delivery of some minimum basic social and economic services through good governance.

LOCAL GOVERNMENT INSTITUTIONS IN INDIA

The institution of local self-government is not foreign to our society. During the Chola period (from 9th to 13th century A.D.) the panchayat system, the institution of local government was functioning in a fairly organized way as an integral part of village administration, economy and judiciary. After Independence, Panchayat Raj Institutions (PRIs) were the institutional expression of the ideal—democratic decentralization below the state level. In Independent India, rural development acquired marked focus and became the part of the overall development strategy. Thus rural development as a strategy includes improvement in the quality of life of rural masses through better infrastructure in terms of health, education, drinking water, roads, housing, sanitation, electricity, etc. PRIs are seen mainly as a means to rural development. This is justifiable even today because a majority of Indian population still dwells in villages.

The first initiative, with the above strategy was made in 1952 through Community Development Programme (CDP) followed by several other efforts. However, over the past half a century, the 'steps' taken to translate the above Constitutional mandate into a reality were limited in scope, lethargic in speed, resistant in commitment and lacking in direction.

INSTITUTIONALISATION OF NEW PRIs

However, for the first time in India, PRI, the third tier gained constitutional status after the 73rd and 74th Amendments to the Constitution. The aim seems to establish democratically elected local self-government to ensure economic development and social justice (Article 243G and 243W). Now, the PRIs must be empowered with transfer of funds and financial autonomy, functions and functionaries. Twenty-nine subjects are listed under the Eleventh Schedule of the Act to be distributed for planning and implementing at the three levels of local bodies. State level election commission and finance commissions have been created.

As per the Constitutional Amendment Acts, regular elections once in five years have to be conducted for the institutionalization of PRIs and the first election should have been held within nine months after the commencement of the state Act. As a result of this, about 2,38,682 local governments at village, block and district levels have been constituted and 2.92 million representatives (of which one-third are women) have been elected. 'This is the broadest representative base that exists in any country in the world'. However, there are some states (Arunachal Pradesh, Assam, Pondicherry, Delhi and new states, namely, Jharkhand and Uttaranchal) where elections have still not been held on one or other pretext and in some other states subsequent elections have been delayed for years (Table 2).

Article 243I of the Constitution provides for the constitution of State Finance Commission (SFC) to decide on the devolution and other aspects of the financial position of local government. Table 3 provides the status of SFC.

Article 243ZD of the 74th Constitutional Amendment Act provides for the constitution of District Planning Committee (DPC) in every district to consolidate the plans prepared by the lower tiers and prepare a plan draft for the entire district. Table 4 gives the status of DPC as on December 2001.

Article 243G of the 73rd Constitutional Amendment Act

TABLE 2

Status of Local Government Elections

Sl. No.	States/UTs	Elections last held	Elections due
1.	Andhra Pradesh	DP-10th Jan., 2001 GP-August, 2001	DP-July, 2006 GP-August, 2006
2.	Bihar	April, 2001	April, 2006
3.	Goa	GP-Jan. 1997 DP-Jan, 2000	January, 2002 January, 2005
4.	Haryana	March, 2000	March, 2005
5.	Himachal Pradesh	December, 2000	December, 2005
6.	Karnataka	GP-Feb., 2000 IP&DP-July, 2000	GP-Feb., 2005 IP&DP-July, 2005
7.	Kerala	September, 2000	September, 2005
8.	Madhya Pradesh	January, 2000	January, 2005
9.	Chhattisgarh	January, 2000	January, 2005
10.	Maharashtra	DP&JP-March, 1997 GP-October 1997	March, 2002 October, 2002
11.	Manipur	GP&DP-31.1.97	January, 2002
12.	Orissa	January, 1997	January, 2002
13.	Rajasthan	January, 2000	January, 2005
14.	Sikkim	October 6, 1997	October 6, 2002
15.	Tamil Nadu	October, 1996	October, 2001
16.	Tripura	July, 1999	July, 2004
17.	Uttar Pradesh	Plains-June, 2000 Hills-1996	May, 2005 (Plains) 2001 (Hills)
18.	West Bengal	1998	2003
19.	A&N Islands	September, 2000	September, 2005
20.	D&N Haveli	October, 2000	October, 2005
21.	Daman & Diu	September, 2000	September, 2005
22.	Lakshadweep	Dec.97/Jan.98	Dec.2002/Jan. 2003

GP—Gram Panchayat, IP—Intermediate Panchayat, DP—District Panchayat.
Source: Ministry of Rural Development, Government of India.

requires the state to endow the Panchayats with necessary power and authority to enable them to function as units of 'self-government' and to devolve powers and responsibility to the Panchayats with respect to the preparation of plans for economic development and social justice and their implementation.

The 11th Schedule of the 73rd Constitutional Amendment Act provides a list of 29 subjects (such as agriculture, small scale

TABLE 3

Status of the First State Finance Commission

Status of SFC	*Name of States*
Constitution of SFC	All States except Arunachal Pradesh and NCT of Delhi
Submission of SFC Report	All States except Bihar
Report accepted in full	Himachal Pradesh, Kerala, Madhya Pradesh, Manipur, Punjab, Rajasthan, Tamil Nadu, Tripura, Uttar Pradesh and West Bengal
Report accepted in Parts	Andhra Pradesh, Assam, Haryana, Karnataka, Maharashtra
Accepted with modifications	Orissa
Report under consideration	Goa, Andaman and Nicobar Islands, Daman and Diu, Lakshdweep, Pondicherry
Report yet to be Placed before Legislature	Gujarat

Source: Ministry of Rural Development, Government of India.

TABLE 4

Status of District Planning Committees

Sl. No.	*States/UTs*	*Status of Constitution of DPCs*
1.	Andhra Pradesh	Not constituted
2.	Arunachal Pradesh	Not constituted
3.	Assam	Not constituted
4.	Bihar	Not constituted
5.	Goa	—
6.	Gujarat	Not constituted
7.	Haryana	Only in 4 Districts. Rest under consideration
8.	Himachal Pradesh	Not yet but it is under consideration
9.	J&K	Not applicable
10.	Karnataka	Yes. In 17 out of 20 districts. After reorganisation there are 27 districts. All DPCs will be reconstituted now
11.	Kerala	Yes. Chairperson of DP is chairperson of DPC
12.	Madhya Pradesh	Yes. District in charge Ministers are Chairpersons. Responsibilities of District Government given to the DPCs
13.	Maharashtra	Not constituted

(Contd.)

Sl. No.	*States/UTs*	*Status of Constitution of DPCs*
14.	Manipur	Yes in 2 districts. Out of 4. Adhyaksha, DP is Chairperson
15.	Mehalaya	Not applicable
16.	Mizoram	Not applicable
17.	Nagaland	Not applicable
18.	Orissa	Yes, Chairperson of DP is Chairperson of DPC
19.	Punjab	Not, yet but its constitution is under active consideration
20.	Rajasthan	Yes, ZP President is Chairperson of DPC
21.	Sikkim	Yes
22.	Tamil Nadu	Yes. Will become operational after election of members from Panchayats & Municipalities. Chairperson, DP is Chairperson
23.	Tripura	Yes. Cabinet rank ministers are Chairpersons
24.	Uttar Pradesh	Yes. Ministers are chairpersons
25.	West Bengal	Yes. Chairperson of DP is Chairperson of DPC
26.	A & N Islands	Yes
27.	Chandigarh	Not in favour as 90% of population covered by Municipality
28.	D & N Haveli	Yes.
29.	Daman & Diu	—
30.	NCT Delhi	State PR Act is under suspension
31.	Lakshadweep	Yes. Chief Development Commissioner is chairperson
32.	Pondicherry	Elections not held

Source: Ministry of Rural Development, Government of India.

industries, rural housing, drinking water, road, electricity, education, poverty alleviation, health and social welfare) to be handled by the panchayats. All are only illustrative and indicative in nature. Any clear-cut demarcation of funds, functions and powers between the state and local governments and among the different tiers has to be done by the state government. For such *inter se* distribution, the principle would be that what can be done at a particular level should be done at that level only and not at a higher level. This rule will facilitate avoiding inter-jurisdictional wrangles. However, many states with some exception, have not fulfilled this satisfactorily.

Article 243G, the most important of the 73rd and 74th Constitutional Amendments Act is very clear about the ultimate purpose of the Amendment—to enable the panchayat raj institutions to function as *'units of self-government'*. Though the Constitution is very clear in letter and spirit in this regard, many states including Tamil Nadu, except Bihar and Punjab, have cautiously avoided committing panchayats as *'units of self-government'*.

PRIs in India, being at its institutionalization stage, cannot be expected to deliver too much as our Constitution or the economists expect. Nothing wrong in being an optimist, but expecting 'to ensure economic development and social justice' and 'self-government' is over-ambitious at this stage. What one can look for, reasonably, at this stage is whether the process of institutionalization has been completed fully? If so, whether the institution can deliver (forget about efficiency, development, empowerment, justice and all that) some basic minimum services like water, primary education, primary health care, roads, etc. Moreover, this is what people, at the least expect from the local government.

However, though we have completed ten years of local self-governance after having created a new formal institutional structure for the third tier of the Indian federation in nineties, still the ground reality is that the process of institutionalisation has yet to be completed in many states. There are several obstacles and the political commitment and sincerity of the state concerned dominate such long list.

To ensure such basic minimum services, the local government should breathe. Commitments of the state government and assured regular flow of funds are the necessary and essential conditions for that. 'Healthy local government' with 'sufficient resources' is too much to expect from the states in view of their own deteriorating fiscal health. At the least, the transfer of 'assigned statutory revenue' meant for the local bodies need to be transferred to keep them 'ticking'. In spite of some progress, the most pressing problem of the local government today in most of the states is their very meagre revenue or absence of any funds.

Table 5 clearly reveals the pathetic state of local finance in spite of the rhetoric of tall claims in some states. Local governments as a whole spend only 12.02% of NSDP. To meet that expenditure, they depend on the higher tiers of government to the tune of 83% (10% of NSDP) and their own revenue collection is less than 5%.

TABLE 5

States of the Local Government Finance

State	Rural Local Bodies				Urban Local Bodies				Total Local Bodies				Per cent of Local Revenue to Total sub-national Revenue
	Revenue Collection	Revenue Accrual	Total Expenditure	% of Own Rev. to Total Rev.	Revenue Collection	Revenue Accrual	Total Expenditure	% of Own Rev. to Total Rev.	Revenue Collection	Revenue Accrual	Total Expenditure	% of Own Rev. to Total Rev.	
	Percent of NSDP				Percent of NSDP				Percent of NSDP				
High Income													
States	0.08	1.81	2.25	4.50	1.52	1.83	33.12	82.94	1.60	3.64	35.37	43.91	10..42
Punjab	0.12	0.30	0.36	39.78	0.91	1.05	0.80	86.62	1.03	1.35	1.16	76.13	6.75
Maharashtra	0.07	2.01	2.79	3.39	2.13	2.42	62.99	88.09	2.20	4.43	65.77	49.64	15.11
Haryana	0.16	0.26	0.44	62.20	0.31	0.54	1.03	58.39	0.47	0.79	1.47	59.63	2.59
Gujarat	0.05	2.96	3.01	1.81	1.08	1.58	1.26	67.97	1.13	4.55	4.27	24.84	7.10
Middle Income													
States	0.10	2.46	2.40	3.92	0.57	1.04	13.21	54.72	0.67	3.50	15.61	19.08	3.94
Tamil Nadu	0.04	0.55	0.63	8.07	0.85	1.58	1.62	53.77	0.90	2.13	2.25	42.06	4.85
Kerala	0.26	2.59	1.92	10.08	0.30	0.69	0.72	43.64	0.56	3.27	2.64	17.13	2.91
Karnataka	0.05	6.50	6.38	0.80	0.28	0.72	0.77	38.96	0.33	7.22	7.15	4.60	1.78
Andhra Pradesh	0.18	3.19	3.18	5.49	0.44	0.83	52.84	52.86	0.61	4.02	56.02	15.25	3.37
West Bengal	0.02	0.60	0.69	4.02	0.77	1.14	0.47	67.57	0.79	1.74	1.16	45.55	6.63
Low Income States	0.04	1.78	1.90	2.24	0.27	0.60	0.64	45.20	0.31	2.38	2.54	13.03	1.75
Rajasthan	0.07	3.28	3.32	2.02	0.82	1.10	1.06	74.54	0.89	4.38	4.37	20.24	4.66

Madhya Pradesh	0.05	2.92	2.93	1.80	0.24	0.79	1.02	30.59	0.30	3.71	3.94	7.96	1.58
Uttar Pradesh	0.04	0.78	0.80	5.28	0.15	0.55	0.54	27.49	0.19	1.34	1.34	14.50	1.23
Orissa	0.03	2.66	2.66	1.09	0.35	0.49	0.57	72.60	0.38	3.14	3.23	12.17	1.95
Bihar @		0.79	1.43							0.79	1.43		
Smaller States	0.03	0.54	0.61	4.84	0.14	0.34	0.52	40.07	0.16	0.88	1.12	18.52	0.38
25 States	0.05	1.35	1.46	3.66	0.53	0.78	10.56	67.73	0.58	2.13	12.02	27.11	4.73

Source: M.G. Rao (2001).

The relative share of the rural local government is still more pathetic. Of the total expenditure of local governments, the rural local government's share constitutes a meagre 12% (1.46% of NSDP) and their revenue collection is 0.05 of NSDP. That is, the revenue collection of rural local governments in India as a whole, is not even one percent of the states' income.

The relative position of some of the individual states, namely, Maharashtra, and Andhra Pradesh is very high but again their share in the case of rural areas is very low. The only exception is Karnataka where around 6.38% is spent for rural local governments out of the total 7.15% of NSDP. As a whole, the state of local government finance is so poor that it needs a lot of encouragement and support from the higher tiers as well as from our policy-makers.

Considering the present pathetic fiscal health of the state governments, it is the responsibility of the Union Government to take required initiative to some extent. Since local self-governments have become the statutory third-tier of our federal system as per the constitutional mandate, the Union government, the Finance Commission and the Planning Commission should come forward to make regular transfers, of course, not directly to the local government but via the state governments, to the local governments. However, it is highly unfair on the part of the Eleventh Finance Commission to disown its responsibility. The Commission declared: The responsibility of sharing and assigning taxes and providing grants to the local bodies rests with the States and does not stand transferred to the Centre. As such an attitude may not serve the interests of local self-government as well as federal democracy, the Union government should come forward to devolve resources regularly to the third-tier of our federal system.

Further, all the centrally sponsored schemes for the provision and improvement of civic services should be transferred to the local governments. A public awareness should be created so that the resources to the local governments are spent without pilferage and seepage and on the subjects for which they are allocated. Then only the ideals of the real local democracy and local self-governance can be realized in the larger interests of the society.

REFERENCES

Buchanan and Brennan (1980): *The Power to Tax: Analytical Foundations of a Fiscal Constitution*, Cambridge University Press, Cambridge.

Dilllnger, William (1994): Decentralization and its implications for Urban Service Delivery, Urban Management Programme, Discussion Paper 16, World Bank, Washington, DC.

Gol (2000): Report of the Task Force on Panchayati Raj Institutions (PRIs), Government of India, New Delhi.

Huther, Jeff and Anwar Shah (1998): *Applying* a *Simple Measure of Good Governance to the Debate on Fiscal Decentralization*, Policy Research Working paper No. 1894, World Bank, Washington, DC.

Kahkonen, S. and Antony Lany (eds. 2000): *Institutions, Incentives and Economic Reforms in India*, Sage Publications, N.D.

Langlois, Richard (ed.) (1986): *Economics as a process: Essays in the New Institutional Economics*, Cambridge: Cambridge University Press.

North, D.C. (1990): *Institutions, Institutional Change and Economic Performance*, Cambridge, Cambridge University Press.

Rao, M.G. (2001): *Fiscal Decentralization in Indian Federalism*, Working Paper 98, Institute for Social and Economic Change, Bangalore.

Educational Initiatives of PRIs and Community in Education Development of Poor

Experience from Kolhapur, Maharashtra

Y. Gangi Reddy

I. INTRODUCTION

Illiteracy and poverty are intertwined in rural India and remains a major challenge for rural development initiatives. While lack of skills is one of the causes of poverty, poverty limits people acquiring skills. Experiences of East Asian countries indicate a minimum of 8 years schooling as a necessary condition for skill acquisition by poor. Hence, to overcome the poverty literacy levels of the poor people have to be enhanced. Poverty being the effect and cause of illiteracy, it is necessary that Rural Development Policies have to lay greater emphasis on the issue of education particularly early childhood care and elementary education that provides the foundation for holistic development of children. The

This paper is part of a research project on "Utilisation of Primary Education and ICDS Infrastructure by the poor: Role of CBOs and PRIs", Thrust Area Group Research Study of NIRD, 2002-03.

economic liberalisation process has further accentuated the necessity for the minimum education so as to equip them with better skills in the emerging competitive environment and to take full advantage of the new opportunities. The role of the state as a provider of all the required resources for social development including education has been found to be inadequate and has been declining under the new economic regime. Given the changing role of state, it becomes obvious that alternative new institutions particularly at the grass-roots are the need of the hour. In this context, it is also imperative to assess the strengths and weaknesses of the existing institutions and equip them with necessary capacities and resources to emerge as alternative institutions for sustainable social development. Since, there is direct relation between the poverty and illiteracy, local initiatives are focused on poorer segments of the population.

Panchayat Raj Institutions are considered as important local institutions, which can ensure people's participation in the overall development. 73rd Amendment to the Constitution envisages a greater role for PRIs in the entire development process at the local level giving equal opportunity to the disadvantaged sections of the society. Apart from PRIs there are many other community-based organisations (CBOs) associated with community development endeavours in several areas. Only in a few areas there is a real organic cohesion between PRIs and other CBOs towards developmental activities. This is necessary that only a symbiosis of all these institutions at the local level would create an environment for equal opportunity to all for their effective participation in the development process.

The State of Maharashtra has been building a strong Panchayat Raj (PR) system even before many other states in India. PR institutions at the grass-root level have been playing a proactive role in ensuring proper support not only in creating necessary infrastructure but also facilitating poor to access and utilise all those infrastructure created not only for education but also for other developmental services. The present paper critically examines the role of the Gram Panchayat and CBOs in the development of education for children, especially children of the poor in the district of Kolhapur, where innovations in primary education are reported.

II. OBJECTIVES AND METHODOLOGY

Objectives

The overall objective of the present paper is to explore various issues that revolve around the role of Gram Panchayat and CBOs in achieving education as a catalyst for the overall development of poor in Kolhapur district of Maharastra. The following are the specific objectives of the paper:

1. To highlight salient features of primary education model in Kolhapur,
2. To study the institutional arrangements and innovations adopted for primary education as well as integrated child development; and
3. To analyse the outcomes of these interventions in terms of quality of education, equity issues including gender, exclusion and inclusion, and public-private partnership.

To examine the above objectives, an intensive field study was carried out in six villages of Kolhapur district of Maharashtra during 2002-03. The following issues that are related to the overall educational development of children of poor communities were examined in this study.

- Role of PRIs (Gram Panchayat) and local community (CBOs) in village development particularly in creating necessary infrastructure and facilitating the poor in availing the services for child development.
- The extent of utilisation of education infrastructure by the poor and gender biases if any.
- The mode and degree of participation of poor in both the maintenance of school and ICDS.
- Motivation, attitude and commitment of children, parents, teachers, officials, community and local leaders.
- Impact of all these measures in improving the quality of education to the children of poor people.

Sampling Design

One block each was randomly selected from the developed and backward areas of the district. Karvir block, which is considered developed, and Radhanagari block that is considered backward were chosen for the study. Six villages were selected randomly for primary data collection and they are Amshi, Bahirashwar and Devale from Karvir block and Saravde, Rashiwade and Arjunawade from Radhanagari block. In order to have an in-depth understanding of the status of primary education, ICDS programme and Child Development, a number of stakeholders were contacted (Annexure-I). Participatory tools such as Focus Group Discussions (FGD), Semi-Structured Interviews, and Timeline were adopted for effective interactions and primary data collection with all the stakeholders.

Background of the Study Area

The district of Kolhapur is considered as a moderate district in terms of levels of overall development. The district has a long history of the great Maratha Emperors, Chatrapathi Shivaji Maharaj and Rajashri Sahu Maharaj. Social development of the district is significantly better compared to several other districts. The great visionary King of Kolhapur Shri Ch. Sahu Maharaj, who is referred as a Royal Revolutionary of the society had initiated a number of socio-economic development programmes in all parts of his kingdom. He has made a law for free and compulsory primary education in the State. He has enacted an Act of Powall in 1917, making primary education as compulsory. He has also established scout movement and number of hostels for various students as part of overall human resource development. Kolhapur is one of the frontline districts of India in the fields of Art, Education, Culture, Music, Sports, Cinema, etc. and in all these fields, the district is represented both at National and International Levels. As per 2001 population census, the district has achieved 77.2% of literacy (87.7% male and 66.4% female) on par with a few developed districts of the country. Literacy levels of SCs (54.3%) and STs (61.10%) are also high compared to many other districts of the country. Kolhapur district is equally good in terms of its education infrastructure.

III. SALIENT FEATURES OF PRIMARY EDUCATION IN KOLHAPUR

There are about 1100 Lower Primary Schools (LPS), 1000 Upper primary Schools (UPS) and 550 Secondary Schools. The implementation of district specific *Rajashri Sahu Sarva Shiksha Abhiyan* has created a good environment conducive for **quality education** at the primary level. Zilla Parishad has a few educational schemes to create and strengthen necessary infrastructure at the village level. Every village in both the blocks possess not only good school buildings but also with all other necessary facilities for the school. Marginal difference is observed across villages in both the blocks. A brief picture of Gram Panchayat's role in primary education and childcare interms necessary infrastructural facilities is presented in Annexure-II.

It was observed in the field that the interventions by local institutions for quality education made for making Primary School and ICDS attractive to the children are significant. Several other measures by the government have also facilitated education for all including poor in Kolhapur district.

IV. INSTITUTIONAL ARRANGEMENTS AND INNOVATIONS

The following are some of the innovations experienced in Kolhapur district.

Historical Background

Village level co-operative organisations such as **Milk Co-operatives, Credit Co-operatives and Farmers Co-operatives** in all the villages extend lot of financial support to various village developmental activities. Extending all these supports through gram Panchayats itself is attributed to the fact that the village Panchayats have been functioning effectively for a long time now.

Environmental Factors

People of this district have realised the importance of primary education since 1910 and ensure Community support to "Education for all". With all the necessary environment, adoption of Innovative schemes for quality education, improvement of teachers' capacity and the active participation of parents **(Rajashri Sahu Serva Shiksha Abhiyan** and **Sant Gadge Baba Swachatha Abhiyan)** have contributed to the overall education development of the district. Apart from the above, frequent interactions of teachers and exchange of ideas at the cluster level **(Monthly**

Cluster level Workshops for Teachers) have created conducive environment for quality education. These interactions are arranged in all the Primary Schools once in a month on rotation basis. Brainstorming sessions are arranged with the help of an outside expert for half a day. Villagers are also involved in the afternoon session to impress upon the guests about their own initiatives in making the school attractive. Towards the end cultural activities of the host school would give a finishing touch to the workshop.

Government Initiatives

The following are a few initiatives by the state government for the betterment of pre and primary education.

- Special schemes for strengthening of primary educational infrastructure.
- Availability of school in all habitations (single teacher).
- Education guarantee scheme of Mahatma Phule (continuous school for dropout children).
- State specific scheme for Girl child adoption by the local people.
- Supply of uniforms to all SC/ST students.
- Inter-connectivity of all the schools with the help of computers.
- Continuous training for teachers of primary schools.
- Supply of concentrate (Therapic food) food to the children between 6-12 months and regular health check up camps for all the children once in three months.
- Supplementary food is served with a fixed schedule from Monday to Saturday with an average weight of 80 grams of Kichidi and boiled gram alternatively.
- All Anganwadi Workers are qualified up to school final and their monthly salaries are increased from Rs. 1,000 to 1,200.

Role of PRIs and CBOs

Local institutions in Kolhapur district have responded well towards achieving universalisation of quality primary education to all including poor. The following are a few broad observations as what these institutions have achieved and how they are able motivate poor to utilise the services.

- Strong Gram Panchayats and their support to Primary Education in terms of providing infrastructure.
- Support of Local Institutions—**Co-operative Societies such as Credit, Dairy and Karshak** in terms of extending financial support through Gram Panchayat.
- Total involvement of Gram Pancliayat in facilitating **Shahu Maharaj Sarvasiksha Abhiyan** by the Zilla Parisliad.
- **Village education committees** are strong and functioning with the support of GP and other village level societies (efforts for convergence).
- **Village education committees** meet regularly under the chairmanship of Sarpanch. The range of issues discussed in VEC are expenditure requirements, need for residential school, scholarship examination, identification of activities under Swachatha Abhiyan (Village Sanitation Programme), etc.
- Constitution of **Mother-Teacher Committees and Parent-Teacher Committees,** which have ensured the parents co-operation for student development including attendance, mannerisms and homework. These measures have helped in reducing the absenteeism among the students and improving the student development in terms of their personality, character, discipline and moral values.
- **Mother-Teacher Committee** consisting of mothers of two girl students from every class, which comes to eight and four teachers one from each class and the head master totalling 13 members per school. Every MTC member mother should contact two other mothers and these two other mothers should contact four other mothers each to discuss various aspects of child development including attendance.
- MTC is to concentrate mainly on girl students while Parent-Teacher Committee (PTC) is for both boys and girls. PTC consists of only nine members (per school) (four parents and four teachers with headmaster as the Chairman). Meetings of PTC are held regularly to identify various issues related the student development (attendance, character, competition, computer facility, Gram Swachatha Abhiyan, homework).

- **Intranet connectivity** of all cluster level schools in the district by Zilla Parishad with the active support from Gram Panchayat.
- GPs meet once in a month to review and discuss about various developmental activities including Primary Education and Anganwadi Centre.
- **Gram Sabhas** are held for six times in many villages of this district (Three are normal and other *three are held only for the purpose of Education and Community development).*
- Gram Panchayat has been very active and extending full support for ICDS.
- GP and Village Education Committee are together extending all necessary support for smooth conduct of Anganwadi Centres in majority villages. ZP provides play items, medicines, teaching equipment, charts, etc.

Awareness Levels of People

It is observed that the general awareness of people in majority of the villages is high in Kolhapur district. The participation of people, particularly poor, in terms of utilisation of several services including Anganwadi centre (AWC) and Primary education is very high. Value of education has been realised by many people in this area. ICDS has relieved many girl children from sibling care and enabled them to attend schools. Enrolment and retention of all children including girl children has increased to a great extent.

Community Participation

The general awareness levels of the people including poor are also high compared to many other areas of Maharashtra and the country. Incidence of poverty can be seen in many villages, but the poor are not poor interms of their social status, accessibility to social infrastructure including ICDS and Primary education. Due to the overall development (Social and Economic) of people the social discriminatory practices could not be noticed in any of the study villages. The following are a few modes of community participation in educational development.

Public-Private Partnership

As it could be observed from the field that lot of support has come from number of private institutions for child development.

They include Credit Co-operatives, Milk Dairy Co-operatives, Karshak Co-operatives, Co-operative Sugar Mills, NGOs and Private Industry. In number of villages many of these institutions are contributing towards the effective management of school systems. Financial support through gram panchayat by the above institutions compensates the cost for inclusion of non-poor sections in all the activities as beneficiaries.

Life Cycle Approach

The concept of Balwadi has been there in almost all the villages for many years and people including poor are habituated to send their small children to those centres. Effective management of all these centres with the total support and involvement of Gram Panchayats and community, the integration of Anganwadi Centre (AWC) and Primary school could be possible in the form of an organic link from one end to the other. All those children who move out of AWC are admitted into the primary school and the same number of children is also enrolled in the upper primary school. On an average one new comer in every month is admitted in AWC. Perfect match between the number of outgoing children from ICDS and number enrolled in the Primary School was evident. Introduction of **extra-curricular activities including cultural and elocution** competitions made the schools more attractive and led to total development of the child.

Most children attend AWC with uniform except on Wednesday. Attendance rate is very high in majority of AWCs (e.g. in Amshi village of Karvir against the eligible 50 children 42 are enrolled and the average rate of attendance is 37, 30, 35 during October, November and December respectively). The share of girl children is nearly 50:50 in many villages in both AWCs and Primary Schools. Number of nursing mothers and pregnant women are very less in many villages due to their awareness on small family norm. Women GP members visit AWC once in a month along with Sarpanch.

Parents' Attitude Towards Education

Apart from the overall awareness levels of people, their attitude towards education is very positive. This could be observed from 100% enrolment and retention in almost all primary schools. It is observed in Arjunawada village that all 45 families belonging to Scheduled Castes are literates except ten females who are above 50 years. Out of fifteen males who are above 50 years are all educated upto second standard. As it is observed that the older generations who are still poor could also be educated to certain level, their attitude towards sending their children will always be positive. This could be observed in all the sample villages.

Gender Equity

Combined efforts of both government and local institutions helped in addressing the issue of girl child education right from the beginning. Almost 100 percent girl child enrolment in both AWC and primary school in many villages indicate that the gender discrimination is not visible in the study area. Further, the constitution of Mother-Teacher Committee and the active participation of women elected representatives of Gram Panchayat in all the matters and activities of both AWCs and primary school have enhanced the girl child participation.

CONCLUSION

Efforts of various stakeholders have resulted in increasing educational levels and standards in the district of Kolhapur. There is a complete change in the societal mind set and attitude towards education. The PRI and other local institutions have taken keen interest in implementing quality education to all. Further, early childhood care has been given importance and necessary support by these institutions. Value of education among young children has relieved many girl children from sibling care. Enrolment and retention of all children including girl children has increased to a great extent. The policies of State Government interim of investment on education and devolution of powers to PRIs have been encouraging in the state of Maharashtra. Above all community participation in supporting education through various means as mentioned above has contributed greatly for children to be the children.

As has been observed in several parts of the country an efficient institutional mechanism would alone help the process of development in rural areas. In view of emerging challenges of decentralised governance, mobilisation of resources and the changing role of government it is essential to build and strengthen the local institutions, which are nearer and closer to the people. The Kolhapur types of model of pre and primary education can be replicated by deliberate policy of strengthening PRIs and Local institutions by the state. And state should play the role of facilitator.

END NOTES

Approach adopted by the District Government (Zilla Parishad) for empowering Gram Panchayais and CBOs in creating the necessary infrastructure and the maintenance of the same at the village level has facilitated for elimination of child labour in majority areas of Kolhapur district.

Primary objective of the study is to identify the constraints in utilising the infrastructure created for primary education and ICDS by the poor and the role of PRIs and CBOs, for effective implementation of compulsory primary education for all.

REFERENCES

A. Abdul Salim (2003), *Educational Development at Micro-level: Case Study of Two Villages in Kerala,* http://krpcds.orspublicafion/Ramohan.html.

Draft Policy: Mainstreaming the issue of Child Labour into Rural Development Programmes, Recommendations of National Seminar-*cum*-Policy Workshop at NIRD, Hyderabad, 28-30 April, 2003.

R. Vidyasagar and K. Simian Chandra (2003), *Globalisation: The Linkages to Poverty and Pushing Children into Work in Rural India,* Centre for Social Developemnt, NIRD, Hyderabad.

ANNEXURE I

District Level

Chief Executive Officer, Deputy CEO (ICDS), District Education Officer, Extension Officer (Primary Education) of Zilla Parishad, Project Director and Project Economist of DRDA.

Block Level

Block Pramuks, BDOs, CDPOs, Extension Officers (Education), Assistant CDPOs (ICDS) of Karvir & Radhanagari Blocks.

Village Level

Sarpanches of Gram Panchayat, Chairmen of Village Education Committee, Members of Parent—Teachers' Association, Members of Mother-Teachers Association, Head Masters (Primary School) and Teachers, Members of Gram Panchayat, Elders of the Village Presidents (Co-operative Society), Anganwadi Workers/Helpers, Parents of a few students, Students of different classes and Members of SC/ST Colony.

ANNEXURE II

Support Services to Primary Education and ICDS by Gram Panchayat

S.No.	Name of the Village	Support to Primary School (PS)	Support to Angan Wadi Centre (AWC)
1.	Amshi	Construction of Compound Wall, Toilets and Additional class room, Supply of Black boards & Saplings Provision of Water connection, Levelling of play ground, Amplifier, Furniture, Slides Projector, VCR, Two in one, Cyclostyle & Sewing Machines	Accommodation Uniforms First Aid Storage Bins Furniture Teaching Equipment
2.	Dewale	3 Additional rooms Painting to 9 rooms 1 computer 65 Benches, 9 chairs & Tables Gate to the school Garden Development Drinking Water Laboratory equipment Teaching Aids & Black Board	One room & Temple Cooking Gas Play Items Tap Connection Uniforms Snacks
3.	Bahiraswar	Compound wall Water point Teaching equipment	All the necessary support
4.	Saravde	Compound wall Toilet facility Garden/Lawn Gate to the Compound wall Distribution of books Computer Electrical material	Accommodation (AWC) Play Items Drinking water facility Own building Support by the teachers Health check-ups Frequent visits
5.	Arjunawada	Uniforms for all SC students Computer Drinking water Repair of electrical appliances Separate toilet for girls Special scholarship Garden development	Uniforms for SCs Storage bins Utencils/dishes Stove Rent (100) for one room
6.	Rashivade	All the support to both the Primary schools (Boys & Girls)	Tables & Chairs, Own building, Support by the teachers, Health check-ups, Frequent visits

Institutional Failure, Corruption and Economic Underdevelopment

Ratan Kumar Ghosal

I. INTRODUCTION

It is well known that institutions are nothing but the rules of the game in a societal structure such that these rules shape the human interaction so as to establish a stable structure. So any type of institution whether it is government or non-government includes certain humanly devised restrictions or constraints, which should be abided by the members of the institutions, particularly by those who are involved in the process of exchange activities performed by the institutions. The different customs, traditions, code of conduct and societal norms certainly affect the functioning of the institution. Thus the most important part of the functioning of institutions refers to the costliness of ascertaining violation and severity of punishment. In any society, which is the congregation of several institutions like government, households and the producers/firms who are intimately related with each other through various types of economic exchange activities, the performance of the economy would obviously be influenced by the effect of the functioning of the institutions on the cost of exchange and production. Interestingly the institutional economists North and Thomas (1973) have treated institution as a crucial determinant of economic performance and the changes in relative price as the source of institutional changes.

Further in a dynamic world institutional structure can't remain unchanged forever. Changes in the rules, formal and informal constraints, societal norms, effectiveness of enforcement would bring about institutional change, which is indeed a complex historical process. In fact, the demographic pressure through change in relative prices of resources will cause change in property right, institutional structure, etc. In course of the functioning of the institutions over time it is likely that the lack of proper enforcement of exchange contracts, the social sanctions, perfect information will cause germination of opportunism in the process of exchange activities performed by the agents. In fact the lack of proper co-ordination and monitoring of the activities will result into institutional failure. As a result of institutional failure opportunism would continue to mount up and lead to the growing use of public resources for private benefit or profit. The manifestation of such opportunism takes place in the form of pervasive or rampant corruption in terms of bribing, transaction cost and rent-seeking activities, etc. All these would lead to the alteration of the institutional framework and modification of the structure of property rights as well as the class configuration within the institutional arrangement. Moreover, the corrupt transaction or exchange will have some externalities. In fact, the pattern of accrual of return to corrupt and non-corrupt transaction in an institutional arrangement is indeed a complex phenomenon such that the complexities arise due to externalities between the corrupt and non-corrupt transactions. The returns from corrupt and non-corrupt transactions reflect the underlying relation between corrupt and non-corrupt agents and also govern the dynamic relation between them. The conventional neo-classical marginal principle can't capture such complex relations between the corrupt and non-corrupt exchange and its dynamism. It is well known that the conventional marginal principles break and fail to render optimum social welfare in Pareto sense particularly when market imperfection leads to generate externalities. Further, the neo-classical rational choice theory is also found to be developed on the basis of some behavioural assumptions which actually do not imply that everybody's behaviour is consistent with rational choice (*North*, 1990; *Winter*, 1986). Interestingly the economists in this tradition have failed to explain the evolutionary process of institutional structure in which the social structure, political environment and cultural belief system play an important role. The literature on New Institutional Economics focuses on the major features of institutional failure especially legal and contractual structures and the rules of third party enforcement which cause sustained economic underdevelopment and so it emphasises the evolution of the more formal (legal contractual) institutions of enforcement (*North*, 1990).

Now the most pertinent question is whether corruption is inimical or congenial to economic growth. In fact, there are two contradictory views amongst the institutional economists. One view, which is based on empirical observations, asserts that corruption in the form of bribing may increase the efficiency of institutional structure as the bribing money is used as speed money or as grease to administrative machinery. In such case the corruption in the form of bribing will remove the administrative impediment (*Theobald*, 1990) thereby raising administrative efficiency. The contradictory view, however, emphasises that corruption may retard economic development by discouraging or crowding out the private investment through high transaction cost, low profitability and rent seeking behaviour (*Bardhan et al*, 2000; *Romer*, 1994; *Shleifer and Vishnu*, 1993). Even a negative association between corruption index and investment rate *vis-a-vis* the rate of growth has been found to persist (*Mauro*, 1995). Karl Marx, a classical institutional economist also emphasized that a given institutional arrangement helps generating different vested interest powerful groups, which in turn act as retarding factor to economic progress. Now whether an institutional structure with corrupt and non-corrupt or honest transaction would help accelerating economic development or hinder economic development would actually depend on the initial condition of the institutional structure especially on the proportion of corrupt to non-corrupt agents or transactions in the institutional structure. The motivation of our study therefore descends from the extensive literature on New Institutional Economics.

This paper is, in fact, a modest attempt to develop an analytical framework for capturing the nexus of inter-relationship between the corrupt and non-corrupt agents involved in a given institutional arrangement and its dynamism and also to highlight its impact on economic development *vis-a-vis* the policy implications. More specifically this paper attempts to develop an analytical structure for determining the dynamic equilibrium of an institutional set-up containing corrupt and non-corrupt transaction and the problem of stability by using an unconventional approach. We actually find the possibility of multiple equilibria of which some are stable and some are unstable depending on the initial ratio of corrupt to non-corrupt transaction within an institutional structure. Our study is completely different from that of Bardhan *et al* (1999) study which is based on marginal principle and establishes two possibilities of stable equilibria either with zero corruption or with fullest form of corruption. This paper is designed as follows. Section II presents the analytical structure of the approach. Section III gives the mathematical model analysing the possibility of multiple equilibria. Finally, Section IV presents the concluding observations and policy implication of the analysis.

II. ANALYTICAL STRUCTURE OF THE APPROACH

To develop an analytical framework for capturing the interrelationship between the corrupt and non-corrupt agents/ transactions involved in an institutional arrangement and its impact on economic development, we consider government as an institution in a federal structure such that the government continues to undertake different developmental projects for the maximisation of welfare of the people in the society. We assume that different officials or agents are involved in the process of implementation of the programmes at the provincial and decentralised local government levels. Thus the government is supposed to coordinate and monitor different exchange activities or transactions, which take place vertically from top to bottom level so that the benefits of these activities reach the target group. One may for example consider the different poverty alleviation *vis-a-vis* employment generating programmes like IRDP, which have been undertaken by the Central Government in India, such that the implementing authority are the states and panchayats at the grass-root level. Now if the government as an institution fails to coordinate and monitor the activities of the agents properly then there is institutional failure leading to corruption and underdevelopment. In fact, this is the problem of principal agent where the principal is the government and agents are the officials. Now, the failure of institution may be due to information asymmetry and lack of coordination, etc. The presence of information asymmetry in such case causes adverse selection and moral hazards. Now, we assume that the relative share of officials/agents involved in such an institutional arrangement constitute a constant faction (*s*) of the total allocation over time (A_t). So the total income/share of the officials (S_t) will be:

$$S_{(t)} = s.A_{(t)} \quad s > 0, t \Rightarrow time \qquad \text{... (1)}$$

The income of the officials/agents involved in the process of exchange/transaction may therefore increase either through the rise in the allocation of the government, which is beyond the jurisdiction of the agents or through the change in the distribution of *A*, i.e. through the change in the value of (s). So we write:

$$\acute{S} = s.\acute{A} + A.\acute{s} \qquad \text{... (2)}$$

Here $\acute{s} \Rightarrow$ change in distribution ratio over time, where dot (.) over the term implies the first derivative with respect to time. The change in the value of (*s*) can only be made through unscrupulous activities say corruption. Now, if we start from a situation of zero corruption then the benefits of '*A*' reaches to the target group. But if there is corruption through change in distribution ratio then, there is leakages and inefficiency into the system and so the target group gets deprived of the benefits and economic progress will be hindered. This is exactly what has happened in India in case of IRDP (see *Rao*, 1994). Now, it is quite likely that the change in the distribution ratio would be possible when corrupt officials or agents can make the non-corrupt and the clients/target group people corrupt. Thus the corruption represents frequency dependent equilibria and the expected gain from corruption depends crucially on the number of other people we expect to be corrupt. So in case of determination of the impact of institutional failure *vis-a-vis* corruption on the economic development in a given institutional arrangement the study of the nature of the inter-relationship between the corrupt and non-corrupt agents/transactions and externalities involved within it matters most.

To capture the relations between the two classes of agents/ transactions, we hypothesise three forms of relations:

(i) Relationship of Mutual Complementarity

In such case the non-corrupt transactions or agents help realising the return from corrupt transaction say through the commitment of not disclosing the process of corruption and the corrupt transaction also help sustaining the non-corrupt transaction by parting with certain portion of bribe money/ margin money. This is actually a relation of symbiotic mutualism such that one species helps other to survive and it can be termed as 'Collusive Corruption'. The outcome of such mutual complementary relation between the corrupt and non-corrupt transactions is the smaller rate of percolation of the development fund for the economic betterment of the target group. Such type of relation between the corrupt and non-corrupt agents eventually leads to economic underdevelopment. However, the degree of corruption in such an institutional arrangement will depend on the extent by which the corrupt agents be able to involve the non-corrupt into such corrupt transaction. This, in turn, will depend on the initial ratio of corrupt to non-corrupt agents/transactions that is relative strength of the two the given institutional arrangement. If this ratio be high initially then the corrupt agents would be able to dominate the non-corrupt and so the degree of corruption will continue to rise. However, the returns from corrupt and non-corrupt which are, of course, influenced by the externalities, matter most in this context. If the return from corrupt transaction be greater than that from non-corrupt transaction at a given ratio of corrupt to non-corrupt transaction/officials then it is likely that corrupt transaction will continue to rise thereby resulting into economic underdevelopment and deprivation of target group. This entire episode is, however, the outcome of institutional failure. The eventuality will be the state of stable equilibrium when the returns per unit of corrupt and non-corrupt transaction be equal to each other. It is the task of the government to bring these two equal when it fails to monitor the agent's work. The standard macroeconomic theory, i.e. the efficiency wage theory can be remembered as a solution to this end.

(ii) Relation of Competitiveness

If the relation between the corrupt and non-corrupt agents be one of competitive, then one will lead to the competitive extinction of other depending on the initial relative strength of the classes of agents and the relative returns from the transactions at a given institutional framework. Such type of relation may result into an unstable equilibrium such that any increase in the ratio of corrupt to non-corrupt transaction will cause more non-corrupt to be corrupt and reverse will be the case otherwise. One example in this context may the commission-based tax collection by the government officials.

(iii) Relation of Partly Competitive and Partly Complementary

The relation between corrupt and non-corrupt agents may be partly competitive and partly complementary such that the non-corrupt agents/transaction may help the corrupt agents to survive but not the other way round. Conversely, the corrupt agent may help the survivality of the non-corrupt but not the reverse be true. For example, the corrupt agents may part with certain portion of bribe money/margin money to non-corrupt so that the non-corrupt agents do not disclose the underground activities and so developmental work continues and this helps the survivality of the non-corrupt.

III. MATHEMATICAL FORMULATION OF THE STRUCTURE OF INTER-RELATIONSHIP BETWEEN CORRUPT AND NON-CORRUPT AGENTS

We now analyse the nature of inter-relationship between the corrupt and non-corrupt agents in terms of mathematical model. We have already mentioned in Section-II that we consider a given institutional arrangement (i.e. government as an institution), which contains both corrupt and non-corrupt agents or officials. Now let the total number of agents/transactions involved in such an institutional set-up conducting the developmental activities be 'T', of which T_C be the number of corrupt transactions/agents and T_N be that of non-corrupt transactions. So the returns accruing to these two type of transactions/agents and their inter-relationship involving the externalities can be presented in terms of the following pay-off matrix.'

Pay-off Matrix of Corrupt (C) and Non-corrupt (N) Transactions/Agents

No. of Transactions	*Return accruing to Transaction*	
	Corrupt	*Non-corrupt*
T_C	a_1	b_1 ±
T_N	a_2 ±	b_2

In the pay off matrix the diagonal elements a_1, b_2 will always be positive as these two imply the respective returns to corrupt and non-corrupt transactions. However, the signs of the off diagonal elements (i.e. a_2, b_1) represent the nature of inter-relationship between the two types of transactions/agents depending on the externalities involved within it. So these two may assume positive values (when there is the relation of symbiotic mutualism) or negative values (when there is the relation of strict competitiveness).

Now, the total return accruing to corrupt transactions (R_C) can be expressed (from pay-off matrix) as:

$$R_C = a_1 T_C + a_2 T_N \qquad \text{... (3)}$$

Similarly the total return accruing to non-corrupt transaction/honest agent (R_N) can be expressed as

$$R_N = b_1 T_C + b_2 T_N \qquad \text{... (4)}$$

Now, we can find out the return per unit of T_C and T_N as follows:

$$\frac{R_C}{T_C} = r_C = a_1 + a_2 \frac{T_N}{T_C} \qquad \text{... (5)}$$

$$\frac{R_N}{T_N} = r_N = b_1 + b_2 \frac{T_C}{T_N} \qquad \text{... (6)}$$

here a_1, $b_2 > 0$. Always.

Now let $t = T_C/T_N$. So equation (5) and (6) can be written as:

$$r_C = a_1 + a_2/t \qquad \text{... (7)}$$

$$r_N = b_2 + b_1 t \qquad \text{... (8)}$$

Now, the equations (7) and (8) will explain the nature of relation between T_C and T_N depending on the signs of a_2 and b_2 and thus give us the possibility of multiple equilibria. However, it is worthmentioning in this context that in the institutional arrangement if $r_C = r_N$ for a particular value of 't', then it will yield an equilibrium solution. But whether the equilibrium is stable or unstable will obviously depend on the initial condition and the relative returns accruing to the respective transactions/agents for undertaking any more or less transaction than the steady state or equilibrium ratio of transaction (t^*). In fact, for any value of $t > t^*$ if $r_C > r_N$ then it will encourage gradually higher and higher level of corruption or more agents being corrupt. The reverse will be the case if $r_N > r_C$ for any $t < t^*$. In such cases, certainly the equilibria will be unstable.

Now we consider that three types of inter-relationship between corrupt and non-corrupt transactions/agents and examine the problem of stability of equilibria in terms of separate diagrams. We consider the first case such that relation between the two agents/transactions (T_C, T_N) is one of complementarity or symbiotic mutualism. So T_C and T_N help each other for their survivality through realization of return. This actually happens in an institutional arrangement where the non-corrupt agents do not directly get themselves involved in corruption but they share the benefit of return accruing to corrupt transaction (i.e. the bribing money, margin money) on the basis of the stipulation that they would not disclose the same. So each helps other to survive and the developmental activities continue with leakage. Thus the extent of development gets reduced. So in such case a_1, a_2, b_1 and b_2 will be positive and there will be stable equilibrium as is shown in the Figure 1 where the schedules r_C and r_N are drawn by following the equations (7) and (8) above.

It follows that t^* gives the steady state or equilibrium ratio of T_C and T_N such that $r_C\ (t^*) = r_N\ (t^*)$. Further it is a stable equilibrium in the sense that for any value of $t > t^*$, $r_N > r_C$. So T_N will rise and t will fall. The reverse will be the case otherwise.

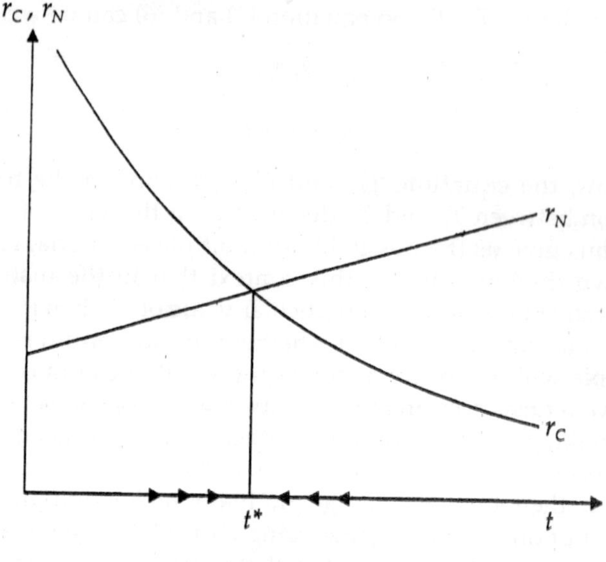

Figure 1

Now, if there is competitive relation between the two types of transactions/agents such that one does not cooperate other then it would lead to the competitive extinction of one of the two agents depending on the initial situation (i.e. T_C/T_N) that is on which class dominates initially. In such case the off diagonal elements in the payoff matrix will assume negative signs (i.e. $a_2 < 0$, $b_1 < 0$). So equations (7) and (8) become:

$$r_C = a_1 - a_2/t \quad \text{... (9)}$$

$$r_N = b_2 - b_1 t \quad \text{... (10)}$$

In fact in such a conflicting situation, if the corrupt agents/transactions dominate the non-corrupt in a given initial institutional arrangements then the corrupt will try to convert more and more of the non-corrupt agents into corrupt either by paying larger share in the bribing money or through intimidation. This process will be completely harmful for economic development and even it may lead either to the disinvestments in public sector projects or to the closure of the scheme. However, if the non-corrupt dominates the corrupt at the initial situation, then the process will lead to zero level of corruption and it will be congenial to economic development. Thus the case of competitive relations between the two types of transactions or agents leads to unstable equilibrium and in such case the initial condition matters most. This is explained in Figure 2.

It follows that $r_C(t^*) = r_N(t^*)$ and so t^* is the equilibrium ratio of T_C to T_N such that for any value of $t > t^*$, $r_C > r_N$ and so the corrupt transaction will continue to mount up and eventually it will extinguish the non-corrupt. Again for any value of $t < t^*$, $r_N > r_C$ and so non-corrupt may eventually lead the extinction of the corrupt. Therefore, any deviation from the steady state value of t^* leads to instability. Thus in such case the equilibrium is unstable.

Now, we consider the third case (i.e. the case of partly competitive and partly complementary relation), which, in fact, implies two separate possibilities of relations viz. (a) a situation when the corrupt transactions/agents act as a retarding factor to non-corrupt transitions but not the other way round and (b) the situation when the non-corrupt acts as an inhibiting factor in a or a parasite to corrupt transaction but not otherwise. Thus the off-diagipnal elements in such case will have mixed signs.

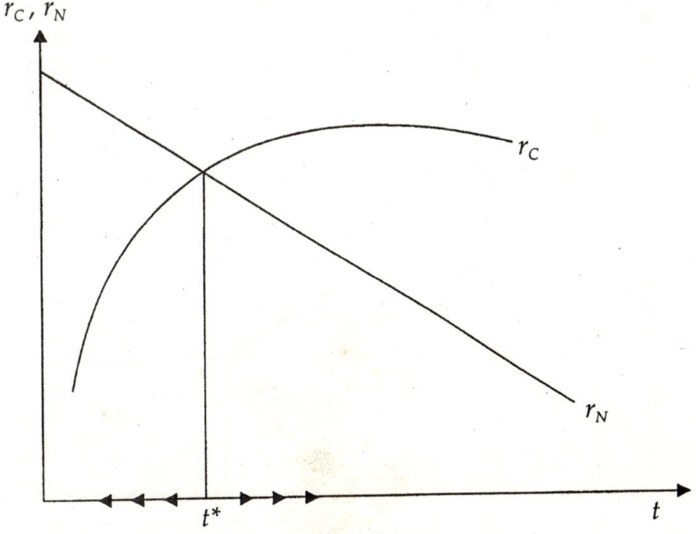

Figure 2

To explain the situation, consider case-a when the corrupt agents/transactions always try to convert the non-corrupt into corrupt but the non-corrupt agents do not like to hamper the corrupt transactions. So in this case $b_1 < 0$ and $a_2 > 0$ such that the returns per unit of T_C and T_N can be expressed as:

$$r_C = a_1 + a_2/t \quad \text{... (11)}$$

$$r_N = b_2 - b_1 t \quad \text{... (12)}$$

So, in this case there is the possibility of two equilibria (as is shown in the Figure 3) of which one with high steady state value of t (i.e. t^*_1) is unstable and there is the possibility of competitive extinction of one class and other with low steady state value of t (i.e. t^*_0) is stable.

Finally, we consider the situation (case-b) when the non-corrupt transactions/agents try to inhibit corruption either by using concilliation machinery or by intimidating the corrupt for disclosing the nature of corruption taking place in an institutional arrangement, i.e. by acting as harmful parasite to corrupt agents but not otherwise. That is, in such case, the corrupts want the

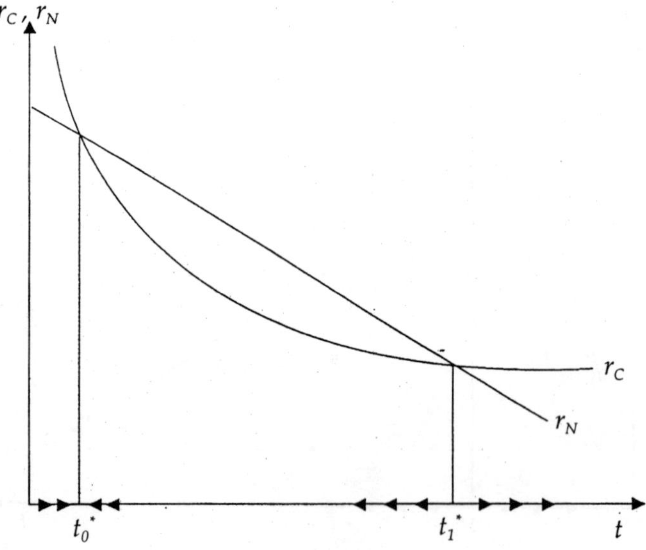

Figure 3

survivality of the non-corrupt transactions for their own survivality. So in such a situation a_1, $b_2 > 0$ but $a_2' < 0$ and $b_1 > 0$.

So the equations presenting the returns per unit T_C and T_N will be:

$$r_C = a_1 - a_2/t \qquad \text{... (13)}$$

$$r_N = b_2 + b_1 t \qquad \text{... (14)}$$

Thus in such a nexus of relations, also there is the possibility of double equilibria (see Figure 4) such that one with higher steady state value of $t = t^*$ giving stable equilibrium and other with a lower value of $t = t^*_0$ indicating unstable equilibrium. Thus the analysis of the nexus of relation between the corrupt and non-corrupt agents gives the possibility of multiple equilibria of which some are stable and some are unstable.

IV. CONCLUDING OBSERVATIONS AND POLICY IMPLICATION

In this paper we have tried to analyse the impact of

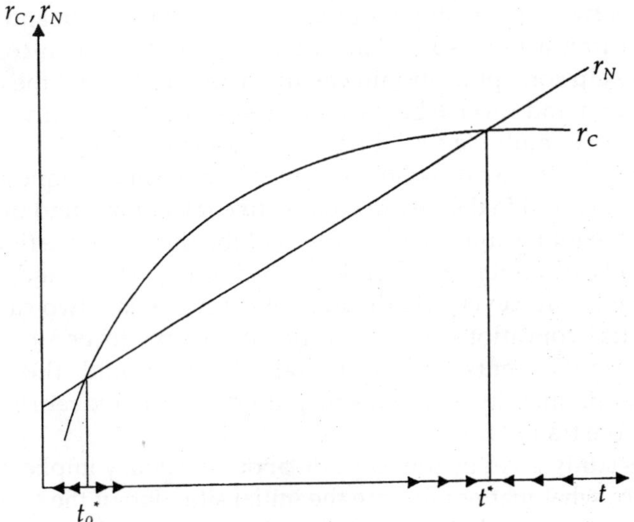

Figure 4

institutional failure and corruption on the economic development in a given institutional arrangement containing corrupt and non-corrupt agents or transactions. It is argued that institutional failure due to lack of proper enforcement of exchange contract, social sanctions and perfect information leads to germinate rampant corruption in form of bribing, rent seeking activities and transaction cost etc., which may worsly affect the economic progress. In fact in an institutional set-up (say government in a federal structure) the corrupt and non-corrupt transactions will involve some externalities, which influence the return accruing to these two types of transactions/agents *vis-a-vis* the inter-relationship between them. The conventional neo-classical analytical methods fail to capture the nexus of relations between the two types of agents and explain the nature of change in the institutional structure over time. So we have used a mathematical model to analyse the nexus of relation between the two types of agents and examine the impacts of it on economic progress. We have actually distinguished between three types of relationship between the transactions or agents viz. (i) relation of complementarily or symbiotic mutualism, (ii) relation of competitiveness and finally the relation of partly competitive and complementary. In the third case, however, we distinguish between two separate types of relation between corrupt and non-corrupt transactions such that in the first situation non-corrupt agents help corrupt to sustain corrupt activities but not the other way round and reverse be the case otherwise. We actually find a possibility of multiple equilibria of which some are stable and few are unstable. In case of symbiotic mutualism we find unique stable equilibrium and in the case of competitive relation we find unique unstable equilibrium. Finally, in each of the third case we find the possibility of double equilibria of which one is stable and other is unstable. However, what matters most in the last two cases is the initial conditions, i.e. the ratio of corrupt to non-corrupt transactions/agents at the initial situation and the class dominating initially as well as magnitude of relative returns per unit of the transaction.

This study gives us some insight about the policy implications. Actually, what matter most are the initial situation of the society/economy, i.e. the relative strength of the corrupt and non-corrupt agents/transactions *vis-a-vis* the hierarchical structure; the relative returns from the two types of transactions and finally, the efficiency of the state or non-government organisation, as the case may be, in respect of governance, i.e. how far the state or the non-government organisation is able to coordinate and monitor the activities through strengthening the legal-contractual structure and the rules of enforcement. In fact, corruption and unscrupulous activities are the instinct feature of any societal structure and institutional arrangement. As Kautiliya wrote in his *Arthasastra* in fourth century B.C. "Just as it is impossible not to test the honey (or the poison) that finds itself at the tip of the tongue, so it is impossible for a government servant not to eat-up, at least, a bit of the king's revenue. Just as the fish moving under water cannot possibly be found out either as drinking or not drinking water, so government servant employed in the government work cannot be found out (while) taking money (for themselves)." (*Kangle,* 1972).

Given this, the major task of the state is therefore to strengthen the legal enforcement structure for the exchange contracts so as to bring about efficiency in the coordination, monitoring and governance, instead of being purchased or controlled by political lobbies, bureaucrats and different vested interest groups so that the corrupt activities may not proliferate and the nexus of relation can be distorted. Further given the three broad types of relations between corrupt and non-corrupt agents and their initial relative strength, it is rather plausible to say that the policy prescription actually depends on the initial situation facing the society. However, for reducing corruption, the return from non-corrupt transaction must be made greater than that from corrupt transaction. Now since return from corrupt transaction is likely to be greater than that from non-corrupt transaction because of the presence of a positive component viz. the expected gain from corruption, this component may be made zero through different rigorous legal enforcements. Finally, one can say that since corruption is ubiquitous and instinct in social structure and institutional arrangements and it may also be the outcome of the inter-generational heritage in dynamic society there must be measures for encouraging 'social consciousness' against the corruption and unscrupulous activities. So, let me conclude with the 'secular' verse of the Rg. Veda:

"SAMVADHAM"
"Let us advance with unity,
Let us speak with unity,
Let us think with unity,
Let us all share the same ideals and follow the same counsel,
Let us have the same desire and inclinations,
Let our prayer be common,
Let our heart be united,
Let our minds be united for the common happiness of all."

REFERENCES

Bardhan, Pranab (1997): "Corruption and Development: A Review of Issues," *Journal of Economic Literature*, Sept., V-35, pp. 1320-45.

—— and Udry, Christopher (1999): *Development Microeconomics*, OUP, New York.

Bhaduri, Amit (1984): *Economic Structure of Backward Agriculture*, Macmillan India Ltd., Delhi.

Ghosal, Ratan Kumar (2002): "Impact of Asymmetric Information on the Allocation of Credit in a Small and Marginal Farm Dominated Backward Economy" (unpublished) Paper presented at the 85th Annual Conference of IEA held at Kerala University, Kerala, Trivandrum, in December 2002.

Kangle, R.P. (1972): *The Kautiliya Arthasastra*, Part-II, University of Bombay.

Mauro, Paolo (1995): "Consumption and Growth", *Quarterly Journal of Economics*, August, 11093, pp. 81-712.

North, C. Douglass (1990): *Institutions, Institutional Change and Economic Performance*, Cambridge University Press, UK.

—— and Thomas, Paul Robert (1973): *The Rise of the Western World—A New Economic History*, Cambridge University Press, UK.

Shleifer, Andrei and Vishny, Robert W. (1993): "Corruption," *Quarterly Journal of Economics*, August, Vol. 108, No. 3, pp. 599-617.

Theobald, Robin (1990): *Corruption, Development and Underdevelopment*, Durham, NC; Duke University Press.

Winter, Sidney G. (1986): "Comments on Arrow and on Lucas," Robin, M. Hogarth and Melvin, W. Reder (ed.), The Behavioural Foundations of Economic Theory, *Journal of Business* (Supplement), Vol. 59, pp. 427-34.

Rao, C.H.H. (1994): *Agricultural Growth, Rural Poverty and Environmental Degradation in India*, OUP, Delhi.

Romer, Paul (1994): "New Goods Old Theory and the Welfare Cost of Trade Restrictions", *Journal of Development Economics*, Vol. 43, No. 1, pp. 5-38.

SECTION III

NIE AND AGRICULTURAL DEVELOPMENT

New Institutions for Meeting Agricultural Development: Challenges under Globalisation

PARAMJIT NANDA AND P.S. RAIKHY

The objective of the present paper is to focus on alternative institutional structure for supporting agricultural development under globalisation in view of the failure and withdrawal of state agencies in the sector. The paper has been divided into three sections. Section I concentrates on New Institutional Economics and changing requirements of the agricultural sector under globalization, Section II is devoted to the building of alternative institutions for agricultural development, while Section III sums up the discussion.

I

In neo-classical economics, market mechanism was given prime importance while the role of state, institutions and property rights, etc. were given some importance only in cases of 'market failure'. New Institutional Economics represents departure in the sense that it questions the efficacy of the market mechanism in conveying of correct information and in the exchange process. It includes the concepts of transaction costs and information costs under market mechanism. Even when markets continue to be most important institutions, non-market institutions have also assumed importance due to prevalence of market failures, especially in developing countries (*Stiglitz*, 1989). The concepts of transaction costs (*Coase*, 1937), imperfect information (*Akertof*, 1970), property rights (*Alchian and Demsetz*, 1972) have largely added non-market dimensions. More such dimensions have now been added due to the polices of liberalization, privatization and globalization.

Globalization, a process through which goods and services, capital, people, information and ideas flow across borders, leading to greater integration of economies and societies, has become the inescapable feature of the world today. It calls for a new set of institutions to meet the emerging challenges, especially in the developing countries. Confidence in the ability of the government to improve welfare through planned development of the economy, creation of barriers to international trade and demand management, etc. has broken down and may erode further in the recent future. Theoretically, the failure has been attributed to rent-seeking, rational expectations and price distortions etc. causing severe handicaps on market mechanism.

However, excessive confidence in market mechanism is equally naive and has more potential for damage in developing world, where small farmers, industries, other producers and suppliers dominate. Small-holder-based model of development requires co-ordination between the small-holders, the large private sector and the government (*Stern*, 2002) and hence requires different type of institutional structure. Small-holders may have great potential if they get correct information from where to get started, large private sector may do the processing and government provides training, extension and infrastructure.

The problems of agricultural sector are more peculiar. Small scale agricultural activities are more vulnerable to adverse investment climate in view of globalisation trends. There is rapid withdrawal of the government from supplies of agricultural credit and inputs and also from marketing. There is much more scope of exploitation of the small farmers by private sector. Therefore, the success of continued liberalization in agriculture is at stake.

In globalised era, developing countries are to meet challenges of availability and efficiency of production of food and other agricultural products. But unfortunately, in emerging liberalized and globalised environment, agriculture in developing countries is becoming weaker. Agricultural productivity per worker was $3680 in Latin America and $2049 in Europe, while it was $568 in South Asia in 1999-2001. The share of agricultural exports of middle income countries decreased from 21 percent in 1990 to 12 percent in 2001. Developing countries are unable to meet sanitary and phytosanitary requirements on more than 50 percent of their potential exports of fresh and processed fish, meat, fruit and vegetables into E.U. (*OECD*, 2001). However, globalisation will increase further the demand for agricultural products, agricultural inputs and hence there will be need for more formal institutions. Developing countries are unable to meet challenges in agriculture as these countries suffer from lack of information and adequate competition. There is weak enforcement of rights, low investment in education and infrastructure, leading to low access to institutions disseminating technological information and lack of effective supporting institutions leading to high transaction cost in marketing. To improve agricultural productivity and to increase exports, public or private institutions are needed that ease information cost, transaction cost and develop new technology. Government has to create an enabling environment for partnership in which the private sector, civic society and all levels of government can contribute. Building effective institutions is a complex task. However, the analysis of country experiences can help policy-makers in developing countries to build effective institutions and modify some existing institutions so that these countries can shorten the development process by learning from other countries.

II. INSTITUTIONS FOR AGRICULTURAL GROWTH

Farming is process of producing outputs using a set of inputs. Outputs and inputs are exchanged through various mechanism and organizations with the goal of achieving positive net margins. For this purpose, specific agricultural institutions for land rights, finance, agricultural technology (developing new technology and delivering existing technology), marketing, production, human resource development, quality, environment and research and developments are required. Importance of marketing, quality and environment institutions will increase in future due to (i) increased consumer demand for qualitative aspects such as food safety, (ii) developments in biotechnology, and (iii) deregulations of agricultural markets.

Building Land Institutions

Land has a number of characteristics that distinguish it from other goods and services that may be traded in the market place. It is essential within market driven economies that land markets are supported by clear legal basis that is administered by regulatory authorities. Land rights should be secure and easily transferable, which can help in raising productivity by transferring land from less efficient cultivators to more efficient cultivators. Carter and Yao (1999) study for China has confirmed that higher levels of transferability were positively correlated with higher levels of farm investment. Further, extensive regulations of land market transactions (restrictions on land sales, high sales cost, restrictions on land sub-division, restrictions on the use of land for collateral and lengthy land registration processes) should be reduced to lower costs of land transactions, to increase transparency, to enhance administrative capacity and to discourage corruption. To create secure and transferable property rights, formal land titles assume importance. Alston (1995, 1996) study of areas of new settlements in Brazil found that formal titles increased productivity by providing clear information about ownership rights in underdeveloped areas. Formal land market institutions include land registries, titling services and land mapping. In building these institutions, three things namely clear definition and sound administration of property rights, simple mechanisms for identifying and transferring property rights, and thorough compilation of land titles and free access to information should be kept in mind. (*Baldwin and Dale*, 2000)

Institutions for Agricultural Technology

No doubt, agricultural innovations such as high yielding seeds, herbicides, fertilizers, agricultural machinery and resource management techniques allowed food production growth to outpace population growth. Global crop yield (wheat, corn and rice) was doubled between 1965 and 2000 and productivity gains in output per hectare of cereal crops averaged 71 percent globally), but liberalization of entry and increased competition require strengthening of existing institutions and innovative institutional designs.

For agricultural technology, mixture of public and private initiatives is needed, as many agricultural technologies are public goods, non-rival and non-excludable, whereas private agricultural technologies are excludable and rival. Public participation is required in weather forecasts, market information, livestock management techniques, fertilizer application schedules and in natural resource management techniques; whereas private participation is required in hybrid seeds, biotechnology products (inputs and seeds), fertilizers, chemicals, agricultural machinery and veterinary supplies. In developing countries, institutional obstacles restrict the delivery of new technologies. To encourage private sector participation, various regulatory barriers should be removed and more flexible approach should be adopted. Gisselquist and Grether (2000) reported that in Turkey, as a result of deregulation of government seed production and sales monopoly, new seed technologies significantly increased, which led to increase in maize yield by 50 percent and income per hectare by $153, equivalent to an annual net economic gain of $79 million. Bangladesh deregulated markets in agricultural machinery, Peru in seeds and Zimbabwe in agricultural inputs. Further, measures like (i) voluntary seed certification system supported by incentives, (ii) voluntary seed varietal registration, and (iii) maintenance of regulations addressing public and environmental externalities are required. To take advantage of TRIPs agreement, developing countries can make use of flexibility introduced in TRIPs. They can (i) narrow the scope of TRIPs, (ii) can use limitations and exceptions of TRIPs to copyrights, (iii) can avoid patenting life forms, (iv) expand IPRs scope to protect genetic resources, traditional knowledge and folklore, etc. In agriculture, they can opt for *sui geneiis* system (Argentina, Chile and Uruguay have adopted this system). To build capacity to manage TRIPs, partnership and development of assistance from private technical producers, should be sought. Kenya and Mexico developed partnership with MNCs (*Qaim*, 1999). Further, to manage water resources efficiently, water markets can contribute to more efficient water allocation and use. The implementation of water market implies government involvement and active water users participation, an administrative system that registers and enforces timely water deliveries, a transparent and accepted measurement system, and a well maintained water delivery infrastructure (*Marino, Kemper*, 1994)

Institutions for Developing New Technology (Agricultural Research Institutions)

Development of new technology assumes importance now-a-days to exploit country's comparative and competitive advantages. The major participants in the agricultural research sector are composed of domestic or non-profit organizations. Historically agricultural research has been usually performed by public sector but in developing countries, agricultural research intensity is very low, which is clear from the following table.

TABLE 1

Agricultural Research Intensity (as percent of GDP)

Country	*Year (1993)*	
	Public	*Private*
Developed countries	1.0	1.5
Developing countries	0.5	0.1

Source: World Bank, World Development Report, 2002.

Due to low research intensity in public sector, private sector should play a major role in agricultural research. Private sector should play a role in basic and strategic biological research. Privatization of agricultural research contributed about 40% of R&D in Latin American countries and 50 percent in Industrialized countries (*Umali-Deininger*, 1997). Private sector R&D can be promoted by encouraging foreign investment, removing barriers to private sector participations and strengthening legal structures to allow private appropriation of benefits.

Agricultural Marketing Institutions

In developing countries, lack of effective supporting institutions lead to failure of agricultural marketing arrangements.

In changed scenario, state has to play role in building better marketing institutions not through state marketing boards but by facilitating private marketing institutions such as contract farming and cooperatives. Contract farming schemes range from agreements between individual traders and farmers in many Asian countries, to more formal systems in Latin America, Central Europe and East Asia. Government can act as information facilitator and by setting complementary institutions (courts) to resolve contractual disputes and ensuring grades and standards. Farmer cooperatives can be helpful in providing information and in bargaining power, thus leading to reduction in transaction cost. For this purpose, Government should stop trying to impose 'top-down' cooperative structures. Various countries experimented with farmer cooperatives (dairy sector in Finland, wheat in Canada, rice in Japan and grain in Argentina). Cooperatives such as Anand in Gujarat (India) or UGC in Mozambique have also been successful. For information about international standards, informal institutions can play important role (as experimented in Ethiopia). Further, policy-makers can enrol poor farmers in certification programs to integrate them into wider agricultural markets (in Guatemala, Mayacert, an NGO enrolled poor farmers). To give Information about prices of products, quality and weights, public sector has important role to play. Major role of public sector will be to help market participants to improve their own information flows by expanding the availability of low cost communication technology. In Ghana, Philippines, and Bangladesh, Governments, while granting license to mobile telephone companies, put condition of rural access.

Agricultural Credit Institutions

To improve formal financial sector, innovations like incentives to loan officers, repayment of loans in small instalments (weekly basis) and information technology can be developed. In Mexico, Compartamos—an NGO, provided inexpensive handheld computers to record data. Certain institutions, like BRI-UD in Indonesia and Bank for Agricultural Cooperation in Thailand, have been successful due to simplicity in financial contracts, transparency in operations and integration across markets. In financial sector, bank privatization should be complemented with institutional changes which strengthen the overall incentive environment. Country experiences suggest that efficient banking system requires sound public finance, stable currency, clean balance sheet, effective regulations, contestable system (one that is open to free entry and exit of banks) and better financial information. Competition in banks requires strong regulator environment because of inherent weaknesses in excess competition and weak competition. These regulations include requirements about banks being audited by certified external auditors, improving banks accounting statements and disclosures and providing market participants with incentives to monitor by eliminating deposit insurance.

In developing countries, rural farmers lack access to formal financial institutions and informal financial institutions still dominate. Informal sources of credit are largely used by poor farmers only. To reduce importance of informal finance, formal and informal sources of lending can be integrated. Some NGOs are working as informal lenders by acting as bridge between poor borrowers and banks. MYRADA—an NGO in Southern India and rice marketers, paddy traders, rice millers, wholesalers and retailers acted as money-lenders in Philippines (*Flora and Ray*, 1997). To give information about urban sources of finance, certain information intermediaries are developing mostly in middle income countries (as Meta-information intermediaries in Argentina) (*Schreiner*, 2000).

Institutions for Delivering Existing Agricultural Technology or Provision (Extension Services)

Extension services help in informing farmers about new products and techniques and in disseminating information from farmers to other participants. Three main types of institutional reforms in provisions of extension services are needed: (i) decentralization, (ii) partial privatization of public extension services, and (iii) separation of funding from extension services (in form of public extension service with private funding or public funding with private extension services). As a result of decentralization, in Colombia, costs per farmer decreased by 10 percent, the area covered by extension services tripled and number of beneficiaries more than doubled (*World Bank*, 2000). Privatisation of public extension services proved successful in Argentina's dairy farming (Umali-Deininger, 1997). Partial privatization in Netherlands reduced overhead expenditure by 50 percent and increased farmers satisfaction rating by 40 percent (*Feder, Willet and Zijp*, 1999). Farmers' associations played role in delivering extension services in Central African Republic during 1970s Privalo funding by farmers for public goods proved successful in Nicaragua and public funding for private extension services proved successful in Estonia, and Madagascar (*Dinar and Keynan*, 1998).

Complimentary Institutions

To strengthen domestic and international competition in agriculture, complementary institutions for investment in education and infrastructure are needed. In education, governments need to create an enabling environment to encourage participation of NGOs of different kinds. Jaganathan (2001), in a study of six NGOs working with school age children in India, showed that NGOs can and do play a strong role in assisting the state to complement the public education system and to improve its effectiveness. To narrow knowledge gap, policies should be adopted for acquiring knowledge (by open trade, foreign investment and technology licensing), absorbing knowledge (by expanding enrolment at all levels, female education and encouraging private investment in tertiary education) and by improving quality of public education. To address information failures in education many countries have adopted approaches like (i) decentralizing administration, (ii) increasing school autonomy, (iii) switching to demand side financing, (iv) increasing information about individual-education institutions, and (v) fostering competition among private, NGOs and public providers. To communicate knowledge, private investment in tele-communication is to be encouraged. Infrastructure provision should be based on three principles (commercial principle, competition and user's involvement). Based on three instruments, three sectors—telecommunication, railways and power-generation should be privatized and be made competitive, roads be operated on commercial principle. Leasing or concessions can be used for ports and airports. Responsibility for local services—such as urban transport, water supply, sanitation and local roads—should be handed over to local governments. Municipal Governments and NGOs should monitor performance, set local standards and deal with customer complaints. To encourage private investment in infrastructure, there is need for regulatory reforms in pricing and efforts to enhance creditability in government's new regulatory framework. Government should see that private investors may get reasonable rate of return, prices be set to cover full cost. If pricing policy is not sufficient, then government can complement it with user fees and subsidies. To deliver infrastructure services to poor, government can adopt regulatory policy in five areas: (i) setting investment target, (ii) being flexible with respect to price-quality combinations in regulatory decisions, (iii) allowing liberal entry of informal infrastructure providers, (iv) involving communities in regulatory process, and (v) subsidies. Different nations (Bolivia, Colombia, Chile, Brazil, Argentina, Mexico, Paraguay, Yemen, Senegal) have adopted these approaches in one form or the other.

Sustainable development is another big challenge. Developing countries are facing threats in international trade due to imposition of environment standards by U.S. and European nations on exports of fish, meat, processed food products, and textiles. Environment degradation can be addressed through either financing or cost sharing by the community within country or from abroad. Costa Rica pioneered a program that allows those who benefit from the environment services of forests to compensate those who bear the burden of maintaining those forests under 'Environment Service Programme' in 1996. To prevent overuse or underuse of any asset, market-based instruments (taxes and subsidies) are more efficient and effective than regulations. Public and civic society can also monitor and ensure compliance with regulations. In Indonesia under 'PROPER' program, polluting firm is disclosed to public and then local community put pressure on polluting companies.

Thus, an expanding and modifying set of existing institutions can assist or complement governments in balancing interest not only in agriculture, but in other areas as well and these can assist citizens in ensuring that their governments are fair and responsive in doing so.

III

It may be concluded from the discussion in the paper that while market mechanism has predominant role under the globalised era, non-market institutions are equally important to prevent market failures, especially in the light of problems of transaction costs, imperfect information and property rights, etc. Many more dimensions have been added due to the policies of liberalisation, privatisation and globalisation. Developing countries face serious challenges in view of the predominance of small holders, who are more vulnerable to new trade and investment policies. Land rights have to be made secure, transferable and formal for maximisation of output. Private sector participation is required in high yielding seeds, biotechnological products, fertilisers, chemicals, agricultural machinery and veterinary supplies. Government participation is required especially in weather, forecasts, market information, livestock management techniques, environmental protection and sanitary and phyto-sanitary standards. State has to play the role of facilitator in developing private marketing institutions, such as contract farming and cooperatives. NGOs can play important role, especially in provision of rural education and health facilities. Users have to be involved in operation and maintenance of agricultural and rural infrastructure.

REFERENCES

Akerlof, G.A. (1970), "The Market for Lemons: Quantitative Uncertainty and the Market Mechanism", *QJE*, Vol. 84.

Alchian, A.A. and H. Demselz (1972), "Production, Information Costs and Economic Organisation", *AER*, Vol. 62.

Alaton, Lee, Gary Libecap and Robert Schneider (1995), "Proporty Rights and the Preconditions for Markets: The Case of the Amazon Frontier", *Journal of Institutions and Theolotical Economics, 151(1)*, 89-111.

Carter, Michael, and Yang Yao (1999), *Specialisation without Regret: Transfer Rights, Productivity and Investment in an Industrializing Economy,* World Bank Policy Research Working Paper No. 2202, World Bank, Washington, D.C.

Coase, R.H. (1937), "The Nature of the Firm", *Economica,* New Series, Vol. IV.

Dale, P., and R. Baldwin (2000), "Emerging Land Markets in Central and Eastern Europe", in Csaba Csaki and Zui Lerman (eds.), *Europe and Central Asia Environmentally and Socially Development Series,* 81-109, Technical Paper No. 465.

Dinar, A. and G. Keynam (1998), *The Cost and Performance of Paul Agricultural Extension Services,* Policy Research Working Paper No. 1931, World Bank, Washington, DC.

Feder, G.A. Willett and W. Zijp (1999), *Agricultural Extension: Genetic Challenges and Some Ingredients for Solutions*, Policy Research Working Paper No. 2129, World Bank, Washington, D.C.

Floro, M.S. and D. Ray (1997), "Vertical Links Between Formal and Information Financial Institutions", *Review of Development Economics*, 1(1), 34-56.

Girselquist, Ddavid, and Jean-Marie Grether (2000), "An Argument for Deregulating the Transfer of Agricultural Technologies to Developing Countries", *World Bank Economic Review*, 14(1): 111-27.

Jaganathan (2001), *The Role of NGOs in Primary Education—A Study of Six NGOs in India*, World Bank, Policy Research Working Paper 2530, World Bank.

Marino Manuel and Kemper E. Karin (1999), *Institutional Framework in Successful Water Markets*, World Bank Technical Paper, 427, World Bank.

OECD (2001), *Agricultural Policies in Emerging and Transition Economies: Special Focus on Non-Tariff Measures*, (Paris).

Quim, M. (1999), *The Economic Effects of Genetically Modified Orphan Commodities: Projections for Sweet Potato in Kenya*, ISAAA (International Service for the Acquisition of Agri-biotech Applications), Brief Series No. 13. Ithaca, New York.

Schreiner, Mark (2000), *Micro Finance in Rural Argentina*, Washington University, St. Louis.

Stern, Nicholas, *A Strategy for Development*, The World Bank, Washington, D.C., 2002.

Stiglitz, Joseph, E. (1989), "Markets, Market Failures to Development", *AER Papers and Proceedings*, Vol. 79.

Utnali-Deininger, D. (1997), *Public and Private Agricultural Extension: Partners or Rivals*, World Bank Research Observer, 12(2), 203-04.

World Bank, *World Development Indicators*, 2001 and 2003.

World Bank, *World Development Report*, 1994, 1998-99, 2002, 2003.

New Institutional Economics and Agricultural Policy Issues

SANDEEP KUMAR

I. INTRODUCTION

This paper presents the potential contributions of the New Institutional Economics (NIE) to agricultural policy research in developing countries. The paper includes specific examples of interest in the area of agricultural market research in such countries that can be analyzed using NIE. Paper describes the potential application of NIE to agricultural policy analysis in this new world environment. Section II presents the importance of New Institutional Economics for economists and its comparative advantages over neo-classical economics. Further the institutions have been defined and different branches of NIE have been sketched in this section. Section III presents the challenges, which the agricultural sector is facing in developing countries. This section includes the discussions about how New Institutional Economics framework can be applied to agricultural policy research in such countries. Section IV discusses the importance of transaction cost economics in the agricultural policy research whereas Section V includes the examples from different areas of agriculture, market; where NIE framework can be used in policy-making issues.

II. NEW INSTITUTIONAL ECONOMICS: IMPORTANCE

The New Institutional Economics is a vast and multi-disciplinary field that includes aspects of economics, history, sociology, political science, business organization and law. Oliver Williamson coined the phrase the "New Institutional Economics" but it is commonly known that the New Institutional Economics emerged with Coase's 1937 article, "The Nature of the Firm". This article and his other famous essay "The Problem of Social Cost" (1960) started what many, including North (2000), considers that the cost of transacting—determined by institutions and institutional arrangements—is the key to economic performance. It is, therefore, argued that the institutions of a country—such as its legal, political and social systems, determine its economic performance, and it is this, according to Coase (2000), that gives the new institutional economics its importance for economists.

Economic agents established institutions to reduce uncertainty inherent in human interaction and/or to overcome market failures caused by presence of risk and imperfect information and the attenuation of property rights. The incomplete information and limited mental capacity by which to process information determines the cost of transacting which underlines the formation of institutions. The costs of transacting arise because information is costly and asymmetrically held by the parties to exchange. The costs of measuring the multiple valuable dimensions of the goods or services exchanged or of the performance of agents, and the costs of enforcing agreements determine transaction costs. Institutions are formed to reduce uncertainty in human exchange. Together with the technology employed, they determine the costs of transacting (and producing). It was Ronald Coase (1937 and 1960) who made the crucial connection between institutions, transaction costs and neo-classical theory. The neo-classical result of efficient markets only obtains when it is costless to transact. When it is costly to transact, institutions matter. And because a large part of our national income is devoted to transacting, institutions and specifically property rights are crucial determinants of the efficiency of markets.

How does this new institutional approach fit in with neo-classical theory? It begins with the scarcity hence competition postulate; it views economics as a theory of choice subject to constraints; it employs price theory as an essential part of the analysis of institutions; and it sees changes in relative prices as a major force including change in institutions. How does this approach modify or extend neo-classical theory? In addition to modifying the rationality postulate, it adds institutions as a critical constraint and analyzes the role of transaction costs as the connection between institutions and costs of production. It extends economic theory by incorporating ideas and ideologies into the analysis, modeling the political process as a critical factor in the performance of economies, as the source of the diverse performance of economies, and as the explanation for "inefficient" markets.

The Role of NIE is crucial in planning both at government and private level. Institutions do matter for best governance. We know that welfare economics is a part of neo-classical economics and in practice the market is not always fully competitive. Some times, the competitive equilibrium cannot be achieved, which leads to an allocation of resources, which is sub-optional, Pareto-wise. In these cases there is loss of efficiency. According to Pigou, these situations are market failures, and hence, are justifications for governmental intervention. New Institutions Economics is an assembly of different approaches. In the determination of best governance structure, which often require more than one coordination model (market, hierarchy or network), NIE is useful in spatial planning.

Institutions

The institutions are a set of formal (laws, contracts, political systems, organization, markets, etc.) and informal rules of conduct (norms, traditions, customs, value systems, religious, sociological trends, etc.) that facilitates coordination or govern relationships between individuals or groups. Institutions provide for more certainty in human interaction (*North*, 1990). Institutions have an influence on our behaviour and, therefore, on outcomes such as economic performance, efficiency, economic growth and development.

NIE operates at two levels—macro and micro (*Williamson*,

2000b). The macro-level deals with the **institutional environment,** or the rules of the game, which affect the behaviour and performance of economic actors and in which organizational forms and transactions are embedded. Williamson (1993) describes it as the set of fundamental political, social, and legal ground rules that establish the basis for production, exchange and distribution. The micro-level analysis, on the other hand, also known as the **institutional arrangement,** deals with the institutions of governance. These, according to Williamson, refer more to the modes of managing transactions and include market, quasi-market, and hierarchical modes of contracting.

Branches of NIE

The literature provides a wide variety of definitions of the NIE. Here we accept the analogy of Olson and Kahkonen (2000) but will also use some ideas from other authors to show the different branches contained under this new paradigm. Fields such as the so-called "new economics history" and the public choice school

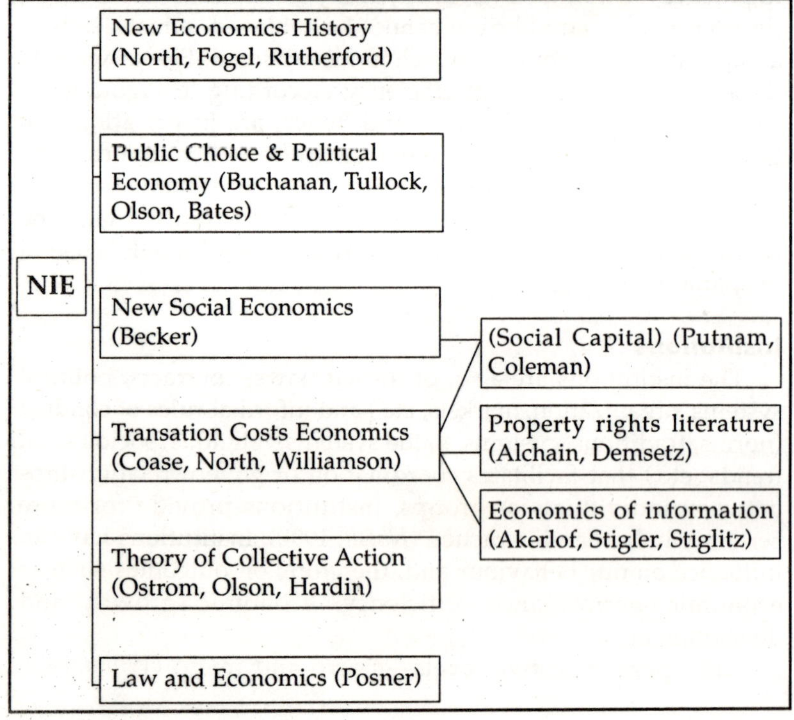

inform the institutional environment at the macro-level while transaction cost economics and information economics for example inform more the micro-analytical aspects of transactions and the forms of governance.

III. NIE FOR AGRICULTURAL POLICY RESEARCH

North (2000) has observed that in the third world countries, cost of transaction is highbe it capital labour or product markets. Since, institutions and the institutional framework provide the incentives for efficient production and/or to engage in economic activity, an institutional analysis is required to explain why the cost of transacting is so high in developing countries. The frequent occurrence of market failure and incomplete markets (because of higher transaction costs and information asymmetries) in developing countries cannot be explained by conventional neo-classical economics and requires an institutional analysis.

The NIE framework has previously been used by a number of authors (see for example *Binswanger and Rosensweig*, 1996; *Binwanger and Mclntire*, 1987; *Stiglitz*, 1974; *Nayami and Otsuka*, 1993) in applications to the problems of developing country agriculture. These studies are amongst a large body of literature that applies aspects of the NIE framework—mainly the cost of information and the lack of property rights—to explain market failures in the main inter-temporal markets (insurance, credit, futures markets) and the labour market. In addition to the many applications of the NIE framework to input market failures it can now also be argued that the rapid changes in the food and agricultural sector in developing countries in the aftermath of market liberalization and government devolution provides an additional and probably much more fertile terrain for the application of the NIE framework.

New Challenges for Agriculture

The trend of market-oriented reforms following multilateral trade liberalization and especially structural adjustment programs in developing countries has led to the increased integration of world markets (*Reardon and Barrett*, 2000). The increased industrialized nature of agriculture in developed as well as in developing countries is largely the result of biological and information technologies (*Schrader*, 1986), economic growth, mechanization, the increasing scale of organization and the modernization of production, processing and distribution systems (*Sofranko et al*, 2000, Drabenstott (1995: 14). There are two powerful forces driving this process of industrialization: a new consumer and a new producer. The new consumer is a highly demanding sort and the new producer is equipped with new technology and management tools that enable him to engineer food from farm to table. This sounds like an ideal situation, but traditional markets do not handle these circumstances well.

The new lifestyles of consumers as well as a growing appreciation for the link between diet and health, has contribution to different eating patterns and has influenced the food purchases of consumers in these countries. Consumers today are demanding much more than choice—they also want quality, consistency and value. New technology now makes it possible to ensure that agricultural and food products do have the characteristics consumers want (*Drabenstoff*, 1995; *Boehlje* 2000). This technology includes biotechnology and information technology. Food production, which include fresh meat, seafood, vegetables and fruits, and with account for half of the value of total food and agricultural exports from developing countries (*Unevhr*, 2000). The need to control for high perishability and safe handing requires specialized production, packing techniques and refrigerated transport. These require large capital investments and also involve investment in research, development, and marketing, which small and medium enterprises cannot easily afford.

Apart from the pressures from consumers and end-use markets, other major drivers and contributors to these changes in agriculture include, increasing competition from global market participants, economies of size and scope in production and distribution, risk mitigation and management strategies of buyers and suppliers, strategic positioning and market power/control strategies of individual business. These changes have introduced different forms of vertical integration and alliances, which are now increasingly dominating the agricultural market chain. The need for increased coordination can also be attributed to the failure of traditional (spot) agricultural markets to deal with this new scenario. Usually, bulk commodities flow through commodity markets to food processors that in turn market standardized products to consumers. Consumers now demand tailored food and to ensure that they get them, food companies want more specific farm products. In addition, food safely concerns have brought increased security and regulation in developed countries. As a result, processors/markets have avoided traditional spot markets and have engaged in more direct market channels such as market and production contracts.

In this context a fresh approach to market access, namely that of economic actors engaging in transactions rather than a large number of atomistic firms constituting a 'market' is imperative to gaining an understanding of market access for small-scale farmers in developing countries. It is often only the well endowed and skilled that have the ability to be part of these marketing chains and alliances. There is therefore a danger that the requirements, quality standards, and food safety rules of the consumers and cooperation (supermarkets) in the developed countries, can act as effective barriers to participation in the high value chains by small exporters and to some extent, small producers.

There are options for smaller firms and farms to still play a role. This role could relate to product differentiation linked to products from region, or organic products and other niche markets. The major route for continued survival will however be through exploiting other factors. One such factor is a reliance on external rather than internal economies of scale through vertical integration, networking/clustering, and other forms of coordination and alliances. This could be amongst small firms, through establishing links or contracts between small firms/growers and larger enterprises that have already overcome the major barriers to market entry, or by acting as ancillary units of bigger export corporations. It is in this context that the NIE can inform agribusiness and policy-markers on the most appropriate organizational form.

Against the background of deregulation and as the vertical coordinating characteristics of global agricultural industrialization increases, there is a need for more specific analytical techniques for contract evaluation using the transaction cost economics paradigm (*Cook and Chaddad*, 2000). This would require the examination of alternative "institutional arrangements" which could minimize transaction costs.

IV. TRANSACTION COST ECONOMICS AND AGRICULTURAL MARKET ANALYSIS

Transaction cost economics is especially relevant for agricultural market analysis in developing countries. As the agricultural sector becomes a more globalize and deregulated industry, the transaction becomes the unit of analysis and, therefore, can potentially offer useful insights to agricultural policy research in these countries. In the context of the greater need for coordination, the role of transaction costs, trust and relationships, formal and informal contracts, vertical linkages, information asymmetries, and strategic alliances will become very important. The transaction costs framework can contribute in explaining the choice of contracts among farmers and traders, and local traders and multinationals.

The transaction cost economics approach, focuses on how the characteristics of a transaction affect the costs of handling it through markets, bureaucracies, and other forms of organization. Williamson identifies the critical dimensions of characterizing a transaction and links these to the institutional governance structure of transactions. The principal dimensions describing a transaction are uncertainly frequency of exchanges, and the degree to which investment are transaction specific. Transaction costs include the costs of gathering and processing the information needed to carry out a transaction, of reaching decisions, of negotiating contracts, and of policing and enforcing those contracts. All transaction costs derive from a combination of bounded rationality (which reflects both imperfect information and a limited capacity to analyze it) and opportunism, which Williamson (1996) defines as "self-interest seeking". Given imperfect information about the future, all contracts are necessarily incomplete. If people were never opportunistic, however, incomplete contracts would lead contract enforcement problems. There have been a number of fairly recent applications of transactions cost economics in different fields of the food and agricultural sector. Examples of these studies are Staal *et. al.* (1997), Frank and Henderson (1992), Key, Sadoulet and de Janvry (2000), Hobbs.(1997), and Loader (1997).

V. EXAMPLES OF USE OF NIE IN AGRICULTURAL ISSUES

(1) Cooperative and Other Farmers' Organisation

Cooperatives and farmer organization are institutional arrangements, the importance of which has re-emerged recently to organize small farmers in developing countries in the wake of agricultural market liberalization. The advantages of organizing farmers into groups include, among other factors, a reduction in the transaction costs of accessing input and output markets, as well as improving the negotiating power of smaller farmers *vis-a-vis* large buyers or sellers. The history of traditional cooperatives, on the other hand, suggests that cooperative have not always been successful at serving the needs of its members. One major problem with traditional cooperatives in developing countries was that members never had a major financial stake in the cooperatives; governments supported cooperatives. Furthermore, cooperative suffered from various organizational problems and a lack of clearly defined property rights assignments resulting in opportunistic behaviour (such as free-riding, moral hazard, agency problems, etc.), bureaucratic inefficiencies, and under-investment in the cooperative (*Cook*, 1995; *Cook and Iliopoulos*, 2000).

The NIE (including property rights and collective action, transaction costs, and the organization/contracting theories of Williamson, Grossman, Hart and Moore) can inform the design of such organizations and cooperative to prevent their failure. Examples of research conducted in the area of agricultural cooperative include Cook and Iliopoulos (2000) for the United State and Staal *et. al.* (1997) covering dairy cooperatives in Kenya and Ethiopia. There is now a renewed interest in a new type or "new generation cooperative" that addresses the weaknesses of the traditional cooperative by strengthening the assignments of property rights to its individual members and reducing the incentives for opportunistic behaviour (*Cook and Ilipoulos*, 2000).

(2) Contract farming and other Vertical Linkages

The increased need for vertical coordination and supply chain management create a potential new role for contract farming as a way to link small farmers to high-value markets in the wake of market liberalization in developing countries. Due to the requirements of the new agriculture, food-markets firms prefer to engage in marketing and production contracts with farmers in developed as well as developing countries to ensure greater coordination of quantity and quality of supply.

Production contracts can vary quite a bit, but in essence under contract farming, a trader contracts with a farmer to buy a specific quantity and quality of produce at a designated price. The price may be fixed at planting time or determined by the market at harvest time. In many instances, farmers benefit from access to technological information and extension services provided by traders. In some cases, traders also provide inputs on credit. Contract farming reduces both production and marketing risk by ensuring a guaranteed source of supply with specific quality requirements to processors or intermediaries and ensuring farmers an immediate market outlet for their produce (as well as access to inputs). This type of contract is common for cash crops such as cotton and coffee, processed and canned vegetables, and highly perishable commodities such as fresh vegetables and diary. Kenya, Ethiopia, Mexico, Mozambique, Peru, etc. have had experiences in contract farming for crops such as coffee, tea, French beans, Asian vegetables, milk, cotton, asparagus, tomatoes, etc.

The literature on agricultural contracts in general, and contract farming in developing countries in particular, provides a good platform to assess the future of contract farming in developing countries. If we accept the premise that contract farming remains an important vehicle to keep small farmers involved in markets for high-value crops and animal products, it is now important to take the lessons from the experience with contract farming and use it to improve the working of this institution. With evolution and increasing prevalence of vertical coordination in agriculture the theoretical framework for evaluating these developments has also evolved. Several aspects in the New Institutional Economics such as contract theory, agency relationships (principle agent problems; incomplete contracts), transactions costs and the boundaries of the firms have now become key focus areas (*Barryu et al.*, 1992). This theoretical framework is useful in analyzing the relationships between the farmer (agent) and the vertical coordination/integrator/agribusiness (the principal), where decisions can influence the financial position and performance of both the principle and the agent. In the context of contract farming, this framework can be used to analysis and address the problems that could typically constrain or lead to the break down of contractual relations in developing country agriculture.

(3) Grades and Standards

The globalized agricultural sector is witnessing an increasing demand for safe, healthy, and high-quality food. This trend results in more stringent and complicated international grades and standards. Grades and standards play a crucial role in proving internationally recognized information and quality assurance about a product, thereby reducing information and transaction costs and facilitating international trade. However, grades and standards can also be used as non-tariff barriers to trade if importing countries impose minimum standards that many developing countries cannot meet. For example, many supermarkets in Europe have strict regulations regarding pesticide residue on fruits and vegetables [formally known as Minimum Residue Levels (MRLs)]. These regulations imposed by supermarkets to meet consumer demand and create market niches, are trickling down to the production level and thereby affect the structure and characteristics of the market downstream.

One can think of grades and standards as the "rules of the game" or as institutions that govern exchange in international markets. Therefore, the use of the transaction cost literature to address the issues revolving around grades and standards would be extremely useful. Now do grades and standards act as barrier to trade particularly for small farmers and firms or do they create a market opportunity to enter high-value produce markets? What are the private and public sectors' capacity in implementing grades and standards? Should grades and standards be used as a national strategy to improve exports sales? Some of these issues have been partially discussed in Reardon *et. al.*, (2001).

(4) Traders' Behaviour and Performance

In most developing countries, especially Sub-Saharan Africa, laws regarding market contracts and property rights are either non-existent or poorly enforced. Consequently, most commodity transactions are based on personalized exchange, markets remain thin and cash-based, and economies of scale in marketing are not fully exploited. Because of high transaction costs in terms of screening for trust-worthy partners, obtaining information about prices or quality, and enforcing contracts, traders have resorted to dealing with a tight network of traders linked either through ethnic group or other social and family relationships. Traders with higher social capital are better able to enter more capital-intensive marketing activities such as wholesaling and long-distance transport, whereas traders with poor social networks face high barriers to entry into the more lucrative market segments. Better-connected traders also seem to have more sales and higher gross profits.

The transaction costs and social capital concepts can help us understand questions such as: Are the institutional responses and contractual choices of traders efficient, or can they be improved? What is the role of the government in cutting down on transaction costs and decreasing the riskiness of market exchange? What institutions are needed to foster the development of north-personalized and more efficient market exchange? The studies by Fafchamps and Minten (1998a, 1998b, 2001) and Gabre-Madhin (2001) analyze some of these issues in the African grain trade context.

(5) Access to Agricultural Input and Rural Credit Markets

In many developing countries, because of high transaction costs (including information costs), inability to enforce contract with farmers, and thin markets, private traders are unwilling to provide input credit to farmers. As a result, there is a market failure in the provision of credit to rural households and farmers are unable to finance the purchase of agricultural inputs such as modern seeds and fertilizers. In Sub-Saharan Africa, the average fertilizer application rate is 9 kg of nutrient per ha, one of the lowest levels in the world, resulting in a decline in soil fertility and rapid soil degradation in many areas.

The literature on the economics of information and agency theory is useful here to identify the types of institutions that would be successful in providing credit to rural households. Some of these older institutions (sharecropping, interlocked contracts, etc.) have been analyzed by Bhardan (1989) and Dorward *et. al.* (1998). However, more needs to be done in this area as the institutional fix for failing rural credit markets has yet to emerge.

(6) Institutions for Risk Management and Market Information

In most developing countries, institutions for risk management and market information are missing. Most farmers and traders rely on informal mechanisms and networks to cope with risk and obtain market information. Price risk is becoming an increasingly important issue in light of public sector evolvement from price fixing policies and price stabilization schemes, and increased reliance on international trade. Obtaining information on prices and market supply and demand is more important in an environment where prices fluctuate with local weather changes, seasonally of supply, world market conditions, and market performance. In liberalized markets, instruments to cope with market risk are essential to increase the commercialization of agriculture. Farmers and traders' performance is as sensitive to price variability as to the absolute level of prices.

The types of institutions needed (either formal or informal) to manage market risk in developing countries is crucial to increase the commercialization of agriculture and encourage farmers and traders to participate in agricultural markets. This includes informal institutions such as contract farming, sharecropping, and other mechanisms that tie input and output markets, as well as formal institutions such as commodity exchanges and financial instruments such as options and futures contracts. It is important to find out under what conditions formal institutions can be created with the help of government policies or public and private investments to replace the informal, and perhaps less efficient, existing mechanisms to deal with market risk. The conditions would include the existence of a legal framework and technical know-how that is necessary before more sophisticated market-based risk management mechanisms can be developed. It is also important to find out what type of market information systems would be most feasible and cost-effective in providing timely market information and price forecasting for market participant. Therefore, more effort and research is needed to design more effective institutions that can reduce the transaction costs of providing information to rural households and help them cope with market risk.

(7) Rural Services Management

Rural input services such as water for irrigation, electricity, feeder roads, and telecommunication networks have traditionally been public goods provided and financed by the government in developing countries. However, in many countries these services were lacking, rationed, or could only be provided at great costs due to inefficiencies and lack of transparency in public utilities. The lack of accountability and transparency of government services in rural areas, and rising fiscal costs, have led to the increased decentralization and devolution of rural services to the concerned communities and user groups. For that purpose, communities have been given the right and responsibility to raise their own funds and spend these funds according to pre-agreed upon rules and regulations. For example, in many instances, institutions such as water user associations have been very helpful in devolving water management to the direct beneficiaries thereby raising efficiency and improving water resource allocation. The same could be applied in the maintenance of feeder roads in rural areas. The studies on the conditions and institutional priors needed for successful collective action would be very useful to determine which user groups are more likely to succeed in these types of schemes (see for example *Meinzen-Dick, Raju and Gulati,* (2000) on the management of canal irrigation system in India).

CONCLUSIONS

With neoclassical economics increasingly being questioned in its ability to provide answers to the many economic problems and issues in low as well as high-income countries, the NIE provide an exciting and challenging new paradigm. The applications of NIE are well suited to the economic problems of world food and agricultural industry. They could vary from studying the relationships in well-developed and highly sophisticated food supply chains to the informal institutions governing grades and standards in developing countries' grain markets. Although various elements of the NIE have already been applied in the context of food and agricultural policy in developing countries, this paper has showed the large potential for further very important applications in the area of agricultural market research. The NIE is particularly poor in Modeling risk and uncertainly related to prices or the environment. These apparent weakness mean that the NIE faces many challenges ahead and much more work remains to be done. This is, however what makes it an exciting and dynamic field with tremendous opportunities for improvement and refinement.

REFERENCES

Akerlof, G.A. (1970). "The Market for 'Lemons': Quality Uncertainly and the Market Mechanism," *Quarterly Journal of Economics*, Vol. 84, 488-500.

Alchain, A.A. (1950), "Uncertainly, Evolution and Economics System," *Journal of Business*, Vol. 59, S358-S399.

Bhardan, P.K. (1989), "The New Institutional Economics and Development Theory: A Brief Critical Assessment," *World Development*, Vol. 17 (9): 1389-95.

Binsnwanger, H.P. and J. Mcintire (1987). "Behavioural and Material Determinants of Production Relations in Land-Abundant Tropical Agriculture?," *Economic Development and Culture*, Vol. 36 (1): 73-99.

Coase, R.H. (1937), "The Theory of the Firm," *Economics*, Vol. 4, 386-405.

Commons, J.R. (1934), *Institutional Economics: Its Place in Political Economy*, Madison: University of Wisocosin Press.

Demsetz, H. (1969), "Information and Efficiency: Another Viewpoint," *Journal of Law and Economics*, Vol. 12, 1-22.

Harness, J., Hunter, J. and Lewis, C.M. (eds.) (1995), *The New Institutional Economics and Third World Development*, London, Routledge.

Lancaster, K.J. (1996). A New Approach to Consumer Theory, *Journal of Political Economy*, Vol. 74, 132-57.

Mueller, D. (1989), *Public Choice II*, Cambridge University Press.

North, D.C. (1981), *Structure and Change in Economic History*, New York: Norton.

North, D.C. (1990), *Institutions, Institutional Changes, and Economic Performance*, Cambridge, Cambridge University Press.

Olson, M. (1965/1971), *The Logic of Collective Action: Public Goods and the Theory of Groups*, Cambridge, Harvard University Press.

Ostrom, E, Burger, J., Field, C. Norgaard, D.B. and Policansky, D. (1999), "Revisting the Commons: Local Lessons, Global Challenges," *Science*, Vol. 281-282.

Ruttan, V.W. (1999), "The New Growth Theory and Development Economics: A Survey," *Journal of Development Studies*, Vol. 35 (2), 1-26.

Sandier, T. (1992), *Collective Action: Theory and Applications*, Ann Arbor, University of Michigan Press.

Sen, A.K. (1991), "Utility: Ideas and Terminology," *Economics and Philosophy*, Vol. 7, 277-83.

Simon, H.A. (1986), "Rationality in Psychology and Economics," *Journal of Business*, Vol. 59, S209-S224.

Tverzky, A. and Kahneman, D. (1986). "Rational Choice and the Framing of Decisions," *Journal of Business*, Vol. 59, S251-S278.

Veblen, T. (1899). *The Theory of the Leisure Class: An Economic Study of Institutions*, New York and London, Macmillan.

Williamson, O.E. (1985), *The Economic Institutions of Capitalism: Firms, Markets, Relational Contracting*, New York, Free Press.

Williamson, O.E. (1996), *The Mechanisms of Governance*, New York and Oxford, Oxford University Press.

Sharecropping: A Rational Institutional Response

Nisar Ahmad Khan

A striking feature of the agriculture in developing countries is the extreme variation in the distribution of land ownership. As agriculture remains the main source of income for a large proportion of population in these countries, the unequal distribution of Iandholdings also implies unequal bargaining power in the process of exchange. The landlord has more than he could optimally cultivate with his own family labour. The tenant has more labour power than he could optimally utilize. So an exchange would be beneficial for both parties. Sharecropping is one such exchange. It is a form of land tenancy in which the payment for the use of land, the rent is a percentage of the total physical output obtained in the crop season. Sharecropping or share tenancy is different from other types of farm tenancy based on fixed annual rent whether in cash or in kind.

COMPLEXITY OF SHARECROPPING CONTRACT

Sharecropping tends to be regarded as an interesting theoretical puzzle by neo-classical economists and as an oppressive form of exploitation by some Marxian economists.

The puzzle of sharecropping resides in the incapability of ordinary economic analysis to explain certain aspects of its existence as an institution, namely:

(a) The fairly strong grounds for suspecting that it may be less efficient and less open to innovation than other kinds of farm tenancy.
(b) Its historical persistence and its coexistence often in the same locations with cash tenancy and capitalist farming.
(c) Customary crop shares between land owner and tenant which can not be explained by optimizing criteria alone.

The exploitation view of sharecropping stems from the way it concentrates economic power in the hands of landowners, and the control this gives them over the livelihoods of tenants and landless workers.

The link between these two angles on sharecropping—the economic riddle and the exploitation—is found in the concept of interlocked factor markets. This refers to the iack of independence between different input markets when multiple transactions are tied together in a single tenancy contract.

New Institutional Economics, which is an extension of neo-classical economics, places relatively greater emphasis on the micro-economic analysis of various interlinkages in agrarian relations, such as patron—client relationships, share tenancy agreements and credit iinkages. It explains that not ail of them are totally exploitative but are rational institutional responses to reduce transaction costs. Such arrangements have incentive effects, risk-sharing effects, and also act as substitutes for missing markets. The interlinked transactions in labour, land and credit markets are contractual arrangements of rational agents to substitute the incomplete or imperfect market situations existing in agriculture. There is scope for the agents to engage in strategic or opportunistic behaviour and there is asymmetry of information. In equilibrium situations they are resolved by institutional arrangements that constrain the behaviour of agents.

ANALYSIS OF SHARECROPPING

There are two opposing competitive models of sharecropping, the first originates in the treatment of share tenancy contained in Marshall's *Principles of Economics* (1890) and is thus referred to as the Marshallian model and the second is attributed mainly to Cheung (1968, 1969). We will examine each of these in turn before considering various other explanations for sharecropping.

In the Marshallian model share tenant is taken to be a profit maximiser in a competitive market subject to the output shares being fixed in advance. It is convenient to refer to the share of the output going to the landowner as S, and the share going to the tenant as (1 – S). The economic position of the share tenant is shown in the following figure.

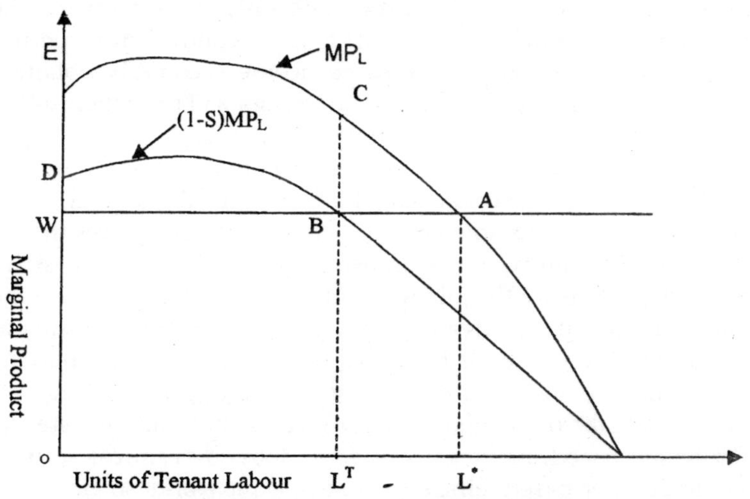

Marginal Product of Tenant Labour

In the figure the marginal product of the tenant on a plot of given size is MP_L, and the market wage is OW. Instead of being the tenant, if he were the owner cultivator he would apply OL* units of labour to the farm (MP_L = OW). He would obtain a net gain over his opportunity cost equal to the area WAE. But in the share contract, he receives only (1 – S) of his marginal product and will be in equilibrium at point B where his marginal cost, OW is equal to his marginal gain, (1 – S) MP_L. He will now employ OL^T units of labour. At B, the marginal product of tenant labour is higher than the market wage and it remains so in the region between OL^T and OL^*. Inspite of this, the tenant will not expend his labour in the farm beyond OL^T as his marginal cost, OW is more than his marginal gain, (1 – S) MP_L. So the share contract results in a net social loss equal to the area ABC. Neither the landlord nor the share tenant is capturing this. In this sense, share tenancy is a socially inefficient institutional arrangement. So the neo-classical economics consider share tenancy an inefficient form of economic organization.

In the Cheung model, the iandowner is a profit maximizer who can vary the amount of land at his disposal, decide the number and size of land parcels distributed amongst share tenants, decide the rent share, and stipulate in the share contract the amount of labour input which is required. The only constraint on the landowner is the market wage: the tenancy contract must permit the tenant to obtain at ieast the same income as couid be obtained by working as a wage labourer or no tenants wiii offer themselves as sharecropper. Since the landowner now sets the labour input of the tenant, profit maximization ensures that this occurs where the marginal product of the tenant labout equal the market wage. Thus, shareeropping now becomes efficient. Cheung says that in a world of certainty where transaction costs are absent, share contract can specify the labour supply of the tenant and also the share of output in advance, and this can result in efficient allocation of resources as in a fixed rent or fixed wage contract.

Neither of the basic models of shareeropping provide an entirely satisfactory explanation for its existence and persistence. The tenant-based, inefficiency, model, does so even less so than the landowner based, efficiency, one since it works so clearly to the landowner's disadvantage and appears socially inefficient compared to other forms of land tenure. However, the landowner model does not solve the riddle either. If the outcome for the landowner is no different from employing wage labour or leasing under a fixed cash rent, then why adopt shareeropping instead of one of the other production arrangements?

One way forward is to drop the assumption of certainty from the analysis. When uncertainty and risk are taken into account the adoption of shareeropping becomes more plausible. This can first be posed in relation to the alternatives. Under a cash rent tenancy fixed in advance of the crop season the risks associated with production in an uncertain environment are borne entirely by tenant; under self-cultivation with wage labour they are borne entirely by the landowner. Thus if either the tenant, the landowner, or both parties are risk-averse a risk-sharing arrangement may be preferred to one in which the risk is entirely borne by one or the other of them. With shareeropping this risk is shared between tenant and landowner in the same proportion as output is shared.

The risk-sharing explanation for the existence and persistence of sharecropping has been criticised by many economists. Yoram Barzel, for instance, provides a purely transaction cost explanation for the prevalence of share contracts even under risk—neutral assumptions. He says that share tenancy contract is an institutional response to minimize transaction costs.

The risk-sharing explanation for sharecropping works better for tenants than for iandowners, depending in part on other assumptions about the nature of markets surrounding production decisions. If these markets are competitive it can be shown for the landlord that there is some combination of cash rent tenancy and self-cultivation which would provide exactly the same degree of risk spreading as a given share contract, while at the same time avoiding the potential inefficiencies of sharecropping. Moreover, this combination would result in the same income shares, between tenants and landlords, as in the Cheung solution to sharecropping efficiency (*Newbery & Stiglitz*, 1979).

So the existence of uncertainty, and the subjective response to it in the form of risk-aversion, do not therefore on their own solve the riddle of sharecropping.

The radical economists are of the view that sharecropping is a non-market (non-capitalist) form of surplus extraction by one class, the landowners, from another class, the landless tenants. This surplus extraction is direct, it is the physical crop share obtained by the non-producing landowner from the producing sharecropper. It is not mediated by prices, and it is therefore, closer to a feudal relation of production than a capitalist one. Sharecropping has been referred to as 'Semi-feudalism' in this context (*Bhaduri*, 1973). To extract further more surplus the landlords very often provide credit and inputs to tenants and also indulge in labour tying.

Pranab Bardhan and Ashok Rudra (1978) surveyed nearly 275 randomly selected villages in West Bengal, Bihar and eastern district of Uttar Pradesh to study the terms and conditions of land, labour and credit contracts. They found that the institution of share tenancy had been largely adopted to the needs of increasing production and profits by enterprising farmers, both owners and tenants. But the economic constraints faced by the small sharecopper or the attached labourer were much more severe, and these frequently pushed them into unequal relationship of mutual dependence with the landlord—creditor—employee.

David Lehmann (1986) in his study of high land in Ecuador found sharecropping compatible with capitalist development. There are several other studies which found sharecropping as non-exploitative. Nevertheless, given the long history of survival of this economic organization in different parts of the world and its persistence even now, it is unlikeiy to be aiways inefficient and exploitative.

Perhaps the most acceptable explanation for sharecropping has been provided by New Institutional Economics. The new institutional economics consider sharecropping as a rational response of both landlords and tenants under conditions of asymmetry of information and positive transaction costs. It identifies factors responsible for the existence and survival of sharecropping within the framework of imperfection of markets. As soon as the causes of sharecropping are sought in the range and nature of market failures in the rural economy 'there is no unanswered puzzle as to the apparent absence of reasons for the common practice of sharecropping. On the contrary there is an embarrassment of riches'. (*Bliss & Stern*, 1982, p. 64). A number of such reasons are: (a) presence of incentive problem, economies of scale and multiple sources of risk; (b) need for costly supervision due to imperfect information about input efforts and need for screening of potential tenants whose abilities are not identical, (c) market imperfections to inputs other than labour, and (d) most recently, the presence of an implicit limited—liability clause which allows a tenant to renege on paying rent under conditions of extreme crop failures. Actually, several alternative combinations of reasons are given to explain the institution of sharecropping.

Newbery and Stiglitz (1979) have showed that share contracts could be superior even when there were no incentive problems or scale effects provided there were multiple sources of risk; but production risk and risk aversion alone would not explain sharecropping. The choice of contract actually conveys information about workers' perception of their abilities. If a worker believed that he was productive, he would choose a fixed rent contract. If a worker believed that his productivity was low, he would choose a wage contract. Those in between would choose the share contract. Economies of scale could also make sharecropping attractive even in the absence of incentive effects.

Neither tenants nor landlords in practice face the competitive labour market alternative which is assumed in both the Marshallian and Cheung sharecropping models. For tenants supplying their labour the market works unevenly and the costs of job search are significant; farm production requires labour seasonally through the year and there is no certainty for landless households that sufficient wage labour could be obtained for survival in a given time period. For landlords seeking wage labour, hiring sufficient workers, with appropriate skills, at the correct time is a problem. So the transaction costs are significant for both parties in the labour market. Sharecropping helps to minimize these transaction costs.

Several different aspects of these labour market problems have been explored in the literature. One way of viewing them is from an *insurance* perspective: a mechanism like sharecropping is required in order to reduce the risks for both landowners and tenants. Another way of viewing them is as a problem of *screening* (*Braverman & Guasch*, 1984): here tenancy permits landowners to select tenants possessing desirable attributes (hard working, agronomic skills), rather than relying on the unknown and variable skills of seasonal wage labour. An offshoot of the screening idea is that landowners select tenants according to their endowments of non-marketed factors of production such as bullocks or family labour (*Shetty*, 1988). A third way of viewing them is as a problem of monitoring the quality and effectiveness of work. Sharecropping is often called as an institutional response to overcome the problem of searching labour and monitoring the quality and effectiveness of work.

The fundamental equivalency theorem mentioned earlier showed that tenants renting some land and also working as wage-earners for other landlords, that is, by mixing rental and wage contracts, could achieve the same results as a share contract in which output risk alone is shared. But a share contract becomes valuable when the labour input is not monitorable, or when the cost of monitoring labour input is very high. By altering the terms of the share contract, the landlord is able to induce the tenant to put in more effort. In other words, by altering the terms of the share contract the landlord provides incentives for the tenant to put in more effort, and, at the same time induces him to share some of the output risks also.

Braverman and Stiglitz (1986) have argued that cost-sharing contracts have a decided advantage over contracts which specify the levels of inputs whenever there are asymmetries of information between landlord and tenant regarding production technologies. Looking at the sharecropping contract in the principal—agent setting, they have stressed the importance not only of the risk and incentive problems but aiso their flexibility and their ability to adopt to changes in environment.

P.K. Bardhan argues that cost-sharing of inputs in the standard 'principal-agent' model would not be rational unless the tenant has more information about production uncertainty than the landlord. He says that imperfections and inter-linkages of transactions in rural markets make the cost of inputs different for the landlord and tenant and that the landlord achieves his goal without being able to observe the tenant's input by cost sharing at the margin instead of a lumpsum transfer.

Mukesh Eswaran and Ashok Kotwal (1985) declare that the view that risk sharing is the main motivation behind sharecropping lacks empirical support. They also hold that the assumption of ignorance on the part of landlord about tenants' abilities is quite inappropriate for most rural communities. They also criticized the screening models as not capable of explaining the change in contractual structures which follow changes in technology or development of markets.

They view share tenancy as a substitute for the absence of a market for some factor inputs besides land. The high cost of quality enforcement can cause the absence or incompleteness of markets. Markets are known to be imperfect for technological known-how, managerial ability, bullocks, credit and family labour. So an effective way of gaining access to such a factor is to provide incentives to such factor owners to enter into a self-monitoring contract with them involving them in the process of production. So Eswaran and Kotwal view sharecropping as a partnership arrangement in which both agents have incentives to self-monitor. Such a contract mitigates potential moral hazard behaviour. Using "management" and "supervision" as the two unmarked resources, they view sharecropping as a partnership in which each partner provides the unmarketed factor input in which he is better endowed.

Kaushik Basu's (1984) analysis covers the risk-sharing, screening and parcelisation of land hypothesis for sharecropping. He has perceptively observed, "an empirical solution to the problem of why share tenancy exists is made difficult by the role of history. It is quite possible that share tenancy emerged in a certain region for economic reasons; but having persisted for many years, it became a part of the society and continues to persist though its economic rational may have disappeared" (p, 125). The historical development could also have created path-dependent processes which might 'lock-in' the system of share-tenancy even in the face of technological change.

In a more recent paper (*Basu*, 1992), he considers the problem of an absentee landlord who can not supervise hired labour. He takes into account the fact that when the weather fails and the harvest is poor, the landlord would not be able to claim his full rent. So he introduces the limited liability clause into the share contract. The limited liability clause is an implicit understanding between the tenant and the landlord that under conditions of extreme crop failures due to natural calamities, the landlord well forego his claim for rents. In the presence of limited liabilities, the tenant would prefer risky projects and the landlord would act as a risk-averse person. Sharecropping could minimize the tension between the two agents. By offering the share-rental contract, the landlord could direct the tenant to choose a less risky project than under a fixed rent contract with limited liability.

CONCLUSION

Neo-classical economics had recognized the widespread existence of sharecropping. Under the assumption of full information and costless transactions, sharecropping was found to be inefficient. So neo-classical economics could not explain the puzzle of its continued persistence over wide areas.

The radical economists has a tendency to equate sharecropping mechanically with the feudal or semi-feudal mode of production, thus ignoring how in the real world the same institution adapts itself to the development of forces of production, with numerous cases of capitalist share-tenant farmers or more widespread cases of cost-sharing and other form of landlord tenant partnership.

Thus, while radical economists have been more vocal in raising the issue of agrarian institutions and their interaction with technological development, the more substantive contribution in development theory in this respect have been carried out with neo-classical methodology looking into the micro foundations of their rational, drawing upon the growing literature on imperfect information, uncertainty, incentive and principal agent games, which is often referred as new institutional economics. The new institutional economics consider sharecropping as rational response of both landlords and tenants under conditions of asymmetry of information and positive transaction costs.

REFERENCES

Bardhan, P. and Rudra, A. (1978) "Interlinkage of Land, Labour and Credit Relations", *EPW*, Annual No., Feb.

Bardhan, P.K. (ed.) (1989): *The Economic Theory of Agrarian Institutions*, Clarendon Press, Oxford.

Basu, K. (1984), *The Less Developed Economy: A Critique of Contemporary Theory*, OUP, New Delhi.

Basu, K. (1992), "Limited Liability and the Existence of Share Tenancy," *Journal of Development Economics*, Vol. 38.

Bhaduri, A. (1973), "A Study of Agricultural Backwardness under Semi-Feudalism," *The Economic Journal*, March.

Bhaduri, A. (1983), *The Economic Structure of Backward Agriculture*, Academic Press, London.

Braverman, A. and Stiglitz, J.E. (1982) "Sharecropping and the Interlinking of Agrarian Markets", *American Economic Review*, Vol. 72, No. 4.

Braverman, A. and Stiglitz, J.E. (1986), "Cost-Sharing Arrangements under Sharecropping: Moral Hazard, Incentive Flexibility and Risk" *American Journal of Agricultural Economics*, August.

Brazel, Yoram (1989), *Economic Analysis of Property Rights*, Cambridge University Press, Cambridge.

Cheung, Steven (1969), *A theory of Share Tenancy*, University of Chicago Press, Chicago.

Eswaran, Mukesh and Kotwal, A. (1985), "A Theory of Contractual Structure in Agriculture," *AER*, Vol. 75, No. 3.

Neelakantan, S. (1992), *New Institutional Economics and Agrarian Change*, Indian Economic Association Trust for Research and Development, New Delhi.

Roumasset, J.E. *et. al.* (ed.) *Risk, Uncertainty and Agricultural Development*, Agricultural Development Council, New York.

Shetty, S. (1988), "Limited Liability, Wealth Difference and Tenancy Contract in Agrarian Economics," *Journal of Development Economics*, Vol. 29.

Stiglitz, J.E. (1986), "The New Development Economics," *World Development*, Vol. 14, No. 2.

Institutional Change, Transaction Costs and Natural Resource Management

FALENDRA K. SUDAN

INTRODUCTION

The motivation for institutional change in use of natural resources has arisen from emerging resource scarcity and greater competition for rights of access and exploitation. The government is shedding some of its responsibilities for management of natural resources and has planned withdrawal from certain area of activity. It is argued that well planned and well executed withdrawal from natural resource management reduces the transaction costs, improves government performance and leads to

* This paper is a part of the research project titled "Participatory Approaches and Environmental and Economic Impact: With Special Reference to IWDP, Hills-II, Jammu and Kashmir, India", completed in May 2003 and sponsored by Ministry of Environment and Forests, New Delhi and World Bank funded "Environmental Management Capacity Building Technical Assistance (EMCaB) Project".

a more equitable diffusion of benefits to more people (*OECD/DAC*, 1995). International lenders have placed a great emphasis on reducing the absolute numbers of public staff, as a cost-cutting measure, and transferring resource management to groups of users (*Carney and Farrington*, 1998). The decentralization measures puts the decision-making in the hands of people who are well informed, accessible to others, and in a position to make decisions, which are fundamental to the lives of many rural people, in a timely manner. The underlying premise of this type of institutional change is that physical proximity of the users is likely to result in better informed, more effective and more transparent decision making (*Hobley*, 1995). The success of institutional change depends on a number of factors such as decentralization of financial and the capacity building of lower level staff to manage the new tasks for which they are responsible (*Bardhan*, 1997; *Carney*, 1995).

The overuse and increasing scarcity of natural resources, and decline in traditional institutions to manage natural resources in *Shivaliks* were the deriving force behind the institutional change under Integrated Watershed Development Project (IWDP), Hills-II, Jammu and Kashmir in early 2000. The agenda for institutional change included: evolving cost-sharing mechanisms for resource development, protection and use; reform of regulatory agencies to act as facilitators in resource conservation; and evolving users' participation in resource management. The underlying intent of the introduction of institutional change was to remove government subsidization of management of natural resources, evolving cost-benefit sharing mechanism, specification of property rights (especially usufruct rights in natural resources) and duties, socially optimal allocation and use of resources, etc. The overall goal of institutional change is a self-maintaining resource management system and minimization of the transaction costs associated with natural resource management. The benefits of institutional change depend almost entirely upon the formal and informal rules in use, and their monitoring and compliance. The well-designed institutional change ensure widely acceptable regulations, better monitoring and compliance, which facilitates in lowering transaction costs. Keeping above in view, an attempt has been made to examine the role of user participation in lowering the transaction costs; and to estimate the transaction costs incurred on institutional change by the project implementing agency and individual resource users in the context of IWDP (Hills-II), Jammu and Kashmir.

STUDY AREA AND METHODOLOGY

In order to prevent and reverse the resource degradation process of the *Shivaliks,* IWDP, Hills-I was undertaken in 1990. Seeing the physical targets being achieved by the participating States, the World Bank decided to further extend the programme in the form of IWDP, Hills-II in 1999, for five years. This was aimed at providing a uniform integrated rural development platform to address the social and natural resource problems of the entire *Shivaliks* in India. The experience gained through implementation of IWDP (Hills-I), J&K encouraged the State Government to extend the watershed development project to other rainfed areas of the State. The main objective of the IWDP, Hills-II is to restore the productive potential of the *Shivaliks*. The focus is on improving *in-situ* moisture conservation, water harvesting and land management practices. An associated objective of the project is to assist with the institutional development and consolidate the progress already made under IWDP, Hills-I. The project design recognizes the need for institutional reforms that will ensure long term sustainability of intended interventions. A "bottom-up" approach is an integral part of the project design and involves all stakeholders during project planning and implementation (*World Bank,* 1999).

IWDP, Hills-II, Jammu and Kashmir covers two sub-watersheds in *Shivaliks,* viz. Ramnagar and Akhnoor and two sub-watersheds in *Karewas,* viz. Rajwar and Rambiyara. The present study was confined to two sub-watersheds of Akhnoor (Jammu district) and Ramnagar (Udhampur district). While Ramnagar is in the inner *Shivaliks,* Akhnoor is on its outer part. Ramnagar sub-watershed is the catchment area of Ramnagarwali *Khad* (ephermal) in the middle catchment of river Tawi. It has an area of 32,630 ha. and is subdivided into 39 micro-watersheds. Akhnoor sub-watershed with an area of 42350 ha. is subdivided into 37 micro-watersheds. It covers about a dozen rivulets *(nallahs)* and a large number of small nallahs originating from *Kalidhar* ridge and draining into Chinab river on the western portion of *Kalidhar* ridge, drains join Manawar Tawi which in turn also meets the

Chinab river. In terms of physiographic features, there may not be 100 per cent similarity between the selected sub-watersheds but, certainly, in term of accessibility, natural resource endowment, infrastructure development and general index of socio-economic awareness, two sub-watersheds are comparable.

The primary data has been collected using well-structured and pre-tested questionnaire, participatory rural appraisal (PRA) techniques and group meetings. Whenever possible and required, secondary data sources have also been utilized. Three Village Development Committees (VDCs each have been randomly selected from the sub-watersheds of Akhnoor and Ramnagar and the sample size has been restricted to the members of VDCs which were in range of 15-25 in each VDC. The data related to the transaction costs in evolving and operationalising participatory institutions has also been collected from the project functionaries at sub-watershed level. In all the focus-group observations, 10-12 stakeholders have been recruited from different settings. Highly formal interviews have been conducted using structured interview schedules. In-depth interviews have also been conducted to elicit opinion of stakeholders with extensive knowledge of the phenomenon under study. The content analysis technique has been used to analyze the data and information qualitatively and quantitatively (using descriptive statistics).

USER PARTICIPATION AND TRANSACTION COSTS

The institutional approach in natural resource management is largely ignored in ecologically fragile areas, which apparently explain the link between environmental resource degradation and rural poverty (*Jodha*, 1986). During the recent past, some kinds of changes in institutional structure are seen to be playing a useful role. Such change in the institutional framework amount to an alternation in the nature of property rights. The group of persons using a resource and the nature of their rights and obligations is laid down by the newly emergent institutions. They aim at laying down a codified set of rules, which by convention or law mediates the nature of the relationship between resources and people (*Blomquist*, 1992). One of the outcomes of such new institutional arrangements is an increase in the capacity of the environment to improve rural livelihoods. A local level "institution creating" focus begins with examination of rights to access, use and ownership of resources by individuals, households and other social groups. It confronts the existing set of social norms and practices and questions whether they are appropriate in the context of efficient and sustainable resource management (*Bromley*, 1989). The local issues led intervention is more flexible in the initial stages. It draws its strength from this ability to improvise rules and conventions and to build on traditional institutions to set-up innovative models of management. However, it may result in conflicts with other institutions that dominate the economy, which necessitate the state involvement to ensure that the seat of local decision-making is not usurped by the politically and economically powerful (*Dasgupta*, 1997).

Organization of rural communities is based on group dynamics in which certain individuals play key roles. Group coordination is required to create institutions to manage the common property resources (CPRs). The high transaction costs involved in coordination and conflict resolutions or negotiations resulted in a deadlock (mainly due to political reasons) and either appropriate institutions fail to emerge or existing ones disintegrate. This leads to open access situations leading to the tragedy of commons (*Hardin*, 1968). The institutional change aims at reducing the transaction costs (*Coase*, 1960; *North*, 1990). Institutions evolve or change when the expected benefits from such changes are greater than the costs involved in undertaking such activities. Thus, the transaction costs are the main force behind the institutional change. Similarly, efficient institutions replace the old and inefficient ones, if the net gains are positive. The collective action outcomes would be preferred when the expected returns are larger than the cost of coordinating institutional change. It is not necessary that all existing institutions are efficient. Imperfect information could block an appropriate institutional arrangement or could lead to degeneration of an appropriate institutional arrangement, particularly in natural resource management where expected benefits are not known. Therefore, information is necessary but not sufficient condition to explain institutional change in the context of natural resource management, where collective action is a prerequisite for institutional arrangements. The costs of obtaining such information are not large compared to collective economic benefits. However, other transaction costs such as the coordination of the group may be high. The coordinating costs act as disincentive for individual initiatives within the group and requires external support.

Neo-institutional economics explicitly considers specific structures of property rights and transaction costs (*Eggertsson*, 1990). A central concern in neo-institutional economics is the structuring of contracts between principals and agents (*Jensen and Meckling*, 1976). The cost of writing, monitoring, and enforcing contracts, which depend on legal and social institutions, determine how much discretion, the principal should optimally delegate to agents. The introduction of transaction costs greatly complicates welfare comparison between alternative organizational forms (*Bromley*, 1989; *Murrell*, 1991). The governance structure of CPRs determines how clearly it allocates rights to members of the collective. Ostrom (1990) identifies a numbers of factors that contribute to long-enduring CPRs: clearly defined borders, congruence between rules and local conditions, representative and collective choice arrangement, agent to monitor use, the graduated application of sanctions, the availability of conflicts resolution mechanisms and reorganization of collective by government authorities. Yet, as she notes, long endurance does not imply that common property is being used efficiently.

The user participation in resource management results in higher efficiency and affects the management costs. User participation contributes positively to the cost-effectiveness of resource management when it lowers costs of information gathering, coordination, monitoring and enforcement. However, the positive contributions of the user groups in resource protection and conservation ultimately depend on resource conditions. If the resources are degraded, the participatory institutions must be evolved before resource conditions decline to the point of scarcity. Effective management of natural resources is difficult because of the conflicts between short-term needs of the stakeholders and long-term objectives of resource sustainability. Individual resorts to use of natural resources without regard to collective benefits. Similarly, collective institutions may be developed in ignorance of the individual needs. Equitable management of natural resources is difficult to achieve, because of divergent interests and value involved. Due to existence of high transaction costs involved in gathering information, monitoring and enforcement, efficient resource management is difficult to realize. However, in favourable and conducive situation, the benefits from resource management may exceed the management costs. The institutions can play an important role in enhancing the outcomes of resource management by lowering the information, monitoring and enforcement costs. They also influence positively the equity and effectiveness of resource management. If the institutions for resource management are fair and effective, the resource sustainability can be achieved, and otherwise, it will result in overuse and degradation of resources. The cost-effectiveness of natural resource management requires that these institutions must be efficient so that the objectives be realized with minimum costs as well as the benefits from resource management must be higher than the costs involved to operationalize the institutions.

Transaction costs of resource management result from the need to describe a resource, and to design, implement, monitor, and enforce a set of regulations. Some transaction costs remain fixed regardless of the type of the process used to make decisions such as the costs related to provision of scientific information. Other transaction costs vary with the process used to make decisions and the quality of data collected. Costs of information gathering, coordinating between user groups, and the programme implementation and enforcement can vary according to the quality of data and the process adopted. Four resource management stages in which variable transaction costs are incurred are the description of the resource context, regulatory design, implementation, and enforcement (*Hanna*, 1995). The implementation of a resource management project requires information on description of resource users, processors, market, and the analysis of social and economic characteristics of all resource interests. The user's participation in information provisioning helps in arriving at accurate assessment of the problem. The project implementing agencies often lack the trained personnel to collect such diverse data to support such assessments. The design phase of the project also requires information describing resource context, which reflects accurate assessment of social and economic conditions. Due to inaccurate assessment of resource context and social and economic environment, the implementation of a regulation failed to control user behaviour in economic, social, and cultural dimensions. Similarly, monitoring compliance with regulations will be excessively costly if the monitoring systems are not designed to be in consistent with resource dynamics or user operations. The same condition applies to the enforcement of regulations. Resource extraction activities often take place over a large geographical area, so the effective enforcement requires some degree of cooperation of those who are regulated. Regulation must also fit within the structure of operations.

Two major costs affect institutional choice: transformation costs, and monitoring and enforcement costs. If the expected costs of transforming the rules are higher than the net benefits to be gained, no further cost calculations will be made. Appropriators will retain their *status quo* rules that produce fewer benefits than would alternative rules, because the costs of changing the rules are higher than the benefits to be obtained. If the *ex ante* costs of transforming the rules are not too high, expected changes in *ex post* costs will also be evaluated including the effects of proposed rules on monitoring and enforcement costs. Transformation costs are the resources devoted to the process of considering a rule change. The number of individuals involved in institutional change, the heterogeneity of interests, and the size of the group minimally necessary to achieve a change in *status quo* rules influence transformation costs positively. Transformation costs are lower when skillful leaders are involved. The total transformation costs is not affected by the presence of individuals who have substantial assets at stake. However, the presence of individuals who will derive substantial benefits from a change in rules influenced the transformation costs positively. The type of proposed rule also affects transformation costs. If the expected benefits from the proposed rules are high and the transformation costs are low, these are likely to be adopted before rules with high transformation costs. Over the period, the resource users can gain experience concerning the costs of changing the rules in their setting before attempting changes that will require substantial transformation costs. If the transformation costs for changing some rules are low enough, one or two individuals may receive sufficiently high benefits from the change to pay the entire costs themselves. The sharing of norms concerning resource use will affect transformation costs directly and indirectly. The transformation costs are high when individuals adopt confrontational strategies (*Scharpf*, 1989). The appropriators who share norms that restrain opportunistic behavior can adopt rules that are less costly to operate than are the rules adopted by appropriators who do not share such norms. The rules instituted at one time will also affect the transformation costs at a later time. The level of autonomy to change their own rules will also affect the transformation costs. Considerable time and investment is required to change rules set by top-down approach. Time is spent in explaining the problem and change required consulting and motivating the stakeholders to forestall their opposition (*Wade*, 1988).

The costs of monitoring and enforcing the new rules under participatory approach are minimal than top-down approach. The users themselves frequently undertake monitoring activities, while attending their normal activities or on rotational basis. The substantial costs are involved in enforcement of rules. The physical attributes of the resources and the proposed rules affects the monitoring costs. The primary cost of exclusion may then be the legal action required for stopping an unauthorized user from continuing to use a resource. The close proximity to the resource tends to lower monitoring and enforcement costs. Alternatively, if appropriation of resources is visible and open for casual inspection, monitoring costs will be low. The shared norm adopted for appropriation will lower monitoring a particular resource. If the shared norms are legitimate and followed will reduce the monitoring costs, and their absence will increase the costs of monitoring. The regular dissemination of information about regulated activities will also decrease monitoring costs. Rules themselves vary in terms of monitoring and enforcement costs. The more frequent the required monitoring, the greater the resources devoted to measurement (*Ostrom*, 1990). Rules specifying the opening and closing dates of seasons are less costly to monitor than the rules specify a quota for resource use. Anyone found appropriating from the resource before or after the specified time is unambiguously breaking the rules. Rules that bring together the intruder and the looser are also easier to monitor than the rules that depend on accidental discovery of a rule breaker by someone who may be indirectly harmed by the infraction. Rules that place limit on the quantity of resource units that can be produced during an entire season or year are more costly to enforce. The use of quota will also depend on regularity of the flow. Besides physical attribute of the resource and the specific rules contemplated, monitoring and enforcement cost is affected by the authorities' recognition of the legitimacy of local rules. In areas, where government fails to recognize the user rights developed by local appropriators, exclusion costs can become very high.

IDENTIFICATION AND ESTIMATION OF TRANSACTION COSTS

The main problem with transaction costs approach is their quantitative estimation. There is general lack of established techniques for empirical estimation of the types of transaction costs associated with decision-making for resource allocation. Unless these costs are measured, there is no way this approach can be tested empirically. Transaction costs are often taken into account without any quantification and their existence is considered as a theoretical possibility. In the following paragraphs, an attempt has been made to estimate the actual transaction costs incurred by project implementing agency and individual resource users in specific situations rather than estimating 'transaction-cost functions'.

(i) Transaction Costs incurred on Institutional Strengthening

The data presented in Table 1 reflect the transaction costs incurred on institutional strengthening by the project-implementing agency in the sub-watersheds of Ramnagar and Akhnoor. The main components of institutional strengthening are capacity-building, policy reforms and human resource development, project coordination and support, and information management and monitoring and evaluation. In 1999-2000, a total sum of Rs. 517.7 lacs and Rs. 428.7 lacs has been spent on various project components respectively in the sub-watersheds of Ramnagar and Akhnoor, out of which Rs. 16.7 lacs and Rs. 16.55 lacs has been spent on institutional strengthening. Thus, the transaction costs incurred on institutional strengthening are very small and work out to be 3.22 per cent and 3.86 per cent respectively in sub-watersheds of Ramngar and Akhnoor during 1999-2000. The proportion of transaction costs incurred in the year 2001-02 has increased to 4.27 per cent in Ramnagar and declined to 3.83 per cent in Akhnoor. Two important transaction costs incurred on institutional strengthening are project coordination and support, and capacity building of beneficiaries and participatory planning staff. The transaction costs on project coordination and support includes travel and logistical costs, hiring of consultants, equipment and supplies and wages to participatory social development functionaries. In 1999-2000, a sum of Rs. 12.00 lacs and Rs. 9.20 lacs have been spent on project coordination and support, whereas in 2001-02, Rs. 11.97 lacs and Rs. 12.82 lacs respectively have been spent in Ramnagar and Akhnoor. Out of total project expenditure, the transaction costs incurred on project coordination and support stood at 2.32 per cent and 2.15 per cent respectively in Ramnagar and Akhnoor in 1999-2000 and 2.07 per cent and 1.91 per cent in 2001-02. (Table 1)

The transaction costs incurred on capacity building of beneficiaries and participatory development staff includes hiring of NGOs services, participatory development coordinators, participatory facilitators at sub-watershed level, and participatory development motivators at village level. Some consensus building/review workshops, participatory assessment planning exercises, training on participatory watershed management, and income generating activities have also been conducted at sub-watershed and village level. In 1999-2000, a sum of Rs. 2.3 lacs and Rs. 4.1 lacs have been spent on capacity building of beneficiaries and participatory project staff in Ramnagar and Akhnoor respectively, which increased to Rs. 8.73 lacs and Rs. 12.17 lacs in 2001-02. Out of total project expenditure, the transaction costs incurred on capacity building stood at 0.44 per cent and 0.96 per cent respectively in Ramnagar and Akhnoor in 1999-2000 and 1.51 per cent and 1.81 per cent in 2001-02. It is significant to note that transaction costs incurred on capacity building increased considerably between 1999-2000 and 2001-02 and recorded at 279.56 percent and 196.83 per cent respectively in Ramnagar and Akhnoor. In the selected sub-watersheds, the project has incurred transaction costs on policy reforms and human resource development only in the initial year, which is also negligible. However, it is pertinent to note that the project has invested a very large sum on data collection and information gathering, particularly in making arrangements for carrying out

TABLE 1

Transaction Costs Incurred on Institutional Strengthening

(in Rs. lacs)

Components of Institutional Strengthening		*1999-2000*				*2001-02*				*Ramnagar Change 1999-2000 to 2001-02 Fin.%*	*Akhnoor Change 1999-2000 to 2001-02 Fin.%*
		Ramnagar		*Akhnoor*		*Ramnagar*		*Akhnoor*			
	Unit	*Fin.*	*%*	*Fin.*	*%*	*Fin.*	*%*	*Fin.*	*%*		
Capacity Building	Rs.	2.3	0.44	4.1	0.96	8.73	1.51	12.17	1.81	279.56	196.83
Policy Reforms and HRD	Rs.	0.1	0.019	1.0	0.23	0	0	0	0	-100	-100
Project Coordination and Support	Rs.	12.0	2.32	9.2	2.15	11.97	2.07	12.82	1.91	-0.25	39.34
Information Management and ME	Rs.	2.3	044	2.25	0.53	4.0	0.70	1.7	0.25	73.91	-24.44
Total Project Expenditure	Rs.	517.7		428.7		578.19		671.44		11.68	56.62

Source: *Physical and Financial Achievements*. *1999-2000 and 2001-02*, IWDP, Hills-11, Jammu and Kashmir.

a number of studies related to policy reforms, which is not reflected in transaction costs incurred on policy reforms at sub-watershed level.

Besides above, the transaction costs incurred on institutional strengthening also includes costs on information management and monitoring and evaluation (ME) by the project staff. The project has incurred transaction costs on hiring of information technology consultants, GIS experts, exposure visits, silt observation posts, and internal monitoring and evaluation system. In 1999-2000, a sum of Rs. 2.3 lacs and Rs. 2.5 lacs have been spent on information and management, and monitoring and evaluation in Ramnagar and Akhnoor respectively, which increased to Rs. 4.0 lacs in 2001-02 in Ramnagar and declined to Rs. 1.7 lacs in Akhnoor in 2001-02. Out of total project expenditure, the transaction costs incurred on information and management, and monitoring and evaluation stood at 0.44 per cent and 0.53 per cent respectively in Ramnagar and Akhnoor in 1999-2000 and 0.70 per cent and 0.25 per cent in 2001-02. Thus, an increase in information and management, and monitoring and evaluation costs to the tune of 74 per cent has been recorded in Ramnagar and a decrease of 24 per cent has been noticed in Akhnoor. It is to be noted that there is in-built monitoring and evaluation wing of the project. However, the focus group discussions held with the project functionaries revealed that the internal monitoring and evaluation was restricted to the component of watershed and protection and very little monitoring and evaluation cost has been incurred on institutional arrangements.

(ii) Transition Costs incurred on Institutional Maintenance

Transition costs are those costs that are expended to bring the institutions into being and to maintain them. The distinguishing feature of transition costs is that the costs would not be incurred in the absence of a change in circumstances, and the costs will not recur after the transition to a new set of circumstances is complete. The types and magnitude of transition costs is determined by the nature of the institutional change as well as the institutional *status quo*. The project-implementing agency has incurred substantial transition costs in establishment of VDC and its maintenance. The main transition costs incurred for the establishment of VDC have been reportedly the costs of information gathering, information dissemination and communication, institutional design, negotiation, bargaining and decision-making and institutions creation. Likewise the transition costs incurred by the project implementing agency on maintenance of VDC includes costs of establishing regulations, capacity building, lobbying with interest groups, financial contribution towards VDC funds capitalization, transportation and logistic arrangement and monitoring and evaluation.

TABLE 2

Transition Costs Inclined by Project Implementing Agency

(*Rs.*)

Transition Costs	*Project Area with VDC*			
	Forested Watershed	*Agricultural Watershed*	*Total*	*Average*
Establishment of VDC				
Information Gathering	28	23	51	25.5
Information Dissemination and Communication	32	26	58	29
Institutional Design	23	18	41	20.5
Negotiation, Bargaining and Decision-making	26	22	48	24
Institutional Creation	28	23	51	25.5
Total	137	112	249	124.5
Maintenance of VDC				
Establishing Regulation	16	13	29	14.5
Capacity Building	17	13	30	15
Cost of Lobbing with Interest Groups	19	16	35	17.5
Financial Contribution towards VDC	22	17	39	19.5
Transportation and Logistics	27	21	48	24
Monitoring and Evaluation	12	9	21	10.5
Total	113	89	202	101

A perusal of data presented in Table 2 makes it evident that the transition costs incurred on establishment of VDC have been reportedly more than transition costs incurred on maintenance of VDC. The participatory institutions require more transition costs for its creation than its maintenance on the part of project implementing agency, as most of the costs of institutional maintenance are borne by the participants themselves. The Table 2 also makes it clear that the transition costs of establishment of VDC and its maintenance was comparatively more in forested watershed than agricultural watershed. This was due to the fact the cost of information collection, dissemination and communication, capacity building and transport and logistics are comparatively high in forested watershed than agricultural watershed. The overall mean values of transition costs on establishment of institution and its maintenance are estimated at Rs. 124.5 and Rs. 10 per beneficiary.

(iii) Static Transaction Costs incurred on Resource Allocation

Static transaction costs are the costs of making decisions for resources allocation within a given institutional structure. Static transaction costs arise through costs of administering an institutional structure, and the costs of decision-making for resource allocation under that structure. In the present context, costs of administering VDC arise through the use of resources in maintaining and administering VDCs such as establishing ownership rights, protecting ownership rights and monitoring and enforcement. The costs of decision-making for resources allocation within a VDC or user group arise largely through costs involved in identifying potential resources users, developing contracts and monitoring contract outcomes. The estimates of static transaction costs is given in Table 3, which makes it clear that the costs incurred on decision-making for resource allocation was comparatively higher than costs incurred on administering VDC. The creation of VDC structure on the existing local institutions has facilitated in bringing down the cost of administering VDCs. However, the idea of participatory approaches in resource management is new to the members of user groups, which resulted in high costs on information gathering, identification of users, designing regulations for resource use and monitoring the outcomes of resources allocation.

New institutional arrangement involves the transaction costs

TABLE 3

Static Transaction Costs Incurred by Project Implementation Agency

(Rs.)

Static Transaction Costs	*Project Area with VDC*			
	Forested Watershed	*Agricultural Watershed*	*Total*	*Average*
Administering VDCs Structure				
Establishing Ownership Rights	13	8	21	10.5
Protecting Ownership Rights	11	16	27	13.5
Monitoring and Enforcement	18	12	30	15
Total	42	36	78	39
Decision-making for Resource Allocation				
Obtaining Information	29	27	26	28
Identifying Potential Users	18	16	34	17
Developing Contracts	17	19	36	18
Monitoring Outcomes	14	11	25	12.5
Total	78	73	151	75.5

of decision-making and exchange to achieve a particular objective with respect to resource allocation and the costs of institutional establishment and maintenance. A new institutional structure will be of benefit to society where the reduction in transaction costs of allocation decision exceeds the costs of establishing and maintaining these institutions. Thus, the efficient set of institutions for governing a particular set of resource allocation decisions will be that which minimizes the sum of transaction costs incurred in making the decisions and in establishing and maintaining the institutions. In the present context, this goal has been realized and cost-effectiveness in institutional efficiency has been achieved, which is clear from the data presented in Tables 2 and 3. For instance, the average transaction costs incurred on decision-making for resource allocation has been estimated as Rs. 75.5 (see Table 3), whereas the average transaction costs incurred on establishment of institutional structure and its maintenance has been estimated as Rs. 225.5 (see Table 2). Thus, the gap between the average transaction costs incurred on decision-making for resource allocation and establishment and maintenance of new institutional arrangements has been very high i.e. Rs. 150. On the other hand, under top-down approach to resource management, allocation decisions are made unilaterally by central agency. The extent to which the resource would be allocated to its highest-valued use would be constrained by transaction costs arising from restriction on the availability and processing of information; problems and costs of monitoring and information collection; and the lack of general consensus to be achieved in allocative decision. Thus, the high transaction costs may result in administrative failure. It is significant to note that project implementing agency has not incurred any cost on conflict resolution/negotiation. This is due to the fact that with the new institutional arrangements in the form of VDC/user groups for resource management, such costs if any were borne by the beneficiaries themselves.

(iv) Ex-ante and Ex-post Transaction Costs

The transaction costs of resource management are affected by process through which the user participation is structured. Management costs are incurred in four stages: two *ex ante* stages (description of the resource context and programme design) and two *ex post* stages (programme implementation and programme enforcement). A participatory process is associated with high *ex ante* and low *ex post* transaction costs. The participatory process generates social and economic information of high quality and quantity through a combination of project staff, secondary data and local stakeholders including the resource users. The user's participation in technical aspects of the project involves greater amount of time and money spent in coordination and information dissemination. Thus, participatory approach is costly approach in establishing the resource context. In the implementation stage, the transaction costs involved are lower under participatory approach (see Table 4). The difference between *ex-ante* and *ex-post* transaction costs is significant in both the forested and agricultural sub-watersheds and estimated on average at Rs. 99 per beneficiary. The local resource users with minimum costs do the monitoring of the programme implementation effectively and enforcement of the regulation compliance is also very high. The lower *ex post* transaction costs is realized through community participation in programme implementation, monitoring and enforcement of regulations. User participation can promote stewardship through creating an assurance of control over outcomes. In brief, the benefits of participatory approaches are end-loaded, with the potential of long-lasting returns.

TABLE 4

Ex-ante and Ex-post Transaction Costs of Resource Management

(*Rs.*)

Transaction Costs	*Project Area with VDC*			
	Forested Watershed	*Agricultural Watershed*	*Total*	*Average*
Ex-ante Transaction Costs				
Description of Resource Context	60	49	109	54.5
Programme Design	246	209	455	227.5
Total	306	258	564	282
Ex-post Transaction Costs				
Programme Implementation	150	124	274	137
Programme Enforcement	53	39	92	46
Total	203	163	366	183
Difference between *Ex-ante* and *Ex-post* Transaction Costs	103	95	198	99

(v) Transaction Costs incurred by Individual Resource Users

Under the new institutional arrangements, the individual resource users have incurred significant transaction costs, which are reflected in Table 5. The data presented in table makes it evident that individual resource users have incurred a very high transaction cost on attending meeting followed by travel costs, which is estimated at Rs. 60 and Rs. 52 in forested and agricultural sub-watersheds respectively. On the whole, the transaction costs incurred by individual resource users were estimated significantly high in forested sub-watershed than agricultural sub-watershed. With new institutional arrangements, the individual resource users were also incurring transaction costs on monitoring and conflict resolution. In total, an individual resource user has borne Rs. 139 and Rs. 111 respectively in forested and agricultural sub-watersheds. It is noted that the total transaction costs incurred by the project implementing was higher, whereas the average transaction costs was comparatively low in case of individual resource users.

TABLE 5

Transaction Costs Incurred by Individual Resource Users

(*Rs.*)

Transaction Costs	*Project Area with VDC*			
	Forested Watershed	*Agricultural Watershed*	*Total*	*Average*
Attending Meeting	60	52	112	56
Travel Costs	32	17	49	24.5
Information Collection	14	12	26	13
Communication	17	14	31	15.5
Monitoring Costs	9	7	16	8
Conflicts/Negotiation	7	9	16	8
Total	139	111	250	125

The benefits of institutional reforms for resource management cannot be withheld from anyone, and also because of their size, most irrigation systems, forests, grazing lands, and other CPRs cannot be managed individually and require coordinated regulation. The coordinated actions are not cost less. The transaction costs are involved to coordinate individual's activities, to develop rules for resource use, to monitor compliance with the rules and sanctions against violators, and to mobilize the necessary cash, labour or material resources. Moreover, natural resources have multiple uses and users and are essential to the livelihoods of the poor. The top-down approach, which focus on resource management to maximize a single use, are not likely to be as appropriate in these situations as rules that are developed locally through negotiation between different users. The new institutional arrangements can be instrumental in finding rules and allocation of the resource between different users in a way that is seen as equitable by the users themselves and help reduce transaction costs.

CONCLUSIONS

In the recent past, resource use entitlements were free and open to all and resulted in severe resource degradation in the *Shivaliks*, which has necessitated immediate restoration of the productive potential of ecologically fragile environment. In the past, the performance of resource management projects has not been encouraging due to lower or virtually negligible participation of the local stakeholders and consequently high transaction costs of implementation of top-down approach. Keeping these in view, the institutional reform has been affected under IWDP, Hills-II by evolving user participation in designing, planning, decision-making, implementing, monitoring and evaluating the outcomes at every stage of resource management to minimize transaction costs. User participation has helped the project-implementing agency to reduce the cost of delivering project interventions and monitoring the outcomes for sustainability. Besides, the active involvement of users has lowered the informational costs associated with project interventions. Further, user participation in resource management has been designed to link investment with returns: for instance, resource conservation, protection, and maintenance with the returns from usufruct sharing. Such a link between investment and returns, secured by assured user rights, is likely to result in higher level of outcomes. But although there is the potential to lower the costs of implementing interventions, it does not necessarily follow that users will always be the lowest cost providers. Many regulated access resource management schemes cannot survive and finally fail. Most permissible use of resources becomes less efficient when the costs of regulation are considered. In the recent past, decentralization and collective action become an important theme in resource management. Institutional change is not cost-less or instant, but the potential costs and time for institutional transformation, i.e. the transaction costs should be carefully considered.

REFERENCES

Bardhan, P. (1997), *The Role of Governance in Economic Development: A Political Economy Approach*, OECD, Paris.

Blomquist, W. (1992), *Dividing the Waters: Governing Groundwater in Southern California*, Institute for Contemporary Studies Press, San Francisco.

Bromley, D.W. (1989), *Economic Interests and Institutions: The Conceptual Foundations of Public Policy*, Basil Blackwell, London.

Carney, D. (1995), Management and Supply in Agriculture and Natural Resources: Is Decentralization the Answer?, Natural Resource Perspectices Paper No. 4, Overseas Development Institute, London.

Carney, D. and John F. (1998), *Natural Resource Management and Institutional Change*, Routledge Research/ODI Development Policy Studies, Routledge, London.

Coase, R.H. (1937), 'The Nature of the Firm,' *Economica*, Vol. 16.

Dasgupta, P. (1997), Environmental and Resource Economics in the World of the Poor, Invited Lecture at Resources for the Future, Washington.

Eggertsson, T. (1990), *Economic Behaviour and Institutions*, Cambridge University Press, Cambridge.

Hanna, S. (1995), Efficiencies of User Participation in Natural Resource Management, in Hanna, Susan and Mohan Munasinghe (ed.), *Property Rights and the Environment*, The Beijer International Institute of Ecological Economics and the World Bank.

Hardin, Garrett (1968), 'The Tragedy of Commons,' *Science*, Vol. 162.

Hobley, M. (1995), *Institutional Change within the Forestry Sector in South Asia: Centralized Decentralization*, Overseas Development Institute, London.

Jensen, M.C. and William H. Meckling (1976), 'Theory of the Firm: Managerial Behaviour, Agency Cost, and Ownership Structure,' *Journal of Financial Economics*, Vol. 3, No. 4.

Jodha, N.S. (1986), 'Common Property Resources and the Rural Poor in Dry Regions of India,' *Economic and Political Weekly*, Vol. 54.

Murrell, Peter (1991), 'Can Neoclassical Economics Underpin the Reform of Centrally Planned Economies,' *Journal of Economic Perspective*, Vol. 5, No. 4.

North, D.C. (1990), *Institutions, Institutional Change and Economic Performance*, Cambridge University Press, Cambridge.

OECD/DAC (1995), *Support of Private Sector Development*, OECD, Paris.

Ostrom, E. (1990), *Governing the Commons: the Evolution of Institutions for Collective Action*, Cambridge University Press, Cambridge.

Scharpf, F.W. (1989), 'Decision Rules, Decision Styles, and Policy Choices,' *Journal of Theoretical Politics*, Vol. 1.

Wade, R. (1988), *Village Republics: Economic Conditions for Collective Action in South India*, Cambridge University Press, Cambridge.

World Bank (1999), *Project Appraisal Document: Integrated Watershed Development (Hills-II) Project*, Rural Development Sector Unit, South Asia Region, New Delhi.

SECTION IV

NIE AND GENDER ISSUES

New and Old Institutional Economics and Gender in India

YASODHA SHANMUGASUNDARAM

I

The remarkable contribution of Thorstein Veblen (1857-1929) whose Centenary (1957) was celebrated by Cornell University and the American Economic Association was that he was a persecuted professor of economics, much ahead of his time, firm enough in his conviction that the scope of economics is ever widening and the profession should keep its door open to the influence of cultural and anthropological institutions, and like Charles Darwin he questioned the established order of uncritical beliefs. His works *The Theory of Leisure Class (1899), Theory of Business Enterprise (1904)* and *the Higher Learning in America (1918)* made him unique. He was strong in philosophy, and it is surprising that he moved into economics, like Adam Smith. Veblen and Richard T. Ely, the *enfant terrible* of Economics, to quote Joseph Dorfman, were friends at John Hopkins, where Veblen studied logic. He laid durable foundation of Old Institutional Economcis (OIE). The broad sweep or holistic, as current diction is known, is the soul of humanities studies, in which domain economics will always remain notwithstanding all the measurements and claims of prediction. His theory of instincts, Marxian moorings, macro-institutionalism, critique of American capitalism's cultural evolution formed the basis of intellectual tributes to him. The leading exponents of New Institutional Economics (NIE) have moved the coins on the chess board of economic logic and in their honour Douglass C. North (b. 6 Nov. 1920, Cambridge, Mass) collected his Nobel Prize along with his counterpart in quantitative studies Robert W Fogel in 1993. Classification cannot be an obsession; OIE and NIE merge on issues and stay apart in some methods and contents.

Ten years later we have opened, on wide acceptance, a new branch of economics tagged to Institutions. This is the philosophic broadening of the excessive obsession with the markets and corporate captains of industry, and the board room diplomacy. Persons like John Kenneth Galbraith (1987) who was not considered sufficiently sophisticated by quantitative economists, paved the way for this era of NIE. Could we affirm that even for pedagogic convenience, OIE and NIE should not be treated in airtight compartments. Did not the prophet of NIE Doughlass C. North himself devote a para on Idle Curiosity which formed the title of an Essay on Veblen Centennial tribute by Norman Kaaplan (*Douglas F. Dowd*, 39-57). History demonstrates the force of ideology, myths, dogmas, bias, as much as rationality, behind economic events. Why and how it happens is our concern in OIE and NIE. In contrast conventional economics is more concerned with current markets and corporate transactions. Long-term or economics over time is best seen in institutional or organizational light. This accounts for the difference between Positive, Welfare, Politics, (*Bughanan*, 1987) Third World (*John Harriss, Janet Hunter C. Lewis*,1995), Health, or Gender-oriented new disciplines of Economics. Classification cannot be an obsession; OIE and NIE merge on issues and stay apart in some methods and contents. We may now consider with this prefatory caution two major institutional forces for sustainable and rapid development of India: Health and Gender.

II

Major institutional problems of poverty ridden, corrupt and stagnant economies are those of the body and the mind: One:

Health Care and Two: Gender Justice, in access to knowledge by education at all levels, for both sexes and for all ages. Let us see how it obtains and how it ought to be firstly in Health Care.

India has made remarkable strides in increasing the life expectancy of its citizens. At the beginning of 1930s, average life expectancy of an Indian adult was only 32 years. (*A.L. Mudaliar*, 1932). As of 2000, average life expectancy was 64 years. This is just half of biological maximum possibility of 120 years for homo sapiens, which no country attempts to reach. And hardly a dozen persons got close to it in the 2000 out of 6215 million world population. The vast medical advances and improvements in sanitation have reduced the incidence and spread of infectious diseases. Better medical facilities, preventive measures using vaccines against diseases such as polio and awareness have contributed to the rise in life expectancy. The health care system in India has deep-rooted institutional problems, waiting for solutions.

In the U.S. Nobel Prize winning economist Robert W. Fogel contrasts the past with the present. In 1875, food, clothing and shelter accounted for 87 percent of the consumption expenditure. By 1995, it was only 30 percent. In 1875, a typical US household spent about 2 percent of its income on health care. By 1995 it was 23 percent And thus long-term income elasticity (percent change in consumption for a 1 percent increase in income) is 1.6 for health care. The growth in per capita income, increasing urbanization, availability of modem biomedical technology, education and overall awareness indicate that demand for health care is bound to increase in India. There is a two-way causality between health and economic development. Table 1 illustrates the pattern of health expenditure in India. The average Indian life expectancy is 15 years less than that of a citizen of a high income country.

The figures, relative quantification in the Table 1 has NEE significance. It is the attitude to health expenditure, which is largely curative than preventive. It is neglect of human resources of the vast majority of the people who constitute oppressive numbers by demographers, rather than potential long-term human capital. NEE is informing social justice-oriented economists at Union and State level planning bodies. (*VSS*, 1972) The low levels of public expenditures on health in India is deplorable. With given resources in current and capital account

TABLE 1

Comparative Health Outlays in India and Rest of the World

Parameter	*Measure*	*India*	*Middle Income Countries*	*High Income Countries*
Life Expectancy at Birth	1980	54	66	74
	1999	64	69	78
Health Expenditure	Public % of GDP 1990-98 a	0.8	2.5	6.0
	Private % of GDP a	4.2	2.6	3.7
	Total % of GDP a,b	5.4	5.0	9.7
Health Expenditure per capita	PPP $ 1990-98 a	94	267	2,587
	$1990-98 a	20	117	2,702
Physicians per 1000 people	1980	0.4	1.2	—
	1990-98a	0.4	1.8	2.8

Data are for available periods. Totals are got by rounding.
Source: HNP Statistics World Bank, Human Development Report of UNDP, Oxford, 2000); Sivaprakasam Sivakumar (2003), *op. cit.*

attitudinal change towards human basic human needs warrants priorities for health and education; instead power, influence, corruption-oriented public sectors have siphoned financial and material resources at the Union and therefore States under over centralized Indian polity. The number of physicians per 100,000 persons remained unchanged in India over the last twenty years. In India it is 48, in contrast to 299 in Sweden and 245 in the USA. (*Sivakumar*, 2002). It is 164 in the UK to which country to maintain its National Health Service, we provide the largest number than any other country. The main institutional change is in mindset; health is a national duty and priority number one for public expenditure; near 300% rise in outlay is the desideratum.

A major health risk factor is affecting 88 percent of the pregnant women found anemic. India has the worst record in the world. The *Lancet* 1996, which evaluated 517 men and women born between 1934 to 1954 in a mission hospital in Mysore, 9 percent of the men and 11 percent of the women had coronary heart disease, low birth weight, short birth length and small head circumference at birth. Birth related coronary heart disease is predicted to become the most common cause of death within 15 years. Low public spending on health, inadequate prevention, low medical standards, checks on quality of medicines, level of medical insurance, neglected research in health economics, and lack of public awareness are the major hazards which institutional change in public economics must countenance.

India does not have any institutional world model to follow. The non-price rationing by queuing in Canada and the price-based allocation in the US are not models are defective. National Health Service in the UK, historically linked to India, is the closest for modification. The number of doctors available in India has to be doubled in a decade, and their services have to be ably supported by para medical personnel. We need many doctors; even more the number of nurses and para-medical personnel should be increased more than proportionately. India which meets the world demand for Indian nurses should know how to meet her own demand.

III

Next in priority are reforms in and reinforcement of education. Tradition, economic monopolies in educational fields, disrespect for social justice, received ideas of male-child preference, and entrenched vested interests, money or/and power grabbers rather than knowledge seekers as teachers, corruption and lack of ethics in general haunt the citadels of learning at all levels—primary to university. Reinforcement of educational ideals primarily, and secondarily supported by monetary incentives Indian education could be rescued by 2020 if started in earnestness right now. These are beyond market mechanism *per se* to control. Prior to economic reforms and financial allocations, social change and cultural revolution should precede.

The 20th century educational evolution is in two orbits. In one catching with the advanced economies, space and nuclear science and technology have been developed. This is in the domain of geopolitical institutions, which could justly and in fairness adjust their sights to national and global possibilities of success. Science and Technology education is blamed for Brain Drain, without national employment perspective. The future career opportunities for science graduates and post-graduates, let alone others is doubtful and not assured with the current employment situation in the country. This leads to more disinterest in science as a career and subject of study. There is no assurance that an experienced researcher will have smooth career in research and teaching. He is nearly 40 when he settles down in life. A good job around 25 after completion of post-graduation/Ph.D. is not a certainty. Limited job opportunities, recruitment procedure and lack of requisite skill and training act as deterrents. A way out of this grim situation is to go abroad for additional studies and research for assured and conducive research and employment climate. A large number of science graduates and post-graduates are satisfied if they get a job in any vocation quite unrelated to the science they have studied. It is high time that science and technology policy as well educational policy in general have a vision of the future and reformulates measures keeping in mind the requirements of teaching and research in science in India.

The other orbit of education for socio-economic justice demands that the government withdraws from outlays in ineffective public sectors and directs them to qualitative universal literacy and basic science education. This implies closing the gap in Science and Technology. Adopting to the demands of industry in the field of sciences Finland and Korea, increase level of human capital, investment and innovation. With additional hurdles at every stage of education and employment, the lot of women in science education is much more severe. Gender balance and equity require that science policy in India gives special consideration for women to sustain their interest in science. In the development programme with science and technology base, women's participation should be encouraged through incentives and concessions.

Twenty first century knowledge society depends upon three factors: (i) strength of basic research, (ii) (R&D), and (iii) mechanisms of technology transfer and diffusion. Basic research in social natural and life sciences which have long gestation in returns is the fundamental responsibility of the Union and State governments. Currently, the major victim is research in universities starved of funds and facilities. To arrest the disinterest of students and indifference of funding agencies strong industry-university-community linkages have to be established. Innovative university courses, apprenticeship/field work and skill training require legislative measures making employers in public or private enterprises to provide training. Future belongs to the youth the world over. India is described as a "poor developed" country. It has many achievements in the field of philosophy, culture and science and technology. The best and worst coexist in the system. India's educational scenario will have to undergo a sea change to make 'education for all' a reality and 'work for all' a certainty.

The new universities are adapting to the new situation and courses are mostly in non-traditional areas which are economically viable. Particular mention must be made of the women's universities which have carefully structured their curricula to make women's studies in-built into the master's programmes in management science, computer science, information technology, social science and fine arts. This model of women's universities in India is also followed world over as for instance in Fatima Jinnah Women's University, Pakistan.

To face the future challenges the trends in Higher Education should have major changes. Universities were the mainstay for research in the pre-independent days. Notwithstanding the populist attack on the Macaulay-oriented education, it stood the test of global high quality and earned three Nobel Laureates and many more of their ilk. A number of national laboratories and institutes took a large share public funds; IIT's have combined high quality teaching and first rate research. Tata Institute of Fundamental Research (TIFR), and Council of Scientific and Industrial Research (CSIR), are the major institutions for scientific research. To a country with massive population these institutions are inadequate. The listing of science institutions in advanced countries runs to pages and pages. To mention only the general natural science institutions—Academy of Natural Science of Philadephia, American Association for Advancement of Science. Buffalo Society of Natural Science, Chicago Academy of Science, Cranbrook Institute of Science, History of Science Society, Maryland Academy of Science, National Science Foundations, Ohio Academy of Science, World Future Society, etc. are but a small proportion of the large number of institutions for science in USA. In India, there are proposals for setting up a Global Institute of Science and Technology (GIST) and a National Science

University (NSU). These proposals, apart the intermediate policy initiative is to strengthen science education in existing Universities and colleges through adequate funding and proper direction.

Excellence is not mere achievement but cultivated habit. The concept of Total Quality Management (TQM) which heralds this concept is highly relevant to educational institutions. The principle behind TQM is that the interest of the customer (student/society) comes first. Continuous innovations, improvement and changes are necessary to maintain quality.

IV

Issues regarding women in science and targeting women for development are interrelated attitudinal and institutional issues. The Constitution of India is one of most forward looking. Its stress on women development needs no mention. Equal opportunities for women, removing of gender bias, empowerment of women are all popular slogans as well as policy actions. Starting from Durgabai Deshmukh Committee (1958) on Women's Education with its recommendation for creating a National Council for Women's Education and Hansa Mehta Committee (1962-62) on common curricula for girls and boys, the emphasis was on equal access to girls in education. Subsequent to the Report of the Committee on Status of Women in India in 1974, a National Plan of Action for Women was initiated in 1976. Guidelines were given by the UN's Plan of Action with stress on employment, education and health of women. The National Perspective Plan for Women (1988) sought to mainstream women's issues and programmes. One-third share in the decision-making bodies from Panchayats to Parliament was recommended. Overall development of women was equally stressed by National Health Policy (1983), the National Population Policy (1993) and the National Nutrition Policy (1983). The National Policy of Education (1986) and its follow-up National Plan of Action have given top priority for women's equality, participation and empowerment. Yet 60% of women are illiterate, while 33% of the total enrolment in higher education is by women. There is a large gap between male-female and rural-urban in all aspects and particularly in educational levels. As per the 2001 census, sex ratio is 933, girls' enrolment in primary, middle and secondary education is 43.6%, 40.4% and

38.6% respectively. Up to the first degree level women's enrolment is 36.9%. With special reference to science education it is still not on par with humanities and arts education. This is a glaring disparity. Every report on education stresses on this aspect and particularly in terms of education of girls and women there is a large gap to be filled in. We reiterate the need for special programmes to promote science among them. Science has to be popularized for girls right from the school level. More infrastructure and funding for science education is a priority measure for educational reforms.

Women's Higher education is for total social transformation, and not sectarian privilege, in the backdrop of low literacy of women and wide disparities and disadvantages. Therefore, these privileged groups of women should take on the responsibility of social engineering. (*Balakrishna*, 1958). Individual's upward mobility is not the only criterion of higher education. 'Cognitive, attitudinal and behavioural' changes are essential for transforming the existing situation of women's invisibility, ignorance and indifference into one of competence, capabilities and creativity. Women's education and particularly at the level of higher education should contribute to both structural changes and generation of new values. This transformation is sequential in terms of investment in human capital, human resource development and social progress.

Towards this end, needless to say, greater coordination of health, education and employment programmes make for a holistic approach in women development. 'Education for all' go hand in hand with 'health for all' and 'work for all'. In development programmes for women, it has been the experience that "a system of well staffed women field workers but without a woman in superior position" could make little basic change. Therefore, education of women requires the "same investment of energy and creative thinking that the women's movement has devoted to community development."

This calls for radical human resource transformation relevant to India than elsewhere. At the end of May 2002, India has 290 universities and university level institutions, over 13,000 colleges, about 7.5 m students and over 3,50,000 teachers. It is a moot question to ask whether the system is well endowed both in terms of infrastructure and human resources. The human resource potential is shown in this magnitude. To use or not to misuse this asset is our challenge. In India enrolment in general education is above 90% whereas in advanced country is 20% to 25%. In other words, the percentage opting for science (including social sciences) and technical courses is higher than for general courses whereas in India it is the reverse. Therefore, a good deal of restructuring becomes essential to put Science, Technology, Humanities, Arts and Commerce courses in proper balance in India to become a source for a meaningful human resource base for national development.

Privatisation and Gender Justice

With special reference to women, there are several objections to privatisation of education. Capitation fees tend to perpetuate inequalities in education through limiting access to women and especially the poor. This will reflect in inequalities in employment as well. This is a long-term cost to the society which cannot be neglected. The high cost of education and differences between fees charged at government and private institutions would cause havoc to the future of student population. The adverse impact on women students is quite real. This is corroborated by the findings of many studies. Malcolm Adiseshiah maintained that the main beneficiaries of higher education come from the top two classes of society. The findings of a survey states that 80% of those who complete university education were from the top 20% of the society. Another survey by the UGC affirms the above findings since it also revealed that 70% of university degree holders are from the top 20% income earners. This also strengthens privatization view point since there is affordability for nearly 80% of the colleges and university students. But the principles of justice and equality demands that 20:80 ratio of poor and rich students must change and disadvantaged classes be given a fair deal in higher education. Though women enrolment in higher education is encouraging in a few states like Maharashtra, Delhi and Punjab there is need for a balanced growth in higher education inter-regions and gender-wise.

Discipline-wise Mapping Essential

Mapping has been continuously done at the school level in India. This helps in planning the location of schools and to assess the adequacy of facilities. Mapping is used as a tool for achieving educational goals of universalization of elementary education in India. Such an exercise in mapping of higher education in India is essential. Presently higher education is urban-biased. There are regional disparities in the access and location of institutions. It is worthwhile preparing an elaborate mapping of higher education in terms of location of the institution and the courses available so that the lacuna in the curricula can be identified and rectified. The Commonwealth Universities Year Book includes a Directory of subjects of study for every country in the commonwealth, and an index to universities and locations list map. A similar mapping is required for Indian Universities from the state level. A science subject-wise index has been prepared for the universities in Tamil Nadu in this study. This is only a limited exercise. It is necessary to have directories of subjects of study for Universities and Colleges in India to serve as a Database in Higher Education. Mapping of higher education is, therefore, suggested to serve as a tool for rational allocation of educational resources and also for reformulating the curricular contents to meet the demands of the local communities and industries.

VI

A recent study of science post-graduate men and women subject-wise, shows that more women join the science post graduate stream than men. Perhaps the choice of engineering and medicine courses in home state or elsewhere is by men, rather than basic science courses which appeal to the parents of women students. They could not opt to study in far off places. Social inhibitions of parents more than women students seem to limit their choice in higher education stream away from their places of residence.

A total of 3793 women and 2755 men is the estimated turn out of science post-graduates men and women by all the Universities in Tamil Nadu during 1999-2000.

The Table 2 is constructed from the data from the Annual Reports of the Arts and Science Universities in Tamil Nadu. All medical, veterinary, engineering and law students study now in Universities for each of the above mentioned subjects. Owing to differences in presentation of data, the figures computed in the

TABLE 2

Science Courses in Universities of Tamil Nadu Gender-wise Strength in Colleges

Universities	*No. of affiliated Colleges*	*No. of Students*		*No. of University Depts.*	*No. of Students*	
		F	*M*		*F*	*M*
Madras University	67	1100	900	19	103	103
Madurai Kamaraj University	63	350	350	11	65	50
Bharathiar University	119	350	210	8	50	30
Bharathidasan University	167	705	645	8	25	25
Manaomaniam Sundaranar University	57	630	150	8	30	20
Alagappa University				6	25	25
Annamalai University				10	150	222
Gandhigram University				7	40	25
Avinashilingam University				11	150	
Mother Teresa Women's University				2	20	
Total	573	3135	2255	90	658	500

Source: Field Study by the author.

table above is a rough estimate, which, nevertheless, reflects the male-female disparities persisting in favour of women over the ten year period under study.

It is evident from the above accounts that the major share of PG teaching in science is from the colleges in Tamil Nadu in terms of number of courses and enrolment. The courses of the universities are mostly special or applied courses in sciences which are not repeated in the colleges. The range of science subjects that are made available to the students is quite comprehensive and wide.

The enrolment and pass details as given in the Annual Reports of the selected universities in Tamil Nadu are presented covering natural and applied sciences. The total number of post-graduate science students made available as human resources in total is 7200 consisting of 3300 male and 3900 female post-graduates. The balance between the outflow of PGs is skewed in favour of female students. In view of the upward trend of female enrolment and passes, concerted efforts have to be taken to keep the balance between male-female composition of the human resource potential which is essential for the long-term sustained development of the system of higher education.

Twenty-first century belongs to the youth the world over. India is described as a "poor developed" country. It has many achievements in the field of philosophy, culture and science and technology. Recruitment of faculty without gender bias and with due credit given to merit, revitalizing the teaching programme to make the complexities of modern science interesting of students, active research in the departments of science in all post-graduate departments, performance evaluation and departmental accreditation, networking of science departments area-wise and subject-wise are among the many suggestions made for meeting the future challenges for science in universities and colleges.

The role of women in science is a grey area in women's studies. Historical accounts of women scientists of India, contribution and impact of women scientists, data base on science institutions, directory/who is who of women in science in India, networking of science education through modern technology, cost effective science education, state-wise and region-wise studies on innovations and inventions for women's development, documenting of post-graduate/M.Phil. level projects/dissertations in science, gender-related issues in access to science learning, teaching and research, economic prospects through application and technology for women employment, are some of the areas for research and further studies.

VII. SUMMING UP

We may conclude that apart from market analysis based on micro and macro economic fundamentals, application of marginal theory, and tools of measurement, there are forces of human behavour embedded in customs and manners, caste and community networks as powerful institutions (for good or bad- there is still present in India as power packs). Events occur within institutional framework, as found by votaries of OIE and NIE. The OIE and NIE theories partake methods of sociology, history, philosophy, logical systems, political science, and in fact all behavioural sciences. The usage is in terms of tools of Positive and Welfare Economics. The goal of economics as art or science is to maximize individual happiness in the context of maximizing societal happiness and welfare. We have argued in the paper that priority areas of institutional attention are health care and education, to ensure health and longevity with skills and education capable of employability and high individual and social productivity. One branch of economics does not replace other branches. They co-exist. Hence the caution to OE and NIE votaries, Thorstein Veblen, Douglass C. North and Robert W. Fogel included, is the old order changeth yielding place to new, only to return another day.

REFERENCES

Arcot Lakshmanaswami Mudaliar (1932): *Infant Mortality in India,* Elizabeth Mathai Lectures, University of Madras.

Balakrishna, R. (1958), *Process of Economic Growth,* Bangalore.

Coase, Ronald (1960), *"The Problem of Social Cost," Journal of Law and Eoonomics* 3(1). 1-44.

Dale, Spender, 'Sex Bias' in Warren D. Piper, (ed.), *Is Higher Education Fair?* 17th Annual Conference of the Society for Research into Higher Education, Guildford, SRHE, United Kingdom.

Feminist Economics, Vol. 1, No. 2, Summer 1005, Rice University, Houston, TX 77005-1892, USA.

Fogel, Robert W. (1967), *The Global Escape from Chronic Malnutrition,* University of Chicago.

Fogel, Robert W., *Economics of Mortality in North America* (1650-1910) NBER Inc.

Government of India: Selected Educational Statistics, 2000-01 Commonwealth Universities Year Book, London, 2001.

Hayek, Friedrich A. (1960), *The Constitution of Liberty,* Chicago University Press.

Hicks, John (1932), *Theory of Wages,* Macmillan, London.

Hicks, John (1965), *Capital and Growth,* Oxford University Press.

Hicks, John (1983), *Collected Essays on Economic Theory,* Blackwell, Oxford.

J.S. Mill (1869), *Subject of Women,* Everyman Edition, London.

Janet Howart (1999), *'Women in Academe: The Transformation of Women's Intellectual Life',* Women Brainpower Conference, Royal Halloway, Universiry of London, July.

Journal of Higher Education, Vol. 1, No. 2, 1975, University Grants Commission, New Delhi.

K. Anbazhagan (1997), *Women Empowerment*, Convocation Address, 18th Convocation, Avinashilingam Institute for Home Science and Higher Education for Women, Deemed University, Coimbatore, January.

Krishnaraj, Maithreyi (1991), *Women and Science: Selected Essays*, Bombay, Himalaya Publishing House.

Malathy Doraiswamy and P. Doraiswamy (1996), 'Sex Discrimination in Indian Labour Markets', *Feminist Economics*, 2(2), pp. 41-61.

North, Douglass C (1993), *Economic Performance through Time*, Prize Lecture, Nobel Foundation.

North, Douglass C. (1990) *Institutions, Institutional Change and Economic Performance*, New York, Cambridge University Press.

North, Douglass C. and Robert P. Thomas (1973): *The Rise of the Western World: A New Economic History*, University Press.

Sivakumar, Sivaprakasam (2003), Fixing India's Health Care System, *Business Standard*, Monday, 4 August.

Social Welfare, Vol. 48, No. 1, New Delhi, April 2001.

Subramanyam, Lalitha (1998), *Women Scientists in the Third World, The Indian Experience*, Sage Publications, New Delhi.

Sudarshan Ratna, M. (2000), 'Educatiqnal Status of Girls and Women, the Emerging Scenario' in Rekha Wazir, (ed.) *Gender Gap in Basic Education, NGOs as Change Agents*, New Delhi.

The Collected Works of K.J. Arrow, Nobel Prize winner along with Sir John Hicks in Volumes 1-6 hold signposts to health economics and social justice based on information and knowledge-oriented society. The volumes are: *1. Social Choice and Justice; 2. General Equilibrium; 3. Individual Choice under Uncertainty; 4. The Economics of Information; 5. Production and Capital; 6. Applied Economics*. Available in Asia Pacific special edition from 2000. (IASR Press, Chennai.

Tripathi, R.S. (1997), 'Access of Female Students to Higher Education in India', *University News*, May 12

Vedagiri Shanmugasundaram (1962, 1974, 2003), *Methodology of Research in Social Science*, Singapore, Madras, Chennai.

Vedagiri Shanmugasundaram (1965), *The Great Famine*, Oxford.

Vedagiri Shanmugasundaram (1972), *Agricultural Development of India*, University of Madras.

Vedagiri Shanmugasundaram (1972), *Social Change for Economic Developmeni*, State Planning Commission,Tamil Nadu.

Vedagiri Shanmugasundaram (1976, 1991, 2003), *Economics of Tiruvalluvar*, University of Madras, IASR, Chennai.

Vedagiri Shanmugasundaram (1979, 2003), *General Theory of Chance from Poverty to Plenty*, IEA, 1979, IASR/Allied, Chennai.

Vedagiri Shanmugasundaram (1983), *Higher Education in the University of Madras*, University of Madras.

Vedagiri Sharrmugasimdaram (1977, 2003), *Indian Economic Thought and*

Policy, S. Chand, New Delhi, IASR, Chennai.

Yasodha Shanmugasundaram (1991), *Studies in Health Economics*, Ethiraj Research Centre, Chennai.

Yasodha Shanmugasundaram (1993), *Women Employment in India*, IASR/ Allied, Chennai.

Yasodha Shanmugasundaram (1994), *Theory and Practice of Health Economics in India*, Allied/IASR, Chennai.

Yasodha Shanmugasundaram (1999), *'Participation of Women in Universities'*, International Association of University Presidents' XII Triennial Conference, Brussels, July.

Yasodha Shanmugasundaram (1999), *Data File on Women in India*, Mother Teresa Women's University Press, Kodaikanal.

Yasodha Shanmugasundaram (1999), *Specialized Higher Education Institutions for Women'* in AIU: Women Participation in Higher Education, New Delhi.

Yasodha Shanmugasundaram (2000), *Women's Studies—Theory and Method*, Mother Teresa Women's University Press, Kodaikanal.

New Institutional Economics Approach to New Household Economics

P. ARUMUGAM AND A. BALASUBRAMANIAN

INTRODUCTION

The new institutional economics (NIE) is a branch of economics that specifically incorporates various institutional constraints into formal economic analysis in order to explain, on the basis of rational choice, observable real-world phenomena that standard neoclassical economics (such as perfect information, zero transaction costs, full rationality absent institutional constraints) is unable to explain, except by assuming irrational behaviour on the part of individual economic agents.

In the words of North (1990), institutions are a set of formal (laws, contracts, political systems, organizations, markets, etc.) and informal rules of conduct (norms, traditions, customs, value systems, religions, sociological trends, etc.) that facilitate coordination or govern relationships between individuals or groups. Institutions provide for more certainty in human interaction within this frame household economics or new home economics can be fit in.

Williamson coined the phrase "New Institutional Economics (NIE)" to distinguish it from the "old institutional economics" pioneered by Commons and Veblen. The old institutional school argued that institutions were a key factor in explaining and influencing economic behaviour, but there was little analytical rigor and no theoretical framework in this school of thought. It operated outside neo-classical economics and there was no quantitative theory from which reliable generalization could be derived or sound policy choices made. Coase (1988), underlined that economic theory has been characterized as an analysis of choice, but in this sense, "economics has no subject matter". He claims that economic theory needs to take a more realistic approach in which the firm, the market, and the law play a crucial role in the functioning of the economic system. For him, economic policy implies a choice among different social institutions that are created by the law or are supported by it (*Coase,* 1988).

In the assessment of Christopher D. Gerrard (1996), the old institutional economics was economics with institutions but without theory; standard neoclassical economics is economics with theory without institutions; and the New Institutional Economics is attempting to provide economics with both theory and institutions.

"BRANCHES" OF THE NEW INSTITUTIONAL ECONOMICS

Kherallah and Kirsten (2001) have discussed the growth of different branches of Institutional Economics. NIE is by definition a multidisciplinary field of study comprising several branches such as New Economic History, Public Choice and Political Economy, New Social Economics, Transaction Cost Economics, Theory of collective action and Law and Economics. The following paragraphs give a very brief summary of each field. North (1990) pioneered the New Economic History in an attempt to explain how economies evolve and develop through time. This is looks at the role of institutional change in fostering overall economic growth. Political and Public Choice branch of NIE carried out the economic analysis of political systems and political decision-making.

One other branch of NIE is New Social Economics which covers the work of Becker on intra-household analysis and family economics. It was a major breakthrough in explaining choices that were made outside the market and that were previously not addressed by neo-classical economics.

TRANSACTION COST ECONOMICS

The general hypothesis of this strand of the NIE is that institutions are transaction cost-minimizing arrangements, which may change and evolve with changes in the nature and sources of transaction costs. This work was pioneered by Coase in his 1937 article, "The Nature of the Firm" where he argues that market exchange is not costless. Coase underlines the important role of transaction costs in the organization of firms and other contracts. Transaction costs include the costs of information, negotiation, monitoring, coordination, and enforcement of contracts. He explains that firms emerge to economize on the transaction costs of market exchange and that the "boundary" of a firm or the extent of vertical integration will depend on the magnitude of these transaction costs.

Williamson has combined the concepts of bounded rationality and opportunistic behaviour (which manifests itself as adverse selection, moral hazard, cheating, shirking, and other forms of strategic behaviour) to explain contractual choice and the ownership structure of firms. In Williamson's framework, a trade-off has to be made between the costs of coordination and hierarchy within an organization, and the costs of transacting and forming contracts in the market. This trade-off will depend on the magnitude of transaction costs.

ECONOMICS OF INFORMATION

The transaction cost economics school and the literature on the economics of information intertwined. Stigler's view is that searching for market information is not costless and that may explain why we may have a divergence of prices between efficient markets and why capital markets are "imperfect". The work by Akerlof on the market for lemons explains how quality guarantees, reputation, and trust are useful tools to ensure the production of quality goods and to project information about it.

Stiglitz also analyzed the role of imperfect information, adverse selection, and moral hazard, on the performance of credit and labour markets, and the behaviour of the firm. The imperfect-information theory has been used to explain the emergence of key agrarian institutions which are seen as substitutes for missing credit or insurance markets in an environment of pervasive risk, information asymmetry, and high transaction costs.

GOVERNANCE

Klein (1999) explained that one should distinguish between the 'institutional environment' and 'institutional arrangements'. The former refers to the background constraints, or 'rules of the game', that guide individuals' behaviour. These can be both formal, explicit rules (constitutions, laws, property rights) and informal, often implicit rules (social conventions, norms). While these background rules are the product of—and can be explained in terms of—the goals, beliefs and choices of individual actors, the social result (the rule itself) is typically not known or 'designed' by anyone. Institutional arrangements, by contrast, are specific guidelines—what Williamson calls 'governance structures'—designed by trading partners to mediate particular economic relationships. Business firms, long-term contracts, public bureaucracies, non-profit organizations and other contractual agreements are examples of institutional arrangements.

INSTITUTIONAL ECONOMIC APPROACH TO HOUSEHOLD ECONOMICS

Definitions of the family and household

Households usually consist of family members linked by blood or marriage, occasionally augmented by unrelated members. Households are defined on the basis of residence, while families are defined primarily by kinship. Shoshana Grossbard-Shechtman says most households are families; household economics can be called economics of the family.

The household is not an undifferentiated unit, but "an economy in microcosm, a system of exchanges, entitlements, and responsibilities allocated among members in a group whose boundaries are far from clear" (*Rogers*, 1990).

THE NEW HOME ECONOMICS

The branch of economics concerned with intra-household or family dynamics is known as the "New Household Economics" (NHE). Prior to NHE, the household was treated as a "black box" (*Pollak,* 1985) and no attempt was made to model the dynamics of intra-household decision-making. The tendency to treat the household as a black box tells us nothing about how its decision-making process is structured by the complex interests and different capacities of family members. The NHE brings economic theory into the microcosm of the household, building on the observation by Becker (1965), "A household is truly a 'small factory': it combines capital goods, raw materials and labour to clean, feed, procreate and otherwise produce useful commodities." NHE redefines household satisfaction in terms of intangible products or utilities. Households are viewed as "consuming" the things that satisfy them, such as the health of their members, bright and successful children, or relaxation (*Berman, Kendall, and Bhattacharyya,* 1994). These ultimate consumption goods are considered to be "commodities."

CONCEPTS IN THE ANALYSIS OF HOUSEHOLD/FAMILY BEHAVIOUR

Some bargaining models apply mathematical game theory to marriage and household decision-making (*Manser and Brown,* 1980; *McElroy and Homey,* 1981). They include models of cooperative conflict (*Sen,* 1990), which address situations in which there are many cooperative outcomes that would be more beneficial to all the parties than non-cooperation, but where the different family members have conflicting interests in the choice among these cooperative arrangements.

A related priority is a more institutional approach to bargaining within the household, one that moves beyond bargaining models with simplistic fallback or threat points in terms of his or her market earnings or individuals assets. But bargaining is obviously affected by legal and institutional factors that determine how household assets are disposed and that define enforceable claims on other individual income flows such as child support.

Family is an institution which has various activities, interaction and decisions take place and have many economic aspects. Till 1973 economists have not focused their attention on the household activities. With the initiative of Becker an economic approach to household activities have come to light. Becker and Robert Michael (1973) have provided a theoretical frame through "New Theory of Consumer Behaviour" to analyze allocation of time which has market, non-market and leisure dimensions as well as decisions on labour force participation, size of the family and investing in quality of children. All these have economic dimensions. This new theory is applicable to family as an institution has been verified in developed and developing countries. In all those empirical studies the findings have supported the theory and justify economic approach to household economic activities.

The concept of household—another institutionally-grounded concept—is useful to illustrate the fruitfulness of formal economic theory for the study of institutions. It is as important to the economy as the firm is. The household is also a non-standard organizational form (of the sort neoclassical theorists have neglected. The increased productivity of the household in recent decades as a result of the new labour-saving devices (not only kitchen appliances but also frozen meals, etc.), improved methods of family planning, better communications, and technological advances in home entertainment has been instrumental in enabling increased female participation in the labour force, which is transforming the economies of the wealthy and even some developing countries. The leading student of household production, Gary Becker, is a formidable theorist. Becker treats household or family as a non-market goods and services producing unit or firm. In this approach household combine market purchased goods with time of the members of the household by applying household technology within the full income constraint covering market and non-market income of the family. It is assumed that the household maximizes the satisfaction of members of the households altruistically. In addition to the above production function activity the family makes decisions such as investing in the children in the form of education, nutrition, health, labour force participation and fertility or size of the family which may be micro-economic in nature but which will have effect on macro economy.

The entire above household activities and decisions have economic aspects and received the attention of economists. Lot of studies has been carried out within the new household economics so far.

RELEVANCE OF NEW HOUSEHOLD ECONOMICS TO ANALYSE HOUSEHOLD DECISIONS

Many studies were carried out by applying the New Household Economic Theory in developed and developing countries. We can mention a few of them here: (a) "Demand for secondary education in Tamil Nadu a household economic approach" by P. Arumugam (1984); (b) "The Effect of Childcare Welfare Scheme on Mother's Participation in Economic activity, Nutrition, Health Status of Children and Consumption Expenditure of Urban Households" by A. Sugirtharani (2002); (c) "Allocation of time, value of non-market work and family income distribution: A study of rural households in Tamil Nadu"—Study carried out by P. Arumugam under IDPAD Project (2002); (d) "Women's allocation of time to market and non-market work: A study of married women in Madras city," by Malathy, R. (1983); (e) "An Econometric analysis of Fertility, Child Schooling and Labour Force Participation of Women in Rural Indian Households" by Duraisamy, P. (1988); (f) "Economics of Marriage: Implications for female age at marriage" by Lakshmanasamy, T. (1997); (g) "Intrahousehold Resources allocation in developing countries" by Haddad *et. al.*, (1997); (h) "A Survey of Theories of the Family" by Theodore C. Bergstrom (1995).

So the above discussion revealed that economic aspect of family can be studied with as household economic theory.

Pollack in his review essay "A Transaction Cost Approach to Families and Households" (1985) argue that the transaction cost approach which recognizes the significances of internal structure provides a broader and more useful view of the economic activity and behaviour of the family. In his essay Pollack examined the advantages and disadvantages of family governance and apply the analysis to two types of economic activity, namely, production for home consumption and production for a market. Then he discussed the internal organization of families and households by focusing on allocation and distribution within the family. Finally he discussed the marriage as a contracting problem by arguing that the transaction cost approach is consistence with bargaining models of marriage. And hence new institutional economic approach can be given to the family. Coase underlined the important role of transaction cost in the organization of firms and other contract. Further he explains the transaction cost covers cost of information, negotiation, monitoring, coordination, and enforcement of contracts. This concept of transaction cost very much one can find in family or household in its organizing household production, investing in children for education and health, decision on labour force participation and fertility. The household incurs cost on information related to market goods and technology, cost of substitutes and availability of jobs and market wage. The head of the household has to negotiate and monitor in organizing the household production. This may incur cost. The head of the household must also coordinate among the members of the family in organizing household production, pooling the market and non-market income as well as deciding how much to invest on which child in the form of education and health and who should go for work and who must attend school. Further within the family implementation of or operation of these activities need voluntary acceptance of different roles for each member of the household either by willing cooperation by all or through bargaining and negotiations within the family.

The transaction cost approach focuses on the role of institutions in structuring complex, long-term relationships. Applied to the family, the transaction cost approach generalized the new home economics by recognizing that internal structure and organizing matter. It treats the family as a governance structure rather than a preference ordering or a production technology. This has two consequences for the analysis of family's ability to provide incentives and monitor performance and on how its ability to do so differ among activities is societies; it clarifies which activities are carried out by the family. Second, by emphasizing the role of institutions in structuring complex, long-term relationships, the contracting perspective of the transaction cost approach elucidates allocation and distribution within family.

The household production approach with its emphasis on

prices and technology, has dominated the analysis of activities in which households or families produce goods for their own consumption. This analysis captures the essence of some household "making-or-buy" decisions, but other households production activities—such as the provision of education, healthcare, and insurance—are better analyzed from a transaction cost perspective. (*Pollak*, 1985)

THE FAMILY AS A GOVERNANCE STRUCTURE

Family as a governance structure provides incentives for various economic activities, monitors the functions of the members of the family keeping the altruistic principle at the center of decisions. Further family plays the role as the provider of insurance against the economic consequences of uncertain and adverse events. Protection against the adverse economic consequences of old age, unemployment or the illness is provided by the family.

CONCLUSION

We have found that under NIE, some of the unrealistic assumptions of neo-classical economics (such as perfect information, zero transaction costs, full rationality) are relaxed, but institutions are incorporated as an additional constraint. The purpose of the NIE is both to explain the determinants of institutions and to evaluate their impact on economic performance.

In this background as explained above family or household economic activity was not explored till 1970s. The contribution of Becker's New Household Economics facilitated for analyses of household economics. Further in this branch of economics many empirical studies were carried out by researchers and found the New Household Economics theory is supported by the research findings. So we attempted to make an institutional economic approach to the family or household which has been subject to household economic theoretical scrutiny. In our analysis production activities within the family and decisions on investment in children in the form of education and health as well as labour force participation faces features of Transaction Cost,

Asymmetric information and Institution as governance. Hence new household economics can be further analysed with new institutional economic approach.

REFERENCES

Arumugam, P. (1984): "Demand for Secondary Education in Tamil Nadu a Household Economic Approach," *Economics of Human Behaviour* Edited by Lakshmanasamy, T. (1997), Allied Publishers Ltd.

Becker, G.S. and Michael, R.T. (1973): "On the New Theory of Consumer Behaviour," *Swedish Journal of Economics*, 75, 178-98.

Bergstrom C. Theodore (1995): *A Survey of Theories of the Family*, University of Michigan, Current version: June.

Berman, P., C. Kendall, and K. Bhattacharyya (1994): "The Household Production of Health: Integrating Social Science Perspectives on Micro-level Health Determinants," *Social Science and Medicine* 38: 205-15.

Bhardan, P.K. (1989): The New Institutional Economics and Development Theory: A Brief Critical Assessment," *World Development*, Vol. 17 (9): 1389-95.

Christopher D. Gerrard, "Introduction to the New Institutional Economics," National TOT Workshop, Harare, Zimbabwe, October 28 to November 1, 1996.

Duraisamy, P. (1988): "*An Econometric analysis of Fertility, Child Schooling and Labour Force Participation of women in Rural Indian Households*," Center Discussion Paper No. 585, Yale University and IIT, Madras, Oct. 1989.

Arumugam, P. (2002), IDPAD Project on, *Allocation of time value of non-market work and family income distribution: A study of rural households in Tamil Nadu*.

Klein G. Peter (1999): "New *Institutional Economies*," Department of Economics, University of Georgia.

Lakshmanasamy, T. (1997): "Economics of Marriage: Implications for Female Age at Marriage," in *Economics of Human Behaviour* Edited by Lakshmanasamy, T., Allied Publishers Ltd.

Lawrence Haddad, John Hoddinott, and Harold Alderman (1997), *Intrahousehold Resources allocation in Developing Countries; Models, Methods, and Policy*, International Food Policy Research Institute, London.

Malathy, R. (1983), "Women's allocation of time to market and non-market work: A study of married women in Madras City," Center Discussion Paper No. 585, Yale University and IIT, Madras, Oct.

Mylene Kherallah and Johann Kirsten (June 2001), "The New Institutional Economics: Applications For Agricultural Policy Research in Developing Countries," *International Food Policy Research Institute*.

Parada J. Jairo (2001), *Original Institutional Economics and New Institutional*

Economics: Revisiting the Bridges (Or the Divide). This paper was written under the supervision of Professor Philip Klein of the Economics Department at Penn State University.

Pollak, A. Robert (1985): A Transaction Cost Approach to Families and Households," *Journal of Economic Literature*, Vol. XXIII, June.

Rosenzweig Mark and Oded Stark (eds.), "A Survey of Theories of the Family," in Mark *Handbook of Population Economics*, Amsterdam: North-Holland.

Sen, A. (1990): "Economics and the Family," *Asian Development Reviews*, 15-26.

Shoshana Grossbard-Shechtman (2001): *Economic Development, Marriage, and the Family: An Interdisciplinary Approach*, Department of Economics, San Diego State University, California.

Sugirtharani, A. (2002): *"The Effect of Childcare Welfare Scheme on Mother's Participation in Economic Activity, Nutrition, Health Status of Children and Consumption Expenditure of Urban Households,"* Ph.D. thesis, Bharathiar University.

Economic Implications of Marriage Institution with Reference to Women's Empowerment

GHANSHYAM UPADHYAY

After the Second World War most of the countries of the world have implemented more or less equal programmes for economic development, but even then the results were considerably different and unequal. Some of the countries could achieve noteworthy development, while some of them remained at the same level development The reason behind the different results of developmental efforts is different forms of institutions existed in the society.

What do 'Institutions' mean? In one sense, institutions are organizations such as school, hospital, firm, club, corporation, etc. These organizations have their objectives, functions, rules, procedures, norms, values, etc. There is a wider sense in which institutions are defined. Welton Hamilton defines institutions as: "It connoted a way of thought or action of some prevalence and permanence, which is embedded in the habits of a group or the customs of people. . . . Institutions fix the confines of human beings. The world of use and want to which imperfectly we accommodate our lives, is a tangled and unbroken web of institutions." According to him, institutions affect nature of wants and needs, allocation of resources. Income distribution, forms of business, savings, investments, innovations, risk taking, factor mobility, factor supply, etc. Individuals are born into institutions and institutions outlive individual, therefore all organizations are institutions but all the institutions are not organizations.

Geoffrey M. Hodgson (1998), enumerates five characteristics of institutions, defined as integrated and systematic social entities as,

(1) Interaction of agents and information feedbacks. (2) Common conceptions and routines and common characteristics. (3) Institutions are sustained through shared conception and expectations. (4) Institutions are durable, self-reinforcing and have persistent qualities. (5) Institutions incorporate values and process of normative evolution. They reinforce their own moral legitimation.

From above points we can say that, institutions are set of rules for human behaviour that are formed or derived through social customs, habits, state-legislations, religious beliefs or concessions of people.

Neo-classical economists believed that human behaviour mainly influenced by economic rationality—a maximizer of utility or gain. According to them autonomous individual as micro-foundation of economic system (methodological individualism) and uniformity of human behaviour governed by motivation for utility maximization (economic rationality) bring an equilibrium through negative feedbacks.

In this view there is a total lack of historical perspective yet Neo-classical Economics has significant achievements to its credit. In its methodology neo-classical Economics draws heavily on the concept of equilibrium from physics. This may be contrasted with the evolutionary methodology adopted by Old Institutional School.

As per Institutional School economic system or theories are run through institutions esteemed in the society. In other words, economic theory can be put in practice only through institutions. These institutions either may be in form of organizations or in form of habits, customs or rules of a game. Evolution as per need and want of society through cumulative self-reinforcing movements, influence of evolutionary biology and positive feedbacks change the old institutions. Science and technology also lead to change in institutional structure. According to Institutional School, institutional set-up imposes a certain aggregative ordering but permits individual variations in motives and behaviour within the limits of tolerance.

There are two Schools of Institutional Economics, the Old and the New. The leaders of the Old School were Veblen, Commons and Clark; while Hodgson and Show are the main leaders of the New School. The Old School emphasized the importance of institutions influencing habits and customs. The new school does not emphasize habits as an influencing factor. In the Old School thinking, institutions are moulded behaviour. According to the New School, economically rational behaviour is confronted with constraints and the institutions emerge to overcome this constraint. According to Hodgson, "definition of an institution in the New Institutionalism do not typically include the notion of habit, they often share with the older institutionalism a broad, rather than a narrow, conception of an institution. Institutions are regarded as general regularities in social behaviour or the rules of the game in society or the humanly devised constraints that shape human interaction."

II. MARRIAGE INSTITUTION AND WOMEN EMPOWERMENT

There is no doubt that marriage is a social institution, but so far as women empowerment is concerned, economic aspect is most affecting factor in marriage life. In this paper I have tried to examine through a case study and through socio-historical consideration of economic implications of marriage institution affecting women empowerment.

A family or a household is an important unit of the society or economy. A family is a link between a person and a society. Therefore, a family can play a vital role for the socio-economic development especially on health, education and socialization sectors. A man and a woman are two main pillars of a family. Generally the man has been earning income for subsistence of the family, while the woman has been responsible for household work and child breeding. Over and above as a housewife, many women in India contribute income from labour in agriculture, construction, mines, etc. The poor families do not have facility of LPG gas for cooking; hence the women have to collect firewood and cow-dung as a free goods from common property of their village.

Place of a Woman in the Family and the Society

Though politically a woman is considered an equal civilian, socially she has got second ranked citizenship. This position is not only in third world countries, but also in the developed countries and socialist countries. There is no doubt that the man has been remaining superior in the important decisions and empowerment in family life.

'A man earns income and the family sustains on it'; this idea has favoured empowerment to the man. 'Can't a woman do labour for earning?' The answer of the question is given with some favourism like this, ' a woman has some biological and physical limitations like mense period, pregnancy and delivery; therefore she can not do labour as a man can do.' In the beginning this thought may be established with the idea of giving protection to the women but then it became a great hindrance for their own development.

Along with performing the duty of earning, the man achieved the right of empowerment. Religious books and priests also supported this view. A woman instead of being a life-companion became a servant or a slave of the husband. Several religions considered and established woman as a property of her husband. The status and importance of the woman declined to the extent that the woman is considered an instrument of sexual enjoyment, a servant of household work and a caretaker of the children. Several communities put the women behind *'pardah'* to protect against invaders or anti-social elements; afterwards this protection became obstacle against women-empowerment and women-development. As a result the status of a woman become inferior to that of a man.

A Case Study for Women-Empowerment

A case study was undertaken to examine empowerment of married women in Bhavnagar city of Gujarat. Through this study an attempt was also made to find out the reasons for lower empowerment of the women. A sample survey of 100 women was conducted. And answers received through questionnaire put in Tables 1 and 2.

Table 1 shows right of decision got by women in household affairs. The degrees of decision right are divided into three categories: (1) Full right, in this category a woman can take decision of purchasing, investment, children's education and day-to-day miscellaneous subjects regarding the household. (2) Partial right, in which important decisions are some time taken with the consent of the woman (wife) and many time the decisions are taken by man and afterward it is informed to the woman. The wife takes most of the minor and less important decisions or the wife is informed in advance or decisions are taken with her consent.

TABLE 1

Woman's Decision, Right in Household

Sl. No.	*Women Group*	*Total No. of Women*	*No. of Women enjoying Decision Right in household*		
			Full	*Partial*	*No Right*
1.	Illiterate	20	0	9	11
	A. House-wife	10	0	4	6
	B. House-wife + Earning	10	0	5	5
2.	Primary Education	20	0	11	9
	A. House-wife	10	0	5	5
	B. House-wife + Earning	10	0	6	4
3.	Secondary Education	20	0	11	9
	A. House-wife	10	0	5	5
	B. House-wife + Earning	10	0	6	4
4.	Graduate	20	1	14	5
	A. House-wife	10	0	7	3
	B. House-wife + Earning	10	1	7	2
5.	Post-graduate	20	5	15	0
	A. House-wife	10	2	8	0
	B. House-wife + Earning	10	3	7	0

Source: A Sample Survey conducted for the information.

(3) No right, in this category, all types of decisions are taken by the husband including purchasing of kitchen items, utensils, and schoolbooks of children.

We can also see from Table 1 that literacy and decision right of women have positive relationship. The illiterate women have no full decision right; out of 20, 9 women have partial right and 11 women have no any right in household decision. The women having primary and secondary education have equal position in decision right. They are little better than the illiterate women. Even then out of them no one has full right of decision. The graduate women can enjoy better position than that of less educated or uneducated women. Out of 20 graduate women, 1 has full decision right, 14 have partial right and 5 have no right in household decisions. The women having education of post-graduation can enjoy maximum right of decision. Out of 20 post-graduate women, 5 have full right, 15 have partial right and no one is without decision right.

Here we can see that education gives honour and decision right to the women in their family, because the educated women are supposed to be wise and with intellect. Secondly, the women who are earning good salary and engaged in mental work have more decision right. The women earning a small income and engaged in body labour have low voice in decisions of family affairs.

As per principle of equality, there should be equal contribution of male and female in child care. The degree of contribution in child care by male is meant to the degree of honour given to female and degree of equality. In Table 2 also the degree of contribution of male in child rearing is divided in three categories: (1) Full contribution means a male fully looks after children and takes care of them, males look after health, education and development of the children. (2) Partial contribution means, whenever the husband is at home, he will inquire about problems and position regarding children. In some cases he will take action and in some cases he will give only instruction and present an action-plan. Then the responsibility of implementation will be on the housewife. (3) No contribution means all the responsibility of child care is upon the housewife. The housewife will take all the steps regarding health, education and development of the children as per her understanding and capacity. In several cases the male does not know, in which standards his children are studying. And

TABLE 2

Woman Getting Male's Contribution in Child-rearing

Sl. No.	*Women Group*	*Total No. of Women*	*No. of women getting male's contributing in child-rearing*		
			Full	*Partial*	*No Right*
1.	Illiterate	20	2	5	13
	A. House-wife	10	0	2	8
	B. House-wife + Earning	10	2	3	5
2.	Primary Education	20	4	7	9
	A. House-wife	10	1	3	6
	B. House-wife + Earning	10	3	4	3
3.	Secondary Education	20	4	8	8
	A. House-wife	10	1	3	6
	B. House-wife + Earning	10	3	5	2
4.	Graduate	20	6	11	3
	A. House-wife	10	2	6	2
	B. House-wife + Earning	10	4	5	1
5.	Post-graduate	20	9	10	1
	A. House-wife	10	4	5	1
	B. House-wife + Earning	10	5	5	0

Source: A Sample Survey conducted for the information.

there are extreme and exceptional cases in which the male does not know, how many children he has.

Here also we can see that out of 20 illiterate women, only 2 get full contribution in child-rearing from their husbands, 5 get partial contribution, while 13 do not get any contribution. The women having primary and secondary education are almost equally getting contribution from their husbands in child care. Their husbands go to their children's school and keep touch with teachers and school management. We can say that male participation in child-care increases along with increase in female education. The women having education of graduation and post-graduation can get more contribution in child-rearing from male. In graduate women group out of 20, 6 women get full contribution, 11 women partial contribution and 3 women do not get any contribution in child rearing from their husbands. While in post-graduate women group out of 20 women, 9 women get full contribution, 10 women get partial contribution and only 1 woman gets no contribution. Here also we can see that working or earning women get much honor and contribution in child rearing

PROBLEMS WITH MARRIED WOMEN IN INDIA

In India women have no equal empowerment in the society, therefore they have to face many types of problems as under:

1. Gender Discrimination in Child Breeding

In most of the family girls are neglected and marginalized. Parents do partiality in favour of male children and female children are deprived from basic needs. 'A male is superior than a female', the informal education is given right from childhood to the children. Therefore birth of male child is welcomed in each and every class of the society. Education, training, nutritious food and so many facilities are diverted towards male children and female children are being deprived from them.

2. No Property Rights to Women

Under the provisions of laws women are entitled for property rights, but they are not implemented in practice. Only sons get succession to fathers property but daughters are deprived from it. At the time of marriage, a woman gets presents from her father and brothers in the form of cash, ornaments, clothes, utensils or domestic appliances, which are called 'Stree-Dhan'. According the law 'Stree-Dhan' is private property of a woman, but her in-laws do not allow her to dispose or invest independently as per her will.

3. Male Dominant Society

Not only in India but also all over world there is male dominance. In the Kerala state there are maternalean families known as 'Moplah' and 'Tharwad'. In these families daughters of the family get succession from their mother. Sons do not get any succession. After marriage a daughter does not go to live with her husband, but the husband has to go to live with his wife. The wife is an owner of all the property of the family. Even then women are considered subject to some biological limitations, hence the brothers of the wife or brothers of the mother do the administration of the property. As a result the economic empowerment is centralized in male members of the family. Therefore, political activities are also lead by male in that region. Thus there is problem of male dominance.

4. Exploitation of Women

Generally women are paid lower wage rates for the same work in comparison with the men. Agriculture, construction, manufacturing, etc. sectors discriminates between men and women and pay different wage rate. In some part of the Uttar Pradesh there is custom of bonded labour. The labourers take debt from the landowner and the labourers have to work for the landowner until the debt is completely repaid. At the time of partition of family property, the debt is also distributed among the sons of the labourer. And each son has to pay his share of debt individually. If one cannot pay the debt of his share, he has to work for the landlord. Some incidents also had taken place in Uttar Pradesh, in which the debtor could not repay the debt of his share, therefore, his wife had to remain as a kept of the lender until the debt was not completely repaid. Thus women are sexually also exploited.

5. Labour without Value

Small and marginal farmers do subsistence farming. They cannot keep labourers. The women of the family have to work as labourers. But their independent output and income is not calculated, therefore, they do not have empowerment in family.

Farmers do cattle rearing along with agriculture activity. The women of the family do most of the work of cattle rearing. They also help as an assistant in agriculture along with the responsibility of household work. But their independent output and income is not calculated, therefore, they have lower empowerment in the family.

6. Deprivation from High Quality Education

So many girls are clever and scholar in education; even then they are admitted in the courses that offer lower income. If women were deprived from qualitative education and higher income, obviously they would be deprived from equal empowerment.

7. Obstacle to the Development of future Generations

Mother's role is very important in development of the child. If a mother is deprived from education, training, nutritious food, health facilities and proper empowerment; she would not be able to give proper treatment to her child for development. As a result, future generation also would be deprived from proper development.

RECOMMENDATIONS FOR IMPROVEMENT OF WOMEN'S EMPOWERMENT

Here some remedial measures are suggested for improvement of women empowerment. The recommendations are presented with reference to the case study and observation as under:

1. Women Education should be made Qualitative

There is no doubt that the Central Government and the State Governments have tried to increase and expand women's education. But the aim of the education remained "women awareness" only. Of course this aim is also useful, but now there should be an aim of 'better employment to women'. Girls should be given vocational training and education for high income earning.

2. Encouragement to Independent Employment to Women

Generally women are housewife and assistant to the males in family business. Their task is just complementary to the work of males. Therefore, their production value cannot be calculated separately. As a result, the status and importance of women in economic, social and political sector is lower than that of the men. Skilled and trained women should be encouraged by government for their independent employment or business and nationalized banks should liberally finance for it.

3. Programmes for Women Awareness

There is a vital role of a mother in child rearing. A mother provides her children education, health facilities, food, socialization, standard of morality, etc. as per her knowledge and understanding. If a mother has not sufficient and proper knowledge and awareness for child requirement for proper development, there will be improper development of the children. Therefore, women awareness programmes should be arranged by governments in large number.

4. Social values should be changed through Literature and Media

Society and literature affect each other and can change their forms, trends and structure. Social environment is often reflected in literature. On the other side, many creation of literature have contributed in changing the social environment. Today there are so many means of media for communication of revolutionary thoughts. The writers and poets should present their creation supporting 'women empowerment, women ability and gender equity'.

5. Implementation of Women's Property Right

According to Indian constitution all the civilians are equal and every one can have property right. Of course this right is also given to the women of the nation, but it remains only on paper. Generally in urban areas the women are given rights to be an owner of immovable property like buildings, plots of land, factories, shares of companies, partnership in business, etc. This type of ownership can be seen only on documents for tax-saving purpose. The decision regarding transfer of property, or investment or sale of property is taken by male persons only. The women should have sufficient and actual rights for disposal of her property. The government should establish proper mechanism for it.

In short if we have will for doing something well, there is certainly a way for it. If we are willing for socio-economic development of our country first we have to achieve true democracy, along with gender equality.

REFERENCES

Eggertsson, Thrainn (1990), *Economic Behaviour and Institutions*, Cambridge University Press.

Gabraith, J.K. (1967): *The New Industrial State*, Boston: Houghton, Miffin.

Gautam Gyanendra and Ruchi Ghosh Dastidar (2000), *Women and Home-based Production*, Rajat Publication.

Hodgson, Geoffrey M. (1993), *Institutional Economics: Surveying the Old and the New.*

Malcolm Rutherford (1996), "The Old and New Institutionalism: Can bridges be built?," *Journal of Economics Issues*, Vol. XXIX, No. 2, June.

Meyhew, Anne (1989): 'Contrasting Origins of the Two Institutionalism: The Social Context", *Review of Political Economy*, Nov.

Miffin David Colander (1996), "New Institutionalism, Old Institutionalism and Distribution Theory," *Journal of Economic Issues*, Vol. XXX, No. 2, June.

North, D.C. (1989), 'Institutions and Economic Growth: A Historical Introduction', *World Development*, Vol. XXXVII, No. 9.

Premlata Pujari and Vijay Kumari Kaushik (1994), *Women Power in India*, Vol. 2, Institutional System for Women's Development, Kanishka Publishers and Distributors, New Delhi.

Rubery (1989), *Women's Wages*, Macmillon Reference Books.

Sheel C. Nuna (1990), "Women and Development," National Institute of Educational Planning and Administration, New Delhi.

William M. Duggar (1995), "Douglass C. North's New Institutionalism," *Journal of Economics Issues*, Vol. XXIX, No. 2, June.

SECTION V

NIE AND FINANCIAL REFORMS

New Institutional Economics: Its Relevance to the Financial Sector

C. THANGAMUTHU

THEORETICAL BACKGROUND

Financial sector consists of financial "institutions" evolved by the society over a period of time. The quality and performance of financial sector (money, credit and capital market) are essentially an institutional performance, conditioned by the institutional interactions, and values and mores underlying the behaviour of agents involved in financial sector transactions. Market is only a subsystem of the society. It only reflects the social institutional character and value pattern. In a society characterised by perfect information, high degree of transparency, identity of interests and symmetry of information between the transacting parties and perfect and efficient legal framework to enforce the contact and punish the guilty. In case of any contractual violation, the transaction costs, market imperfections, and incidence of market failure would be minimal. The significance of the above non-market variables in determining transaction cost and, in effect, the market performance has been duly recognised by the institutionalists, especially the New Institutionalist Economists, including Douglass C. North, Joseph Stiglitz, Clive Bell, Oliver Williamson, George Akerlof, Pranab Bardhan, Kaushik Basu, T.N. Srinivasan and others. New Institutionalists would believe that market reforms should transcend boundaries of the market and reach out to the institutional parameters, because it is the latter group which ultimately influences transaction costs. Under institutionalist paradigm, the market-reforms, in fact, seek the intervention and toning up of state and its governance in order to tackle the problems of information asymmetry, adverse selection, moral hazard, principal-constraints that structure political, economic and social interaction. They consist of both informal constraints (sanctions, taboos, customs, traditions and codes of conduct), and formal rules (constitutions, laws; property rights). Throughout history, institutions have been devised by human beings to create order and reduce uncertainty in exchange. Together with the standard constraints of economics they define choice set and therefore determine transaction and production costs and hence the profitability and feasibility of engaging in economic activity. They evolve incrementally, connecting the past with the present and the future; history in consequence is largely a story of institutional evolution in which the historical performance of economies can only be understood as a part of sequential story. Institutions provide the incentive structure of an economy; as that structure evolves, it shapes the direction of economic change towards growth, stagnation, or decline" (*North*, 1991).

The importance of institutional factors in explaining the differences between the levels of income and rate of growth between MDCs and LDCs has been rightly emphasised: "The differences (in income levels and growth rate between developed and developing countries) can be attributed, perhaps tautologically, to differences in economic organisation, to how individuals (factors of production) interact, and to the institutions" which mediate those interactions. Among the most important of these 'institutions' are markets. It is now well recognised that there are many instances of market failures in more developed economies. . . . In some cases, market failures may be ameliorated by non-market institutions. . . . Market failure is more prevalent in LDCs and the non-market institutions that ameliorate its consequences are, at least in many instances, less successful in doing so" (*Stiglitz*, 1989).

In this context, the present paper seeks to examine the institutional dimensions of financial sector reforms underway in India and other parts of the world.

LIBERALISATION Vs. REGULATION

The story of institutionalist approach to financial sector reforms was preceded by theories of liberalisation of the financial sector by Mckinnon (1973) and Shaw (1973). These theories argued against financial repression brought about by government controls and that directed credit to favoured sectors would adversely affect resource mobilisation and resource allocation. Artificially suppressed interest rates would discourage savings and distort the choice of investment projects. Under these conditions, financial sector liberalisation/marketisation would increase efficiency and growth by eliminating distortions created by government interventions.

The liberalisation theories were challenged by institutionalists (*Stiglitz,* 1993) (particularly the advocates of information theoretical approach). The institutionalists argue that if financial market is fully deregulated there would be greater incidence of market failure thanks to imperfect and asymmetric information, adverse selection and moral hazard. The basic point (made by institutionalists) is that in the presence of asymmetric information, competitive credit markets may not clear, equilibria being characterised by credit rationing. The reason is that the interest rate plays a dual role: it affects the excess demand for loans but it also affects the average quality of a lender's loan portfolio. As the interest rate rises, the quality of the portfolio worsens because (a) sound borrowers are discouraged relative to unsound borrowers (the adverse selection effect), and (b) all borrowers have an incentive to undertake riskier projects (the moral hazard effects). Hence, a divergence can arise between the interest rate that clears the credit market and the interest rate that maximises the lender's return. If the latter is less than the former, there will be credit rationing and some borrowers (including some good borrowers) will not receive loans.

So far there is no dispute. But does this constitute case for administered control of interest rates? The argument so far has shown that in the presence of asymmetric information, the free market outcome is inefficient relative to situation where the information constraint is absent. But the operational question is whether it is possible to improve the situation. Prima facie, this seems very doubtful since the government usually faces the same or worse constraint. Moreover, the government dearly can worsen the situation by imposing an interest rate ceiling lower than the loan rationing equilibrium.

The credit-rationing literature can, however, be employed to construct a case for interest rate control in the following way. The above argument pre-supposed that moral hazard applies to borrowers but not to lenders. But this assumption may not hold in the case of banks, if there is deposit insurance or government assurance of bailout (widely prevalent in modern economies) and if, in addition, prudential supervision and regulation are weak or absent. Banks then become risk-lovers. If outcomes are favourable, they stand to make large profits since they do not face the costs imposed by provisioning and capital requirements or high deposit insurance premia; if outcomes are unfavourable, they can walk away from the losses as these are borne by the monetary authority, (this is true a fortiori if there is implicit protection of both deposits and equity. But the danger exists even if bank owners bear their share of the losses. Indeed, in a nationalised banking system, equity losses are borne by the state and may not constrain the behaviour of managers). These dangers are exacerbated during liberalisation since banks have increased freedom with regard to interest rates and the direction of credit, and all the more so if there macro-economic environment unstable and the variance of project outcomes is higher than in more stable times. In such circumstances, temporary imposition of ceilings on deposit and loan interest rates may well be desirable (*Joshi and Little*, 1997). It should be noted that the above is not an argument for interest rate control in a 'long-run' equilibrium but a sequencing argument about the order of liberalisation, particularly in the context of macro-economic instability. A particular worry along these lines is that real interest rates may rise excessively during financial liberalisation, leading to acute difficulties for companies in the real sector, and eventually distress and even collapse of financial institutions. This phenomenon has been observed in several Latin American liberalisations. But it was product not only of bankers' moral hazard in the presence of weak regulation but also of high inflationary expectations, exchange risk, oligopolistic financial markets, and wrong sequencing as regards opening of the capital account. One would have to be careful in drawing lessons for India. A material difference is introduced by the fact that India is not a high-inflation country in the Latin American sense. Nor does India suffer from the close ownership links between banks and firms as was the case in, for instance, Chile. Even so, India's regulatory apparatus is currently in its infancy. So the moral hazard/weak regulation argument for interest rate ceiling is not devoid of relevance (*Joshi and Little*, 1996).

It is generally argued that the capital market facilitates the process of disintermediation and that the capital market establishes a direct relationship between the savers and the users of funds. On the other hand, banks and other financial institutions act as intermediaries between the savers and users of the funds.

Rationales behind financial intermediation include the minimisation of information and transaction costs and the diversification of risks, in a world in which assets are imperfectly divisible and both asset returns and wealth holders' cash-flow positions are imperfectly correlated.

Notwithstanding the deficiencies of the agency system, the principals have to engage the services of agents, because their gains are likely to outweigh the possible losses. Jenson and Meckling (1976) use the theory of property rights, agency and finance to develop a theory of ownership structure of the firm. Specification of individual property rights determines how costs and rewards will be allocated among the participants in any organisation. Agency costs are the sum of (a) the monitoring expenditure by the principal; (b) the bonding expenditures by the agent; and (c) the residual loss. The separation of ownership and control, first explored by Berle and Means (1932), in modern business corporations allows the agency theory to operate there. Organisation is effected through contract, and individual behaviour will depend on the nature of these contracts. When owners employ managers (agents) in controlling positions, they may attempt to get a stream of non-pecuniary benefits such as air-conditioned office space, office car, luxury travel expenses, rent free housing, etc. This necessarily reduces the value of the firm. But these costs are an unavoidable result of the agency relationship. The owners are responsible for creating the relationship and bear the costs because the benefits from their creation outweigh the costs.

In a modern mature society specialisation requires increasing percentages of the resources of the society to be engaged in transacting, so that the transaction sector rises to be a larger percentage of gross national product. This is so because specialisation in trade, finance, banking, insurance, as well as the simple co-ordination of economic activity, involves an increasing proportion of the labour force. Of necessity, therefore, highly specialised forms of transaction organisations emerge. International specialisation and division of labour requires institutions and organisations to safeguard property rights across international boundaries so that capital markets (as well as other kinds of exchange) can take place with credible commitment on the part of the players (*North*, 1991).

BANKING SECTOR

Interest rate regulations and direction/rationing of credit to preferred sections lead to inefficiencies and distortions because of institutional problems. The Principal-Agent problem in the Indian Context of financial market, particularly in the directed bank credit towards preferred sections, has a peculiar and more complex ramification. Between the principal (Depositor) and the agent (Bank Manager), there is another middle-agent, a political power-broker who actually controls the decision as to who should be lent and how much. Hence, even if the bank manager has the information that the loan applicant and his proposal are not credit-worthy, he has no choice but to grant loans as per the dictates of the politicians. The incidence of benami loans and loans to undeserving non-target groups (but economically and politically influential) cannot be ruled out. Further at the recovery front also, the bank manager has to play soft and wink at the wilful default and desist from serious recovery proceedings. These institutional bottlenecks (partly socio-politico) have added on to the mounting non-performing assets (NPA) with the nationalised banks. Although there may be some salt of truth in the argument of the pro-poor that but for such political armtwisting, the banking bureaucrats would shut their doors completely on the underprivileged. But this should not lead to the other extreme, a mad game of "loan melas" just to suit the whim of the politicians of the ruling party.

Another spill-over of this principal-agent problem is the prevalence of rampant corruption at various stages of loan sanction. The so-called subsidy is considerably eaten away by the political agent and bureaucrats and some times the bank officials. The government policy of reserving 33 per cent of loans to the weaker sections at subsidised rate of interest is partly responsible for the NPA of the nationalised banks soaring to 24 percent of the total assets. Another area of target loan was the SSI sector. The loan locked in the SSI sick units and the sick medium and large units accounted for 16 per cent of the total volume of loans in mid-nineties. These loans, though technically a bad-dept, could not be written-off because of the inherent legal bottleneck in closing-down the sick units. The industrial Dispute Act forbids the termination of workers, without the permission of the Government, which seldom gives approval for such termination even on genuine economic grounds. Similarly, the Urban Land Ceiling Act (ULCA) does not permit the sale of the lands of sick units. Many such sick units can settle their dept claims and make some surplus, if their lands in valuable urban areas are permitted to be disposed by the government. Only in the recent budget, some attempt has been envisaged along these lines. Because of these legal (institutional) bottlenecks, the banks could not optimise their performance on purely market considerations. These non-market, institutional bottlenecks call for immediate legal/institutional reforms.

The problem of moral hazard is almost endemic to the financial sector, under the existing system of legal/judicial dispensation. The scope for moral hazard exists at the bankers' end as well as at borrowers' end. Poor law enforcement machinery and a weak, time-consuming and costly process of judiciary inadvertently encourage the incidence of moral hazard. The borrowers take advantage of this situation and escape the repayment obligation partly or fully. The bankers indulging in illegal advances such as the one made to stockbrokers resulting in the notorious scam involving a mindboggling loss of Rs. 5000 crores in 1992 occurred because of absence of scope for quick punishment in the present system of judiciary. Here, there is no question of information asymmetry between the banker and the fraudulent borrower that facilitate the crime. Such crimes may recur because neither the social stigma against economic crimes is very powerful, nor there is quick and surest scope for punishment. The judicial system provides for unimaginably long delay for the final award of punishment.

Under such conditions, besides improving the machinery of law enforcement and streamlining the system of judiciary, transparency in transactions may reduce, if not preclude, the possibilities of crime. The transparency in procedures, details of transaction and the performance profiles of the banks, stock exchanges and other institutions are an institutional pre-condition (promoting information symmetry) for achieving market efficiency.

Bank supervision and regulation can be seen as an answer to the moral hazard problem. What is the scope of desirable supervision and regulation? Controls on Interest rates and credit allocation and micro-monitoring of bank decisions are, in general, undesirable. The current international consensus favours imposing minimum capital requirements. The underlying idea is simple: not only is adequate capital a cushion against unforeseen losses but banks are less likely to take risks the greater the loss that shareholders might suffer. But capital adequacy requirements are not enough because bank managers may not act in the interest of shareholders. (Ironically, this may be particularly true in a nationalized banking system where there is a single shareholder with 'deep pockets'!). It is therefore generally agreed that banks must also be subject to rules concerning income recognition, provisioning, and portfolio concentration. Audit and disclosure requirements are also necessary so that the accounts of banks are transparent to outsiders. It is dearly important that bank supervisors should be independent and possess adequate enforcement powers.

Liberalization will increase the complexity of the financial environment and the use of instruments such as swaps, forwards, and options. It is clear that both the RBI and the banks have to make a massive effort in terms of training and improvement of skills. Technical assistance will have to be sought from foreign central banks and financial institutions.

In the recovery side, the banks needed legal support in their recovery efforts; this was to be provided by special recovery tribunals which could dispose of cases expeditiously. Recovery was to be facilitated by special tribunals. The Recovery of Debts Act was passed in 1993 and tribunals were set-up in several major cities. But they have not functioned because their constitutionality has been challenged in both the Delhi and Madras High Courts. Even here the endless process of litigation is the serious bottleneck.

Under regulated financial market wherein administrated interest rates are the rule, the banks have little scope for price competition but only non-price competition. The quality and type of service and the procedures and modalities of transactions are substantial the same from bank to bank. There is no reason why one should shift his account from one bank to another, excepting perhaps for the proximity to his work place or residence. Here the institution of government through its regulation and regimentation throttles the free market play in banking sector. It is important to note that there should be some range of functional freedom (given the overall framework of accountability) for the banks to innovate product differentiation in terms of services.

UNORGANISED MONEY LENDING

As there is always a market for second hand cars with incidence of adverse selection, in the financial market also, there is an unorganised segment left with the character of adverse selection. The role of money lenders, pawn brokers and informal discounters cannot be completely replaced or regulated fully. They have evolved as a social institution to cater to the risky, non-creditworthy clients. Moneylenders in India are able to charge very high rates of interest, but yet grant loans to those who would otherwise get no loan at all. The organised money market charges much lower rate of interest, but offers credit only to "credit-worthy" persons. Moneylenders are able to grant loans to "high risks" because their (a) a personal knowledge about borrowers, and (b) special ability to enforce the contracts. If any other person (or bank) attempts to lend at the same high rates of interests without those qualifications, he is likely to attract "bad risks" and may end up becoming bankrupt. Inherent in the business world is the difficulty of distinguishing good quality from bad. In such conditions "adverse selection" is a consequence of the asymmetric of information (*Neelakantan*, 1992).

INTER-LINKED CREDIT

Similarly, prevalence of inter-linked transactions is again an institutional arrangement. As it is well observed (*Neelakantan*, 1992) When two are more independent exchanges are simultaneously agreed up, then interlinked markets develop. When a mundy merchant agrees to buy a farmer's output, and also agrees to lend him credit, then an interlinked deal is struck between them. The presence of interlinked contracts might explain the existence of a wide spectrum of interest rates for rural credit at the same time. "An interlinked transaction is one in which the two parties trade in at least two markets on the condition that the terms of all such trades are jointly determined. There is a "package" or "bundled" deal in which each element in the deal is connected with every other in an essential pay.

CAPITAL MARKET

Capital market suffers from principal-agent problem, among others. "In principal-agent relationships, the agent is likely to have move information than the principal because (a) he will have more information about his own actions, preferences and abilities; and (b) it will cost him less to acquire information about the particulars affecting the individual tasks assigned to him by the principal. Hence information is distributed asymmetrically between the two. It is costly for the principal to measure the characteristics and performances of agents. So agents could engage in shirking and opportunistic behaviour. Agents may have informational advantages In the form of "hidden actions" and "hidden information." Hidden actions cannot be accurately observed or inferred by others. The information asymmetry and conflict of interests between principal-agent in capital market can lead to two-fold problems; (a) misuse or inefficient use of capital supplied by the investors, and (b) the problem of moral hazard, i.e. the investors being cheated by the unscrupulous spurious principals, for instance, chit-fund companies.

The incidence of information asymmetry, adverse selection and moral hazards has become a serious problem in the Indian money market, both organised capital market and the NBFI. The promoters in the stock markets are observed to engineer incomplete and wrong information with strategies such as inflating project costs, fixing high premia and raising money for companies which exist only on paper. This is observed to take place under the collusion of merchant bankers, underwriters, advertisers, financial weeklies and other sundry marketeers under the very nose of regulatory bodies. It is estimated that about Rs. 10,000 million have been defrauded in this way during Jan.-June of 1994 alone. The legally allowed preferential allotment of stocks and insider trading (informational asymmetry) by promoters and companies is observed to have caused misappropriation of capital anywhere between Rs. 10,000 million to Rs. 50,000 million (*Bhole*, 1995). Furthermore, the high transaction costs in clearance, settlement and share allotments and transfers work against small investors (*Patibandla*, 1997). That the working of stock exchanges in India is far from satisfactory is graphically described in the following lines: The Bombay Stock Exchange, the premier exchange in the country, was well known for its murky practices. An investor could not be sure he got a fair deal because trading methods were not transparent. Deals were not time-stamped and brokers' contract notes did not clearly separate price, commission and carry-forward charges. Trades were often executed outside the exchange. Brokers did not distinguish between personal and client accounts. Exchanges were closed down whenever it suited the interests of brokers. There was a significant amount of insider trading. Brokers were undercapitalised. Margins were inadequate and, in any case, not enforced. The 'badla' or carry-forward system made the market prone to speculative instability (*Joshi and Little*, 1996). The recently established Stock Exchange Board of India (SESI) and the consequent regulations have partially succeeded in streamlining the working of the stock exchanges in the country.

Another related issue stems for the principal-agent problem which is the characteristic of private corporate sector and public sector as well. The dichotomy of interests between the managers who manage the funds and the investing public (share holders) who actually own the funds, go against the interests of the latter. The squandering and wastages of capital (euphemistically reflected in high capital/output ratio which in fact indicates inefficient use of capital) by the corporate managers are detrimental to the interests of shareholders. Lack of transparency, accounting gimmicks and legally permissibly window-dressing tactics facilitate the continued exploitation of the vulnerable shareholders.

When it comes to moral hazard, the case of sudden 'disappearance' of spurious chit fund companies and mutual fund institutions virtually cheating the investing public who were mostly the salaried sections lured by the fabulously high interest offers, is a sickening case in point. These defaulting chit fund promoters cleverly manage to escape any punishment, thanks to the inefficient/corrupt/time consuming administration of law and justice. As a result of this cruel institutional failure, the market for funds crumble and the genuine fund managers/fund savers are unable to enter into transaction.

PATH DEPENDENCY

The institutions have tendency to be path-dependent. They resist changes. There is a time-lag for a change to be assimilated by every one. All over the world, financial intermediaries, by natural disposition tend to zealously preserve and protect profits that spring from non-transparent business practices. They have, therefore, been found to be too slow to accept changes and new technology that lead to greater transparency in the way they do their business. The foreign exchange market, for instance, in the beginning, grudgingly welcomed the entry to computers for dissemination of information. Today the computer screen is facilitating small order execution but many foreign exchange dealers are not very happy about it. They still talk in glowing terms about the advantages of negotiating deals on the telephone. Institutionalists would call this tendency a path dependency. People who are skeptical about transparency in financial transactions should realise that if all the deals that took place in early 1990s had been brought on a transparent screen and settled the NSE's clearing corporation settles all equity transactions today by offering settlement guarantee, the scam would not have taken place and the banks would not have lost thousands of crores. It is strange that even today several active market players refuse to accept the proposition that, modern financial markets with huge dally turnover should adopt transparent practices and they need to be closely monitored to prevent possible frauds (*Patil*, 2000).

INTERNATIONAL CAPITAL FLOW

International capital flow as it has been facilitated in the current scenario of liberalisation/globalisation, is to be explained in terms of institutional approach. The sudden and momentous migration of short-term capital (FDI) which established the liberalised economies of East Asian and Latin American countries is a phenomenon of special case of information asymmetry or rumour-mongered misinformation. The existing reporting systems fall to capture significant part of potentially reversible short-term components of capital flows. Significant omissions include investments in developing country assets by international mutual funds and non-BIS banks, non-resident deposits and inter-firm cross-border flows. The Inter-Agency Task Force on Finance Statistics with participants by the BIS, the IMF, the OECD and the World Bank, has recently been established to improve the quality, frequency and coverage of debt informatlon (*Dadush*, 2000). It is paradoxical that the new information technology and telecommunications, improved information sharing, reduced transaction costs and government facilitated frequent trading in short-term investments, which helped and hastened the massive flow of short-term capital flows to developing countries, have themselves facilitated in the reverse direction also. Moreover, the short-term FDIs act under "herd instinct" and incomplete information propelled by group irrationality. The problem assumes crisis proportions, spreading from country to country, like wildfire. This contagion effect (*Rangarajan*, 2000) is mostly a function of misinformation about the health of the economies wherein the FDIs have staked their short-term investments. If every investor takes the wild rumour seriously and draws out his funds suddenly, then the economy, however, sound it might be otherwise, has no escape from the collapse. This is nothing but a self-fulfilling fallacy. Thus the volatility and imperfection in the International short-term capital market are partly the creations of information asymmetry.

CONCLUSION

Thus institutlonalist interpretation of financial sector reforms suggests that, notwithstanding the syndrome of liberalisation of financial sector, there is a genuine case for state regulation and controls, but with a different thrust. These state regulations are not restrictive but proactive in promoting the institutional efficiency. These measures would include transparency in transaction, information collection and dissemination and avoiding the problems of principal-agent and moral hazard. The improvement in the quality of governance including streamlining of legal-judiciary system for effective enforcement of contracts are on the top of the institutionalist agenda. This approach becomes all the more relevant because in most of the financial transactions, there are inherent problems of risk and uncertainty, information asymmetry and moral hazard, which are more institutional than just market specific.

REFERENCES

Bhagwati, Jagadish and T.N. Srinivasan (1993): *India's Economic Reforms*, Govt. of India, New Delhi.

Bhole, L.M. (1995): "The Indian Capital Markets at Cross Roads" (*Vikalpa*, 20) Quoted in Patibandla, 1997).

Dadush, Uri *et al.* (2000), The Role of Short-term Debt in Recent Crises, *Finance & Development*, Dec.

Jensen, M. and Meckling (1976): "Theory of the Firm, Managerial Behaviour, Agency Costs and Ownership `Structure," *The Joumal of Financial Economics*, Vol. 3.

Joshi, Vijay and I.M.D. Little (1996): *India's Economic Reforms*, 1991-2001, *OUP*, Delhi.

Mckilnnon, R.I. (1973): *Money and Capital in Economic Development*, Washington D.C. Brookings Institute.

Neelakantan, S. (1992): *New Institutional Economics and Agrarian Change*, Indian Economic Association Trust, New Delhi.

North, Douglass (1991): *Institutions, Institutional Change and Economic Performance*, CUP, New York.

—— (1991): "Institutions," *Journal of Economic Perspectives*, 5(1).

Patibandla, Murali (1997): "Economic Reforms and Institutions," *EPW*, May 17-14.

Patil, R.H. (2001): Industrial Finance and Capital Market—Changing Scenario," *EPW*, Jan. 27.

Rangarajan, C. (2000): "Capital Flows: Another Look," *EPW*, Dec. 9.

Shaw, E.S. (1973): *Financial Deepening in Economic Development*, OUP, New York.

Stiglitz, J.E. (1989): "Markets, Market Failures and Development," *AER*, Vol. 79).

—— (1993): The Role of State in Financial Markets," *Proceedings of the World Bank Annual Conference of Development Economics*, Washington D.C., World Bank.

Financial Sector Reforms in India: An Institutional Economics Perspective

M.K. Datar and Parikshit K. Basu

I. INTRODUCTION

During the last two decades several economies in the world have deregulated their financial sectors though to different extent. A strong and efficient financial system is generally considered a prerequisite for establishment of market-driven, productive and competitive economy. The aim of financial sector reforms in India has been to create such a financial system (*GOI*, 1998). Financial sector reform measures initiated in India since mid-1980s, mostly affected external factors such as increasing competition by permitting private (including foreign) entrants, removing price restrictions such as interest rates and exchange rates and instituting a system of prudential regulations. Very rarely reform measures so far dealt with organizational aspects of the processes internal to financial institutions. The organizational and governance structures of individual institutions are important for efficient decision-making and that, in turn may affect the efficacy of the market system itself. Moreover, financial institutions in

India are mostly owned by the government, which increases the importance of non-market objectives, tactics and working practices.

The New Institutional Economics (NIE) approach has sought to explain the relative efficacy of markets and hierarchies. Initially it seeks to explain existence of firms in terms of efforts to minimize transaction costs. Subsequently, the approach became deeper as the analysis was broadened to include factors that result in transaction cost differences, links between transactions and governance structures and differences in processes that have a bearing on economic organizations. While the NIE approach has evolved mainly in the study of industrial organization, it also witnessed wider applications *inter alia* in explaining workings of labour and financial markets. The problems of corporate finance, i.e. choice between debt/equity, corporate governance and risk sharing are certain areas that have attracted attention. It has also found useful in the context of problems faced by less developed countries. (*Harries et al.*, 1995)

Financial systems in different countries do exhibit significant differences in terms of relative importance of capital markets and banks and such differences are considered crucially important in explaining inter-country differences in the working of financial systems.[1] The differences in stock market-based financial systems (USA and UK) and bank-based financial systems (Germany and Japan) are well recognised. NIE may therefore provide a useful perspective to understand the efficacy of the financial system, in terms of factors affecting the workings of financial markets and financial institutions.

This paper makes an attempt to assess the progress of financial sector reforms in India from an institutional perspective. The importance of the NIE is also heightened due to significant government ownership of financial institutions, a factor that has important bearing on internal working of such institutions. The thrust of the argument here is, unless there are improvements in internal processes within the financial institutions, the reforms would remain incomplete. The financial sector reforms in India have been more successful in improving workings of financial markets while the success as regards improvements in internal working of lending institutions has been rather limited. The rest of the paper is divided in five sections. Section II explains the concepts of efficient financial market and the possibility of an inherent imbalance when reforms are introduced. Section III presents a brief overview of financial sector reform measures in India. Section IV explains the gaps in the reform process in India and their impact on risk behaviour of the financial institutions. Concluding remarks are in section V.

II. EFFICIENT FINANCIAL SECTOR AND DANGERS OF INHERENT IMBALANCE

Efficient working of a financial market necessitates sound institutional background, effective market procedures, transparent accounting standards, efficient price dissemination and settlement procedures (*Andrews & Lynch,* 1994). External environment of a country must provide adequate support to implement and maintain these conditions. At the same time, individual financial institutions need to restructure their internal organisations to obtain the maximum value of this efficient operation. Shortfall in either part would lead to a sub-optimal financial system. Viewed from a slightly different perspective, all countries have distinct business (corporate) cultures. The concept of efficient market is primarily based on Western business culture and standards. Structural reform programs in the present context imply the necessity of transforming the business culture of individual institutions within the system as well. When a particular country with a predominantly non-Western business culture attempts to introduce structural reforms, there is every possibility of an imbalance being created in the process.[2] If introduction of regulatory (and deregulatory) measures do not match initially with, internal structures and work cultures of individual organizations, it would be desirable that the differences are resolved sooner. If commonly accepted measures of differences in national and business cultures are considered[2], Indian situation when reform measures were initiated, was quite different from that in the US, Western Europe, Australia or New Zealand. Thus with introduction of market reforms, institutional imbalance was expected in different sectors at least initially. Such imbalances, if persists, may result in inefficiencies if not a crisis in the financial system.

The process of economic reforms gained momentum in different economies since early 1980s. The world economy had seen at least four serious financial crisis affecting the less developed world since then viz. Mexican crisis (1994), South-East Asian and subsequent Japanese crisis (1997), Russian crisis and Brazilian crisis (1998). In all of these events, the role of the imbalance created in the process of introducing reform measures was apparent (*Motamen-Samadian*, 2000).

An analysis of the Asian crisis provides a good example. Indonesia is one of the worst affected economies of the crisis. It had achieved tremendous economic growth over the three decades prior to the crisis of late 1990s. However, it had a weak and politically controlled central bank (*Harvie*, 2000). To maintain financial health of a country a strong central bank in terms of supervision and regulation is essential. Bank Indonesia reportedly failed to enforce rules that could keep borrowers and lenders healthy. As a result, non-performing loans of the state owned banks expanded very rapidly.[3] At the same time, a number of insolvent institutions were permitted to continue operations with subsidies. The central bank failed to monitor the build-up of high corporate debt as well.[4] At the same time, financial derivatives facilitated efforts by some entities in raising their risk-to-capital ratios, dodging regulatory safeguards, manipulating accounting rules and evading taxation (*Dodd*, 2000). The severe financial and economic crisis followed and the country is yet to recover from the downturn.

Japan is another example which demonstrated that such imbalances can create serious financial and economic disorders even at a very mature stage of growth. The Japanese economy is the world's second largest.[5] After experiencing very high and satisfactory economic growth for decades, stagnation started in early 1990s and downfall since late 1990s. Structural inefficiencies and non-performing loans are identified by researchers as major problems for the Japanese economy (DFAT Online). The failure to clear bad loans is still preventing the financial sector from supporting new economic initiatives through lending and prolonging oversupply problems. Structural reform programmes initiated by the Japanese government include measures such as market restructuring, revision of banking regulations, reduction of restrictions on access to the banking sector and measures to encourage cross-border business by reducing barriers to foreign direct investment.

III. FINANCIAL SECTOR REFORMS IN INDIA

While financial sector reforms are generally associated with the Narsimham Committee Report (*RBI*, 1992) that charted a road map for reforms of the banking sector, the capital market reforms were initiated from mid-1980s.[6] Over the past decade series of reform measures have been introduced that have significant impact on workings of stock exchanges, commercial banks, development financial institutions, mutual funds, insurance companies and non-bank finance companies. The technological changes in computing and communications technology have facilitated upsurge of competitive forces unleashed by entry of new, private players, removal of different price and non-price controls and creation of a regulatory structure.

Several participants in the financial system have responded by product diversification and entering new business segments. Non-banks entered banking operations while banks entered in insurance, mutual funds and stock broking. Simultaneous reforms in trade and foreign exchange markets have facilitated opening of financial system to foreign capital, foreign participants and their business practices. The reform process began with stock exchanges and then spread to banks, mutual funds, NBFCs and of late insurance companies. However, the spread of reforms has been rather uneven. For example, while co-operative banks and NBFCs have remain largely unaffected, the state level institutions which performed a significant role in funding of small and medium enterprises are yet to adjust to the effects of competition. While the reforms in those sectors where participants are comparatively bigger and therefore visible remain at the center of public discussion, the weaker links in the financial system become apparent in different irregularities (scam) in the financial system in recent years. A snapshot of different segments of financial system with certain characteristic features in terms of ownership, competition and regulatory process is presented in Annexure.

Capital Markets Reforms

Though reforms in capital markets commenced in mid-1980s, these were confined initially to equity market. Since 1990s these have gained momentum and gradually covered debt markets. The capital market reforms present a case where a judicious combination of competition, deregulation and regulation has led to sustained reforms and increased efficiency.

Traditionally, stock exchanges were governed by brokers leading to conflict of interest situation between the interest of common investors and those of brokers/owners of stock exchanges. With the establishment of National Stock Exchange, a new institutional structure was introduced that could ensure smooth functioning of market through a combination of new technology and efficient market design. The Securities Exchange Board of India (SEBI) was set-up as a market regulator with statutory powers to control and supervise operations of all participants in the capital market viz. stock exchanges, stock brokers, mutual funds and rating agencies. The development of debt market is another significant development, which has been facilitated by deregulation of administered interest rates. Opening of stock exchange trading to Foreign Institutional Investors (FIIs) and permission of raising funds from international market through equity linked instruments have introduced a degree of competition to domestic exchanges and other market participants. Operations of FIIs have facilitated introduction of best practices and research inputs in trading and risk management systems.

Such institutional-organizational changes have resulted in significant and visible improvements in working of the capital market. The reforms period has also coincided with crisis situation arising from boom/burst cycles in prices and other irregularities among the operators in the financial system. Initially such crisis situations were linked to market design and settlement processes. In subsequent years the causes were related to ill-functioning of financial institutions (mutual funds, stock broking firms, commercial banks, etc.).

BANKING SECTOR REFORMS

In contrast to the reforms in capital market, banking sector reforms are dominated mainly by deregulation, decontrol and increasing competition. This was partly because banks were subjected to elaborate micro-regulation, and the institutional changes were limited by dominance of government ownership.

Banks are now free to set most of deposits/lending rates. The rates could defer across client categories depending upon risk associated or volume.[7] While commercial banks were regulated elaborately in the pre-reform period, the focus of regulation has now changed to prudential regulations. Banks are now subjected to uniform accounting standards, provisioning requirements, asset classification and capital requirements. Subject to such prudential regulations banks are left free to decide about micro-decisions of credit assessment and disbursement. An element of competition was introduced with permission to set-up new banks in the private sector. Such new private banks could start using new technologies from a clean state and compete with existing established banks. These banks have carved out a niche for themselves and have been instrumental in forcing other banks to adopt modern technology, offer wider product range and adopt a customer centric approach. However, the ownership, organization and internal work process of government owned banks and other financial institutions have largely remained unchanged so far. There has not been much change in systems of nomination of directors on bank boards, appointment of chief executives and other senior managerial professionals. Similarly, in the area of credit policy, banks are now required to adopt an independent professional approach based on risk appetite and existing industrial and commercial outlook. Such a transformation will require major changes in human resource policies followed by the commercial banks. A more professional and flexible performance-based set of policies need to be introduced. This requires significant departure from existing policies and practices followed by the public sector banks.

Reforms in Non-bank Financial Institutions

This sector consists of Development Financial Institutions (DFIs)[8] largely owned by government and small firms in private sector providing specialized financial services.[9] Deregulation of interest rates and phasing out of low cost funding support from the government made the traditional model of DFIs unsustainable. As interest rates are now market determined, long-term lending rates are higher than short-term rates and banks have natural advantage in offering loans at lower rates as these have access to low cost retail deposits. The relative disadvantage of DFIs in offering loans at competitive rates coupled with industrial slow down has resulted in higher non-performing loans and lower volumes of fresh business. In such a situation, DFIs need to redefine their roles and reposition themselves in the competitive financial system. This process, however, is subject to government policies, as the government owns most of these institutions. Except for ICICI, which entered the area of commercial banking, other DFIs are yet to be restructured. While the problems of all-India institutions are publicly discussed those of state level institutions, which are no less serious often, go unnoticed.

NBFCs, mostly the private sector, are operating in diverse areas. Here the problem appears to be lack of effective regulation. As noticed in several instances, regulatory failures to control the activities of errant NBFCs had resulted in depositors' being taken for a ride. They have recently been brought under prudential regulations.

Mutual Funds Reforms

Mutual funds market has recently witnessed entry of several private players. With the public sector Unit Trust of India facing serious problems on more than one occasion, private sector players have increased their market share. Mutual fund activities are regulated by SEBI and improvements in the working of the capital market as a whole have helped in brining higher competition in mutual funds sector as well.

Insurance Reforms

Insurance sector was perhaps the last sector to be impacted by deregulation and competition. Although the public sector operators in life insurance and general insurance segments are still dominant, new private sector players should improve their market shares in the near future. As the market becomes more competitive problems could crop up if the public sector participants are unable to respond to the challenges of competition.

IV. GAPS IN REFORMS PROCESS

Along with stock markets, financial institutions also play an important role in allocation of capital. This is done by collecting and analysing information on client performances. It becomes more relevant for large unlisted clients. The essence of financial intermediation is to match the different risk profiles preferred by savers and investors. Savers may be comfortable with short maturing instruments while loan borrowers may need long maturing loans. Financial intermediaries manage such mismatches by maintaining them at reasonable levels. The need for proper supervision and regulation of financial system arises mainly from the importance of maintaining stability. Measures such as deposit insurance are primarily aimed as confidence building measure so that depositors are not unduly worried about safety of their deposits. Government ownership of financial institutions also provides such safety. In times of crisis, mere announcement that government or monetary authority would provide financial/ liquidity support to a troubled institution is sufficient in most of the cases to restore investor confidence.

Equally important are the processes of project identification and evaluation. These processes are beset with problem of information asymmetry and the institutions need to choose between different risky projects. Certainly there is a clear trade-off between risk and return. Each lending institution would need to decide its business strategy by formulating its risk preferences and ways to diversify them.

Financial institutions have internal rules about acceptability of different projects. Managers of the institutions assess viability of individual projects after taking into consideration of different types of risks. The process of project selection would be most efficient and optimal if objectives of the managers are aligned with interests of the owners. Otherwise, agency problems arise and the institutions may end up with a sub-optimal situation—either with disproportionately higher very risky projects or with predominantly low risk low earning projects.

The risk-taking behaviour of the managers of a financial institution is a function of its institutional policies on acceptable risk profile and human resource policies on performance management and incentives schemes. Only those institutions that are well equipped to handle risk assessment and mitigation can compete efficiently in the market.

In India, the government owns most of the financial institutions. The government decides most of the important aspects of human resource policies in these public sector institutions and, they are not performance-oriented. As compared to pre-reform period, the financial institutions in India now work within a more competitive environment with much higher risk. With liberalization of interest rates and foreign exchange rates market price risks have become more relevant. Moreover, as Indian industries now face a more open and competitive business environment, credit risks faced by the financers have only gone up. In such a scenario internal systems of banks should be more risk sensitive while at the same time flexible enough to be appropriate for a competitive business environment. This would require quite a bit of overhaul of human resource practices followed by the public sector institutions. Unless financial sector reforms start addressing these aspects the spread of next stage of reforms would remain limited. In absence of such reforms public sector institutions may remain unable to compete effectively and would loose market share in the process.

V. CONCLUSIONS

Indian financial sector reforms have led to increased competition and, inevitably, enhanced business risk. The risk assessment, monitoring and control systems become therefore more important. External measures such as prudential and regulatory changes provide a trigger. But internal measures such as complementary organizational and institutional changes are also equally important. An uneven process of external and internal reforms creates an imbalance within the system and that may lead to a financial crisis. There are several global examples in this regard. The financial sector reforms in India so far have been more successful in improving working of financial markets while the success has been limited as regards improvements in internal working of participating institutions. Bulk of major institutions such as banks, insurance companies and development financial institutions, are owned by the government. The question of organisational reforms in these segments thus is linked to the nature of government control, operational autonomy enjoyed by such organisations and human resource policies in the public sector. In order to improve the efficiency of the financial system the reform measures should impact the internal decision-making processes and governance standards within such institutions in addition to improve the efficiency of external working standards. Due to organizational limitations the large majority of the financial institutions are still not in a position to respond effectively to the risk sensitive competitive environment although they are being forced to operate within it. If left unattended, this may pose a serious threat to financial stability and economic growth, as it happened in several other less developed economies in the past.

NOTES AND REFERENCES

1. See Zysman (1983), which analyses financial systems in USA, Japan, Germany and France and its effect on respective industrial sectors.
2. Such as Hofstede's dimensions of national culture (*Hofstede*, 1994) and Fletcher and Bohn's index of psychic distance ratings (*Fletcher & Bohn*, 1998).
3. During 1992-97 bad debts in Indonesia increased by an average of 32% per annum (*Harvie*, 2000, pp. 110).
4. By the end of 1997 Indonesia's total private sector debt stood at US$ 74 billion with average tenure of 18 months for most of the loans. Indonesia's value of total exports in 1997-98 was about US$ 56.2 billion (*Harvie*, 2000, pp. 109).
5. In 2001, its economy accounted for around 15 per cent of world GDP and over 60 per cent of East Asian GDP (DFAT Online).
6. G.S. Patel Committee (1988) presented agenda for reforms of stock exchanges while R.N. Malhotra Committee (1992) unveiled insurance sector reform agenda.
7. The proportion of funds that can be deployed by banks at their discretion has substantially increased from 47% in pre-reform era of their deposits to 71% at present. However, most of the commercial banks continue to hold large proportion of their portfolio in the form of Government securities that are far in excess of statutory requirements. It is a result of their risk return preferences rather than a regulatory requirement.
8. DFIs used to provide term loans to industrial concerns often at administratively kept low rates. The category includes large institutions operating at all-India level and smaller one operating at state levels. These institutions are fully/partly owned by central/state governments. Irrespective of proportion of ownership, government has the right to appoint board of directors and chief executives.
9. They provide services like higher purchase, leasing, stock broking, etc. The number of such firms is quite large.

REFERENCES

Alexander, Kern (2001), 'The need for efficient international financial regulation and the role of a global supervisor', *Journal of Money Laundering Control*, London, Vol. 5, Issue 1, pp. 52-65.

Andrews, Peter and David Lynch (1994), *Financial Markets*, Oxford University Press, Melbourne

Dodd, Randall (2001), 'The role of derivatives in the East Asian financial crisis', *Financiar, Philadelphia*, Vol. 7, Issue 1-4, pp. 28-44.

Fletcher, Richard and Jenifer Bohn (1998), 'The impact of psychic distance on the internationalisation of the Australian firm', *Journal of Global Marketing*, NY, Vol. 12, Issue 2, pp. 47-68.

Government of India (1998), *Report of the Committee on Banking Sector Reforms.*

Harris John, Hunter Janet and Lewis Colin M. (Eds.) (1995), *The New Institutional Economics and Third World Development*, Routledge, London.

Harvie, Charles (2000), 'Financial Crisis in Indonesia: the role of good governance', in Tran Van Hoa and Charles Harvie (ed.), *The causes and impact of the Asian financial crisis*, Macmillan, UK.

Hofstede, G. (1994), *Cultures and organisations: International cooperation and its importance for survival*, McGraw-Hill, UK.

Motamen-Samadin, Sima and Celso Garrido (ed.) (2000), *Emerging Markets: Past and present experiences, and future prospects*, Macmillan Press Ltd., London.

Rao, Bhanoji (2001), *East Asian Economies*, McGraw Hill, Singapore.

Reserve Bank of India, *Report on Trend and Progress of Banks in India*, various issues.

Williamson Oliver E. and Winter Sidney G. (Eds.) (1993), *The Nature of the Firm Origins, Evolution and Development*, Oxford University Press, New York.

Williamson Oliver E. (1975), *Markets and Hierarchies: Analysis and Antitrust Implications*, Free Press, New York.

Zysman, John S. (1983), *Governments, Markets and Growth: Financial System and Politics of Industrial Change*, Cornell University Press.

ANNEXURE

Structure of the Indian Financial System

	Assets/Market Capital (Rs. crore) (end-March 2002)	*Characteristic features/Impact of reforms*
Stock Exchanges (Market Cap of equity and Debt securities on NSE)	13,93,655 (37.3%)	Free pricing of public issues. Setting up of SEBI to regulate all market participants. Establishment of professionally managed, National Stock Exchange leading to modernisation of all stock exchanges; Introduction of screen-based, paper less trading and settlement system
Scheduled Commercial Banks (Total Assets)	15,35,513 (41.1%)	Reduction of level of preemptions through SLR, CRR. Freeing of interest lending and deposit rates. Entry of new banks. Regulatory and prudential structure created. Reduction in government ownership through public issues of government owned banks. Infusion of additional capital by Government to weaker banks Limited moves towards reorganisation through Mergers and Acquisitions. Banks enter in term lending, MF, stock broking and merchant banking
All India DFIs (Total Assets)	1,75,520 (4.7%)	Deregulation of lending rates. End to concessional funding, Corporatisation of and reduction in government holding, level playing field with commercial banks in fund raising and competition with commercial banks in lending activities.
State level DFIs (Estimated)	30,000 (0.8%)	Owned by State governments, end to concessional funding, no focused measures for reorganisation or recapitalisation

Co-operative Banks (Deposits with Urban, State and Dist. Co-op banks)	1,93,898 (5.2%)	In the private sector. Dual control by RBI and Cooperatives department of respective state governments; obvious links with politicians
Mutual Funds (Assets under Management)	1,00,594 (2.7%)	End of monopoly of public sector Unit Trust of India (UTI) as private MFs enter the scene. Regulatory framework created. Private sector MFs account for 41% of AUM.
Insurance Companies	2,54,583 (6.8%)	Private entry allowed. Regulatory authority set-up. Government owned institutions still dominate.
NBFCs	53,878 (1.4%)	Supervisory and regulatory set-up strengthened. Predominantly private owned
Total	37,37,641 (100.0%)	

Formal Financial Institutions and Rural Credit Provisioning in India:
A Micro-economic Model of Default Mitigation

ASHUTOSH KUMAR

The rural sector is still the largest employer in Indian economy with more than two-third of the population depending on agriculture, while the contribution of agriculture and allied services to national GDP is around 25% (1999-2000). These facts underline the importance of the rural economy in India. Despite having enough room for development in the rural sector, it has been largely ignored in the recent years of economic growth. I would like to discuss in this paper one particular aspect of the rural economy and institutions, rural credit, in the context of present day financial reforms. My objective in this paper is to analyze some approaches for rural credit institutions, which primarily aim to reduce default and thus increase the viability of credit, for extending credit delivery in an efficient manner. The issues addressed here are quite specific, in the definitional sense (deliberately so). I categorize defaults into two main types:

*Acknowledgement: I would like to thank Mr. Chandra Kiran, B.K., Research Scholar, IGIDR, for his great help and support in writing the paper.

- That owed by those who are willing to pay, but are unable to (rather, those who are unable to pay, irrespective of their willingness).
- That owed by those who are able but unwilling to pay, either due to:

  (1) Inappropriate monitoring/supervision
  (2) Attitudinal problems.

I am deliberately omitting an analysis of type I defaulters, since the problem and their solutions, are outside the domain of what, I consider, purely economic analysis, since the solutions require many policy prescriptions, all of which are subject to value judgment.

RURAL FINANCIAL INSTITUTIONS AND CHARACTERISTICS OF RURAL CREDIT

Rural credit is significantly different from other categories of credit. The basic characteristics of rural credit are uncertainty in production and high transaction costs, which often lead to a high rate of delinquencies. Uncertainty in production, however, (being a prime reason for differential treatment of rural credit) cannot be overcome by economic and policy measures by Rural Financial Institutions (RFIs). Though insurance and other similar approaches could be put forward to address this concern, the importance of this factor does not diminish. It is important to note that the rural sector, in addition to agriculture as its main occupation, is also composed of non-farm occupations that are as vulnerable as agriculture to same shocks. The existence of these uncertainties in the rural sector decreases the viability of institutional credit operations and makes it more risky, which in turn can explain some of the reasons for the lack of interest in rural credit by some credit providing institutions (e.g. Commercial Banks).

The high default rate in rural credit is one of the factors primarily responsible for this lack of interest. High default rate (ranging from 30 to 95%) is observed (*Braverman & Guasch*, 1989) in the studies around developing world (with exception of East Asia). For RFIs to be self-sustainable and rural credit, *more* viable, one has to look for ways to reduce the default rate as well as increase the credit base, in consonance with the process of financial reform.

Growth Rates of Rural Population, Rural Bank Offices, Rural and Agricultural Credit for Scheduled Commercial Banks, India, 1973 to 1999 (in percent per annum)

Period	*Rural population*	*Rural bank offices*	*Credit from rural offices*	*Rural + semi-urban branches*	*Credit from rural + semi-urban branches*	*Credit to agriculture*
1973-81	1.78	15.54	23.46	12.32	16.72	18.76
1981-91	1.84	7.15	9.97	5.95	7.91	6.64
1991-99	1.66	–0.86	2.51	0.13	2.88	2.16

Source: Chavan (2001) cited in Ramchandran & Swaminathan, 2001.

Given the pace of the financial reform process, and the pressure there from on the banks to be competitive and productive, rural financial institutions must explore some new approaches consistent with the changing scenario, such as:

- Group lending
- Saving mobilization
- Enhanced supervision
- Support service facilitation.

The successful experiment of lending through Self Help Groups (SHGs) is an example of group lending (and of saving mobilization as well), NABARD being the flag bearer in India of the SHG movements. The following information indicates the effectiveness of bank lending through its linkages with SHGs. (*Seibal*, 2001)

364,000 SHGs established as autonomous financial intermediaries,
5.8 million SHG members,
30 million rural poor covered as household members,
194,000 SHGs credit linked to banks,
380 banks and 8000 bank branches involved as bank partners,
Non-performing bank loans to SHGs: 0%

750 NGOs and many GOs involved as social mobilisers and facilitators.

It is interesting to see an impressive 0% default rate, even when there is no interest rate restriction. The profitability of financial institutions is high also due to the fact that there is low transaction cost for the lender (and also for borrower).

The latter two approaches viz. Enhanced supervision and Support service facilitation are mainly concerned with ensuring efficient utilization of credit given and decreased intentional default in repayment. In this context it would be worthwhile to have a look at the results of a comprehensive survey, one of the few of its kind, undertaken by Central Bank of Ceylon in Sri Lanka.

The Sri Lankan Experience and the Reasons for Default

This survey was undertaken in 1971 for inquiring into the reasons for default in agricultural loans disbursed during 1967 to 1970 (*Padmanabhan*, 1988, *Sanderatne*, 1974). Though I am quoting the quantitative result of the survey, my emphasis is more on the identification of the potential reasons for default among borrowers; the significance of various reasons might well be different in the Indian case.

Category of default	*% of loans*
Defects in farm production	17
Variability in incomes	33
Defects in credit organization	12
Attitudinal conditions	18
Misallocation	15
Miscellaneous	5

The first two reasons for default viz. defects in farm production and variability of incomes are cases where the farmers are willing to pay but are unable to, due to either poor production condition or to some external shock (seasonal or market fluctuations, etc.). These are the same as the uncertainty factor discussed in the earlier section. The lending institution has little or no control over these factors. Misallocation of the credit by the borrower to some other uses, which is illiquid or unproductive, is another reason of default. In World Bank categorization it is termed as failure of farmers to use borrowed fund for production.

Whereas the third reason for default is purely institutional, occurring due to poor supervision and lack of interest on the part of the employees of the institution in recovery efforts. In the result of the above survey, the reason attributed by the borrowers was that the officers did not particularly insist on repayment of the loan and were indifferent to loan recovery. In Indian studies too (*Kher & Jha*, 1979), lack of proper supervision and follow-up was found and regular check and supervision was suggested for proper utilization of credit. Therefore, it is reasonable to assume that enhanced monitoring and supervision may completely convert this proportion of default into recovery. Regarding the fourth reason, that is, unwillingness of the borrowers to repay their loans, one can infer that this type of default can be converted into repayment, at least up to some extent by providing proper incentive to farmers to repay. The requirement of incentives can also be understood with the help of "triadic interaction" argument (*Basu*, 1994). In this regard one approach would be that banks or RFIs should work as support service facilitators to the rural people (*Dhawan & Kalhan*, 1997 also see *Padmanabhan*, 1988, p. 115). Here the basic argument is that the borrower would like to reap the benefit of the support services available with the institution, and in this way find an incentive to repay. The quantum of cost incurred to provide such services can be decided on the basis of probable conversion of default into recovery. The nature of support services may be providing technical know-how, marketing facilities and information thereof, warehousing facility, access to cheaper inputs, etc.

The model

In the framework of the model we have basic assumptions taken from previous analysis:

1. The proportion of default with the reason as defects in the credit providing institution could be completely converted into repayment by employing more efforts on supervision and monitoring. This additional effort will, it is surmised, increase cost, which will in turn increase the cost of funds for the lender institution. The

relationship between the additional cost incurred and conversion of default into repayment is taken to be monotonically non-decreasing and concave* in nature and institutions try to convert the maximum possible of this category of default into repayment.

2. A proportion of default due to reasons of attitudinal condition can be converted into repayment by providing incentive in terms of support service facilitation. However, it is again reasonable to assume that the relationship between the cost incurred due to providing support service facilitation and recovery generated there from (conversion) is, as in the previous case, monotonically non-decreasing and concave.

Assume a Rural Financial Institution seeks to recover the default due to lack of supervision.

Let,

Amount of credit lent : C
Rate of interest charged to borrower by lender : r
Cost of fund (rate at which the lender institution get the fund + Transaction cost per unit of credit to the lender institution) : P
Total time of repayment (years) : T
Rate of default (as % of amount of credit delivered) : q
Percentage of total default due to institutional defect : α^0
Cost of additional supervision to decrease the default rate by α., where $\alpha \in [0, \alpha^0]$: ω
(α is proportion by which default is reduced and new default rate will be $(1 - \alpha)$ q.)

$$\frac{\partial \alpha}{\partial \omega} \geq 0 \; ; \; \frac{\partial \alpha^2}{\partial \omega^2} \leq 0$$

*The monotonic non-decreasing function implies that (*Chiang*, 1984):

If $x_1 > x_2 \Rightarrow f(x_1) \geq f(x_2)$

In above context it explains that any increase in cost due to enhanced supervision will, at least, result in same level of recovery. The concavity of the function explains the *diminishing marginal recovery with additional supervision cost.*

Gain/loss to institution (after additional supervision) : Π

Now consider the usual case with less supervision

Expected return to lender (institution)* : $(1+r)^T C$
Realized return to lender ** : $(1+r)^T (1-q)C$
Cost of fund lent : $(1+p)^T C$
Gain (loss) to lender (institution) : $[(1-q)(1+r)^T - (1+p)^T]C$ ... (1)

Now consider another case where institution is willing to convert the default, occurring due to institutional defect, into repayment and therefore increases the supervision, incurring an additional cost ω.

Cost of fund lent (with enhanced supervision) : $(1+p+\omega)^T C$
The new rate of default : $(1-\alpha)q$
The realized return in this case will be : $(1-(1-\alpha)q)(1+r)^T C$
New gain/loss to lender (institution)

$$[(1-(1-\alpha)q)(1+r)^T - (1+p+\omega)^T]C \qquad \text{... (2)}$$

Gain to institution (from additional supervision) (subtracting 2 from 1)

$$\Pi = [(1-(1-\alpha)q)(1+r)^T - (1+p+\omega)^T - (1-q)(1+r)^T + (1+p)^T C$$

$$= [(1-q)(1+r)^T + \alpha q (1+r)^T - (1+p+\omega)^T - (1-q)(1+r)^T + (1+p)^T C$$

$$= [(1+p)^T + \alpha q (1+r)^T - (1+p+\omega)^T] C \qquad \text{... (3)}$$

Let, the institution tries to maximize its "gain" with respect to the additional cost ω. The maximization exercise would be:

$$\frac{\partial \Pi}{\partial \omega} = \frac{\partial \alpha}{\partial \omega^2} q [(1+r)^T] C - T(1+p+\omega)^{T-1} C$$

we should recall our assumption which says a is monotonically non-decreasing and concave function of ω, i.e. $\partial\alpha/\partial\omega \geq 0$; and $\partial^2\alpha/\partial\alpha^2 \leq 0$.

+Also, to avoid complexity in analysis, we are assuming the future value of the credit after T period as the amount to be repaid. We are indifferent to the structure of repayment within the time period T.
**It is assumed that the institutions recover the non-defaulted portion of the credit during the stipulated time period T. Thus it gets full return on (1–q) C, which is $(1+r)^T (1-q)$ C.

Using the first order condition of maximization exercise w.r.t. ω, we get

$$T\,(1+p+\omega)^{T-1} = \frac{\partial\alpha}{\partial\omega}\, q\,(1+r)^{T}$$

$$\omega = \left[\frac{\dfrac{\partial\alpha}{\partial\omega}\, q\,(1-r)^{T}}{T}\right]^{\frac{1}{(T-1)}} \qquad \text{.... (4)}$$

But for the institution to undertake the additional supervisory effort, gain obtained there from should be non-negative.

i.e. $\Pi \geq 0$;

from (3) this will be:

$[(1+p)^{T} + \alpha q\,(1+r)^{T} - (1+p+\omega)^{T}]\,C \geq 0$

substituting the value of ω in above from (4), we get:

$$[(1+p)^{T} + \alpha q\,(1+r)^{T}\,] \geq \left[\frac{\dfrac{\partial\alpha}{\partial\omega}\, q\,(1-r)^{T}}{T}\right]^{\frac{1}{(T-1)}}$$

$$\Rightarrow T\,[T[(1+p)^{T} + \alpha q\,(1+r)^{T}\,]]^{(T-1)} \geq \left.\frac{\partial\omega}{\partial\omega}\, q\,(1+r)^{T}\right]^{T} \qquad \text{... (5)}$$

Also,

$$\frac{\partial^2\Pi}{\partial\omega^2} = \frac{\partial^2\alpha}{\partial\omega^2}\, q\,(1+r)^{T}C - T\,(T-1)[1+p+\omega]^{T-2}C$$

this satisfies the sufficient condition for maximization.

Apart from the usual interpretations, the above results could also be explained as follows (for the credit delivery institution). Expression (5) gives primary condition for an institution to go for enhanced supervision, failing which it would not be possible to gain from this approach. In case the condition (5) is satisfied, expression (4) gives the optimum level of the supervision cost to be incurred for maximum gain to the institution.

Now assuming

Percentage of total default due to attitudinal condition : β^0

Cost of additional supervision to decrease the default rate by β, where $\beta \in [0, \beta^0]$: η

$$\frac{\partial \beta}{\partial \eta} \geq 0; \quad \frac{\partial^2 \beta}{\partial \eta^2} \leq 0$$

we can get similar expression as (4) for η as:

$$\eta = \left[\frac{\frac{\partial \beta}{\partial \eta} q\,(1+r)^T}{T} \right]^{\frac{1}{(T-1)}} - (1-p)$$

and the condition as

$$\Rightarrow T\,[T[(1+p)^T + \beta q\,(1+r)^T]]^{(T-1)} \geq \left. \frac{\partial \beta}{\partial \eta} q\,(1+r)^T \right]^T \qquad \ldots (5)$$

It is to be borne in mind that the additional cost, ω, may be considered as the cost of providing what the banks already ought to have (in the first place). These costs may, thus, not to be considered *new*, rather, they are merely those components that have not been provided (probably) due to lack of information regarding the nature of the task being undertaken by the commercial financial institutions in the rural areas.

If even after provisioning for these costs, the banks do not improve their profitability, it would indicate that they either have inefficient operations given their present institutional set-up, or their portfolio of loan is not ideal (with a major proportion of lending going to that section not willing to repay their loans; this is because, other than those who do not pay due to the lack of supervision, the major category would be of those who are deliberate defaulters) or indeed a combination of both. In such a scenario banks may undertake institutional restructuring so as to enable them to reduce cost and yet be profitable.

I would like to conclude by pointing out that the present scenario of rural finance in India calls for innovative solutions, not merely working by rote, to ensure that credit is not denied those in dire need of it merely due to the inefficiency of the delivering institutions.

REFERENCES

Basu, K. (1994), "Rural Credit & Interlinkages; Implication for Rural Poverty, Agrarian Efficiency and Public Policy", Development Economics Research Programme, London School of Economics, London UK.

Braverman, A. and Guasch, J.L. (1989), "Rural Credit in Developing Countries," Working paper, Agriculture and Rural Development Department, World Bank.

Chiang, A.C. (1984), *Fundamental Methods of Mathematical Economics*, 3rd Ed. McGraw Hill Book Company, Singapore, p. 172.

Dhawan, K.C. and Kalhan, A.S. (1978), "Adequacy and Productivity of Credit on Small Farm in Panjab," *Indian Journal of Agricultural Economics*, cited in *Institutional Finance for Rural Development*, Veerashekharappa, (1997), Rawat Publication, New Delhi, p. 46.

Kher & Jha (1979), "Credit Utilization Pattern in Respect of PACS," *Indian Cooperative Review*, cited in "Institutional Finance for Rural Development" by Veerashekharappa (1997), Rawat Publication, N. Delhi, p. 49.

Padmanabhan K.P. (1988), *Rural Credit*, Intermediate Technology Publications Ltd., London, UK, p. 75, p. 115.

Ramchandran, V.K. and Swaminathan, M. (2001), "Does Informal Credit Provides Security? Rural Banking Policy in India," International Labour Office (ILO).

Sanderatne, N. (1974), "Analytical Approach to Loan Default by Small Farmer", *Savings and Development*, Vol. 2, No. 4, pp. 290-304.

Seibal, H.D. (2001), SHG Banking: A Financial Technology for Reaching Marginal Areas and Very Poor", Working paper, International Fund for Agricultural Development (IFAD), Rome.

Yaron, J., Benjamin, M.P. and Piprek, G.L. (1977), "Rural Finance; Issues, Design, and Best Practices," The World Bank, Washington, D.C.

Address by Dr. Y.V. Reddy, (2001), Deputy Governor, Reserve Bank of India at Conference of Indian Society of Agriculture Marketing at Vizag on Feb. 3.

International Financial Institutions, European Central Bank and the International Monetary System

DEBESH BHOWMIK

OBJECTIVE

The paper, firstly, emphasizes on the role of conceptual issues of institutions and secondly, it evolves a debate whether the reform of IMF is necessary or a new international financial institution is required to stabilize the international monetary system in the emergence of regional institutions like European Central Bank (ECB).

CONCEPTUAL ISSUES

Institutions not only affect the economic prospects of nations but are also central to the distribution of income among individuals and groups in society. It is true that the fundamental causes of differences in prosperity between countries are geography and institutions. So institutional reform is the first step towards significant progress in rapid growth in many areas of the world (*Doran Acemoglu*, 2003).

The role of institutions in economic development during the last twenty years in the domain of New Institutional Economics, has attracted a lot of attention in the development policy debates in which the analysis of institution is not some optional extra but is essential in underlying the workings of the market economy where the following regulations are of very much important, such as,

1. What can be traded
2. Who can trade
3. What constitute fair trading
4. How much price can vary

D.C. North (1990, 1997) explained that institutions are the rules of the game in a society. That institutions affect economic performance is hardly controversial. That the differential performance of economies overtime is fundamentally influenced by the way of institutions evolve is also not controversial. He argued that the institutional and organisational structure of a country is the primary source of economic growth and development. Experience clearly indicates that efficient institutions reduce uncertainty and transport cost, affect the performance of the economy by their effects on the costs of exchange and production, promote economic growth and welfare. The existence of efficient political market is necessary to create efficient economic institutions minimising informal constraints which require the stability of the consequent political-economic system. Relatively efficient institutions have strong effects on gains from trade. But the stability is not the sufficient condition for efficiency. The institutional economists put institutions at the center of their analysis in economic development, structural change and the process of policy reform. So, the institutional framework of market economies has to be adjusted with cost associated with the changes in environment, individual perception and technological change.

There are rule setting or rule making institutions such as WTO or IMF and there are also development-oriented institutions such as UNDP or UNICEF. There is a distinction between treaty-based inter-governmental organisations which constitute the United Nations System and informal consultative groups of countries within or even outside the United Nations System. Again, there is a distinction between inter-governmental organisation and non-governmental or private sector institutions.

The evolutionary process of institutions are not completely random, rather, historical and comparative institutions are essential in understanding the evolution of institutions.

In the development experience, we can identify three types of institutions, namely,

Institutions of co-ordination and administration.
Institutions of learning and innovations.
Institutions of income redistribution and social cohesion.

For category one, we need to look at,

The constituent institutions that make up the market and the state.

Non-market, non-state institutions that perform the functions of co-ordination and administration.

The interrelationship between different types of institutions of co-ordinations.

The category two matters for the process of learning and innovations. It concerns the knowledge generating institutions, namely educational system, public research institutions, corporate R&D laboratories etc. The types are,

Property rights.
Institutions for human resource development.
Financial institutions.
Rules of competition.

Financial institutions are critical for mobilising and allocating resources needed for productivity growth in general but especially for innovations, which often involves large scale investments and a long gestation period. Legal framework is needed for widening up national as well as international financial institutions.

INSTITUTIONS AND DEVELOPMENT

Dani Rodrik, A. Subramanian, Francesco Trebbi (2002)

explained that if the extent of integration and quality of institutions are endogenous and geography is exogenous, then we should rethink that these variables determine the economic growth. In diagram 1, it explains that geography influences directly on income affecting agricultural productivity and morbidity (1). It has also indirect effect through its impact on distance from markets and the extent of integration (2), or its impact on quality of domestic institutions (3). The direct impact on integration on income and the indirect impact through institutions are shown by (4) and (5) while (6) and (7) are reverse feedback from income and institutions. Institutional environment are an independent determinant of income (8) and are not simply the consequence of higher income (9) or of greater integration (5).

Diagram 1

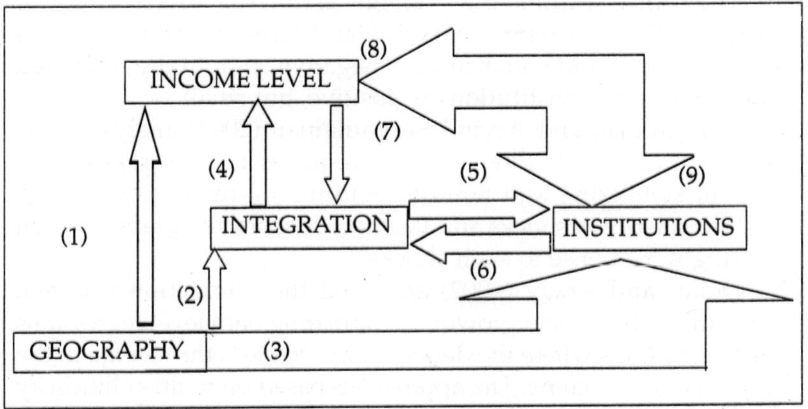

There is a causal effect from trade and institutions to income. If institutions are controlled, then integration has no direct effect on income, while geography has at best weak direct effects. Institutional quality has a positive and significant effect on integration that also has a (positive) impact on institutional quality.

Therefore, they estimated the following equations:

$$\text{Log } Y_i = \mu + \alpha \text{ inst}_i + \gamma \text{ int}_i + \gamma \text{ geo}_i + \varepsilon_i$$

where Y_i = per capita income, $inst_i$ = institutions, int_i =

integration, geo_i= geography, ε_i = Error, α, β, γ, are co-efficients and positive, μ = constant,

$$inst_i = \lambda + \delta\, sm_i + \Phi\, const + \psi\, geo + \varepsilon_i \text{ , and}$$
$$int_i = \Phi + \sigma\, const + \in\, sm_i + \omega\, geo + \varepsilon_i$$

where sm_i = Scattler mortality, const—trade/GDP and δ, Φ, ψ, σ, $\in$, and ω are co-efficients.

They verified that a unit increase in institutional quality increases the trade share by 0.77 units, while a unit increase in trade increases institutional quality by 0.23 units. Again, a unit (positive) shock to the institutional quality equation ultimately produces an increase in log incomes of 2.15, and a unit (positive) shock to the trade equation ultimately produces in increase in log incomes of 0.2.

They also studied that (1) the estimated direct effect of institutions on income is positive and large, (2) the estimated direct effect of trade on income is negative, and (3) the estimated effect of trade on institutions is positive, but small.

Dani Rodrik and Arvind Subramanian (2003) analysed that long-run economic development requires market regulating, market stabilizing and market legitimizing institutions which build resilience to shocks and facilitate socially acceptable burden sharing in response to such shocks.

Dollar and Kraay (2002) analysed the interaction between institutions, trade, and growth by estimating both level regressions and regressions where the dependent variable is the change in the growth rate of income. The approach is based on multi-collinearity between instrument for institutions and trade that militates against a proper discontangling of the two effects. The estimated coefficients on institution and trade are both insignificant which is allegedly a reflection of multi-collinearity.

BRETTON WOODS INSTITUTIONS AND INTERNATIONAL MONETARY SYSTEM

Bretton Woods Institution (IMF) introduced the Gold Exchange Standard Mechanism in International Monetary System to outstrip the Sterling domination as a Post-war reconstruction of world financial stability. Later on, by creating SDR, it could not solve the crux of the problem of international liquidity because SDR are less reliable and predictable resource in times of crisis but its desire of setting up a World Central Bank and circulating a international money clearly nipped in the bud. International Monetary System cracked down after the collapse of the Bretton Woods in 1973 due to suspension of gold dollar convertibility when the dollar hegemony was dethroned.

Hence the monetarist felt that whether the new institution would be created or the existing institutions should be reformed?

The Halifax Summit in 1995 indentified three key areas of action, e.g.

Enhancing transparency and accountability.
Strengthening national financial system.
Managing international financial crisis.

So, their proposals for reforms constitute:

Limiting capital account convertibility.
Introducing an international lender of last resort.
Proposal for reforming debt market institutions and debt market instruments.

On the other hand, Basle Committee on Banking Supervision Working Group agreed to set-up a large international financial institution. But they could not throw any light on the instability of world monetary system and the framework and functions of such institutions.

Joseph Stiglitz emphasised on the reform of existing institutions and he also analysed the issues of emerging need of new institutions.

But, the Chiang Mai Initiative in May 2001, proposed to set-up an Asian Monetary Fund to create Asian SDR as a reserve asset to meet up the liquidity crisis. This proposal could not clear whether AMF would be a substitute for IMF.

To make the IMF as the new international architecture, the following set of reforms are summarised below (*IMF Report*, 2002),

(1) To reduce external vulnerability of member countries, IMF developed in 2001,
   (a) Guidelines for public debt management

(b) Guidelines for foreign exchange reserve management

(2) In July 2001, IMF set-up
  (a) Special data dissemination standard
  (b) General data dissemination system

(3) IMF agreed to co-operate with Financial Stability Forum.

(4) It emphasised the Financial Sector Assessment Programme.

(5) It has undertaken 19 Offshore Financial Centers to gather information providing technical support at the end of April 2002.

(6) It strengthened capital account liberalisation programme.

(7) It laid down 4 point work programme to strengthen the framework for crisis management resolution.

(8) IMF takes steps to counter money laundering.

(9) IMF will evaluate its programme effectiveness.

(10) Following the crisis of the 90s, IMF developed early warning system in which it has focused on identifying potential indicators of vulnerability, finding the most way to synthesize the information from these indicators, and assessing their predictive performance. (*Abdul Abiad*, 2003)

(11) To improve the function of international lender of the last resort,
  (a) IMF, in 1997, introduced Supplemented Reserve Facility which made large short-run loan at penalty rate to countries in crises.
  (b) IMF executive board, in 1999, established the Contingent Credit Line Facility, preventing from contagion effects.
  (c) For strengthening macro-economic facility, the flexible exchange rate policy would be adopted at a quicker pace.

To consider the redefined role of IMF, it is important to note the following measures which are going to be implemented;

(i) Better international financial governance including restructuring of voting representation, transperancy and accountability are necessary.

(ii) Conditionality should be reformulated.

(iii) Review its position on macro-economics and liberalisation mechanism which facilitate consultation, consistency and surveillance. Countries must have freedom of choice of exchange rate regime. To improve institutional framework such as Financial Stability Forum that can regulate risk and instability.

(iv) Alternatively, World Financial Authority can be set-up, that can manage systematic risk associated with international financial liberalisation, co-ordinate national action against market failure or abuse, and act as a regulator in international financial markets (*WIDER*, 2002)

IMF INTERNATIONAL MONETARY SYSTEM AND ECB

Will the regional financial institutions be the supplier of international lender of last resort in comparison with IMF? Or, will these regional institutions be the complement or substitutes to the multilateral institutions to stabilize international monetary system and to solve the basic problem of international liquidity?

First of all, if we recall the evolutionary process of Bretton Woods Institutions, we will find that Keynes wanted his International Clearing Union to be an International Lender of Last Resort. In contrast to Keynes' Plan, White's Stabilisation Fund would not have the means to be an international lender of last resort. White's understanding was that International Monetary System should be based on dollar and its link to gold. He insisted on multilateralism on international finance in designing a multilateral institution. But after the collapse of the Bretton Woods, White's vision on the interest of US monetary dominance through gold convertible dollar was ended. Present IMF could not be the international lender of the last resort since it is neither a world central bank nor is an institution of issuing a gold convertible dollar as an international unit of account. "The IMF was smaller than the Keynes wanted and lacked an automatic mechanism for rising in line with the growth in world trade, it could not realistically fill the function of a lender of last resort, and the Fund would have to ration its scarce resources by imposing condition on their use." ($40 billion rescue packages!), (*J.M. Boughton*, 2002). Naturally, in the process of globalisation without a global currency, IMF inspite of being a international lender of last resort, seems to intensify the instability of international monetary system under the emergence of new regional financial institutions such as ECB. ECOWAS countries' Economic and Monetary Union and West African Monetary Zone, Asian Monetary Fund, etc. as effects of regional trading blocs with their regional currencies for increasing international trade. Morris Goldstein (2003) stated that the Fund loans under prequalification criteria generate serious moral hazard problems and the Fund does not lend to countries against collateral while the lender of the last resort should lend freely and the lending should be done on "good collateral".

Secondly, IMF will clearly irritate the international liquidity shortage because regional trading arrangements may be solved by regional currencies and the uses of SDR would be narrowed down and the inconvertible dollar would be supplemented by currencies introduced by the regional payments mechanism as the regional trading systems are supplemented by multilateral trading order.

Thirdly, the floating exchange rate mechanism along with capital account convertibility as advocated by IMF in the reform measures, may produce higher growth rate but enhance inequality in wealth and creates unequal trade flows with a non-monetary system dominated by unbacked dollar.

Presently, there has been a polarisation of monetary policy dominance in the world. A dollar bloc exists in Latin America and in Asia. Euro bloc has been forming in Europe as the monetary policy has been increasing overtime in Euro area. Japanese monetary policy has been little influence in Asia.

The introduction of Euro may be the most important event in the history of the international monetary system. It will profoundly affect the external relation of the USA and pose serious challenges to US and international community on both policy and institutional issues ranging from international money, exchange rate regimes, international finance, liquidity and capital flows. EMU will be the most far reaching transformation of the international monetary system in at least a generation (*Randall Henning*, 1998).

It is clear that Euro will provide the first real competitor for the US dollar to global currency dominance. Robert Mundel, C.F. Bergsten and many others believe that the Euro will move quickly to challenge the dollar. The developing countries are influenced by the rivalry between Euro and Dollar. Most influence may well turn out to be political rather than either trade or financial although the significant changes will occur in the choices of exchange rate regimes of the developing countries.

The reasons are many-fold. EU consists of 300 million people having 16% of world GDP which is 6% less than USA. The share of EU exports is 13% of world exports and the share of Euro area exports is 19% in comparison with 15% of USA and 9% of Japan. The exports/GDP of Euro is 35%. The Euro occupies 25% of worldwide money market activity and 35% of international bond and notes. Euro denominated debt securities stayed 15% lower than the 43% share of US dollar. The Euro official reserve accounts 13% in contrast with 68% of the US dollar. The share of international transactions of Euro stood 15-17% (www.ecb.net). The Euro has reduced the volatility of world commodity prices (*John, T. Cuddington and Hongliang*, 2000) and the EMU increased FDI in many folds within EU and in the rest of the world (*Harry Flam and Per Jausson*, 2000). The strong monetary integration were found in unsecured money market, repo market and government bond market considerably with EMU convergence process. (*Philipp Hartmamy, Augela Meddaloni, Simone Manganelli*, 2003)

This unique development of Euro becomes possible due to successful functioning of monetary integration of European Monetary System which was ratified in Maastricht Treaty. And the ECB is the sole responsible of implementing the following policies successfully since the treaty.

The Stability and Growth Pact of ECB.
Creation of Pan European payment System with TARGET policy.
Independent two pillar monetary policy.
Coping with parameter uncertainty.
Following ECONIA principle.
Maintaining stable exchange rate of Euro/Dollar under floating regime.
Adopting collaterisation to access liquidity.
Transformation of financial system with unique supervision.

The institutional framework and co-ordination of ECB is so unique and scientific that the Euro System and the European System of Central Banks (ESCB) are governed by the decision-making bodies of the ECB: the Governing Council and the Executive Board. The General Council is constituted as a third decision-making body of the ECB. The functioning of the decision-making body of the ECB is governed by the Maastricht Treaty establishing the European Community.

The Governing Council formulates the monetary policy of the Euro Area and establishes the necessary guidelines for their implementation. The Executive Board implements the monetary policy in the Euro Area and manages the current business of the ECB. The General Council carries out those tasks taken over from the European Monetary Institute which will have to be performed by the ECB in the stage III of European Monetary Union.

On the basis of bimonthly meeting of the Governing Council, ECB undertakes the interest rate decisions. ECB has been able to draw upon the new emphasis on transparency and openness when it developed its communication and disclosure policies. It is surprising that as a relatively young institution, the predictability of ECB policy decisions should be acknowledged uniquely. (44% reliable on ECONIA rates). (*Kelvin Ross*, 2002). Even, the monetary policy decisions of the ECB have been accurately predicted 87% of the times when the one month rate is used to assess the expectations of market participants. (*Gabriel Perez-Quiros and Jorge Sicilia*, 2002).

In the world's institutional space, Japan's Asian Monetary Fund proposal was in essence a threat to the authority and effectiveness of the IMF itself. The US administration opposed to the idea, perceiving it as an attempt to challenge its regional hegemony.

Moreover, the APEC forum agreed to establish a Manila framework for enhanced Asian Regional Co-operation to promote financial stability at the 5th APEC Summit in Vancouver in November 1997, where the initiatives were:

* A co-operating financing arrangement that would supplement IMF resources.
* Enhanced economic and technical co-operation particularly in strengthening domestic financial systems and regulating capacities.
* A mechanism for regional surveillance to complement the IMF's global surveillance.

Last but not the least, the Chiang Mai Initiative extents and expands upon the little known ASEAN Swap Arrangement to encompass all ASEAN countries including China, Japan and Korea. This attempt is the first step towards the establishment of Asian Monetary Fund (*Chang Li Liu and Ramkishen Rajan*, 2001).

Therefore, US-based multilateral international financial institutions began to face a series of evolving regional financial institutions which emerge to encounter IMF surveillance to monitor institutional autonomy regarding international liquidity problem, to equalise international capital flows changing institutional lending practices and enhancing regional trading shares to improve regional financial instability.

Thus, we cannot nullify the emergence of a new international institution for reforming international monetary system in which it requires a world money with a world central bank to ensure the international financial stability under multilateralism *vis-a-vis* under emerging regionalism. It is hoped that the new institution must stabilize international payment mechanism mobilising unequal trading partners towards sustainable equal exchange system in future global economy where political and economic dominance would be insignificant to the world institutional harmony.

CONCLUDING REMARKS

The surveillance of international financial institutions will be working in a well behaved manner if the world governance functions properly along with its needs, where the redistribution is in normal shape.

The cluster of regional financial institutions should aim at regional as well as international monetary stability where national sovereignty should be given prime importance as per its environment but national domination should be vehemently prevented.

The new international financial institution should confirm the progress of sustainable development process with more equity, justice and welfare.

References

Abiad, Abdul (2003): Early Warning System, *IMF Research Bulletin*, Vol. 4, No. 2, June, www.imf.org

Acemoglu, Daron (2003): Root Causes—A Historical Approach to Assessing the Role of Institutions in Economic Development, www.imf.org

Ahrens, Joachim (1997): Prospects of Institutional and Policy Reforms in India: Towards a Model of the Development State? *ADR*, 15(1), pp. 111-46.

Asian Development Bank (1999): Strengthening the International Financial Architecture, *EDRC Briefing Notes No. 12*, May.

Balladur, Edward (1999): The International Monetary System: Facing the Challenge of Globalisation, Institute of International Economics, 25th May.

Bank for International Settlement (1998): Report of the Working Group on Strengthening Financial Systems: Executive Summary of Reports on the International Financial Architecture, October, 1998.

Bergsten, C.F. (2000): The coming rise of Euro. Speech delivered on 28th January, www.ecb.net

—— (2002): The Euro *versus* the Dollar: Will there be a Struggle for Dominance? Speech delivered on 4th January, www.ecb.net

Bhowmik, D. (2002): *Essays on International Money*, Deep & Deep Publications Pvt. Ltd., New Delhi.

Bird, Graham and Ramkishen S. Rajan (2002): The Solving Asian Financial Architecture, *Essays in International Economics No. 226*, February, Princeton University.

Boughton, J.M. (2002): Why White, not Keynes? Investing the Postwar International Monetary System, *IMF, WP 02/52, March*, www.imf.org

Buiter, William H. (2000): Targets, Instruments and Institutional Arrangements for an Effective Monetary Authority, RBI, 7th Memorial Lecture, 16th October, Mumbai.

Chang, Ha-Joon (1998): The Role of Institutions in Asian Development, *ADR*, 16(2), pp. 64-95.

Cuddington, J.T. and HongLiang (2000): Will the Emergence of the Euro Affect World Commodity Prices? *WIDER WP 178*, March.

Debrun, Xavier, Paul Massion and Catherine Pattillo (2000): "Monetary Union in West Africa: Who Might Gain, Who Might Lose, and Why?", *IMF, WP/02/226*, December, www.jmfprg

European Central Bank (2001): The Institutional Framework of the Euro-System and the European System of Central Banks, *Annual Report 2001*, Ch. 12.

—— (2001): Annual Report 2001, www.ecb.net

Fischer, Stanley (2000): On the need for an International Lender of Last Resort, *Essays in International Economics*, No. 220, November, Princeton University, New York.

Flam, Harry and Per Jausson (2000): EMU effect on International Trade and Investment, *WIDER WP 180*, April.

Goldstein, Morris (2000), 'Strengthening the International Financial Architecture: Where Do We stand? www.iie.com

Hartmann, Philipp, Augela Meddaloni and Simone Manganelli (2003): The Euro Area Financial System, Structure, Integration and Policy Initiative, *ECB WP-230*, May.

Henning, C. Randall (1998); Europe's Monetary Union, the US and International Co-operation Institute for International Economics. Speech delivered on 18th April, www.ecb.net

TMF (2002): IMF Report 2002, Chapter-3.

Issing, Otmer (2002): Various speeches collected from www.ecb.net

Kumar, Nagesh (2002): Towards an Asian Economic Community—Vision of Closer Economic Co-operation in Asia: An overview. *RIS, DP 32/2002*, July, New Delhi.

Liu, Chang Li, and Ramkishen Rajan (2001): The Economics and Politics of Monetary Regionalism in Asia, *CIES, DP No. 0'107, March*, Adelaide University, Australia.

North, D.C. (1990): Institutions, Institutional Change and Economic Performance (Cambridge University Press).

—— (1997): The Contribution of the New Institutional Economics to an Understanding of the Transition Problem, *WIDER Annual Lecture-1*, March, wivw.wider.unu.edu.

Perez-Quiros, Gabriel and Jorge Sicilia (2002): Is the ECB Predictable? *ECB WP-192*, November.www.ecb.net

Ramcharan, Rodney (2003): Assessing IMF Programme Effectiveness, *IMF Research Bulletin*, Vol. 4, No. 2, June, www.imf.org

Rodrik, Dani, Arvind Subramanian and Francesco Trebbi (2002): Institutions Rule; The Primacy of Institutions over Integration and Geography in Economic Development, *IMF, WP /02/189*, November.

Rodrik, Dani and Arvind Subramanian (2003): The Primacy of Institutions (And what this does and does not mean), www.imf.org

Ross, Kelvin (2002): Market Predictability of ECB Policy Decisions: A Comparative Examination, *IMF WP/02/23 3*, December.

Solan, Eugenio Domingo (2002): Various speeches collected from www.ech.net

Srinivasan, T.N. (1998): Strengthening the International Financial Architecture, *ADR*, 16(2), pp. 1-17.

WIDER (2002): Governing Globalisation: Issues and Institutions—A Policy Brief, www.wider.unu.edu

Index